ZHENG HE'S
ART OF
COLLABORATION

"Professor Hum's venture to provide a new approach to business management through Admiral Zheng He's Art of Collaboration rather than an Art of War merits attention. Admiral Zheng He is an eminently suitable candidate to draw lessons from. He was the CEO designated by the Ming Emperor Yongle (永乐) in the early fifteenth century to build a super fleet and to assemble a multi-ethnic crew to undertake a total of seven voyages spanning a period of twenty-eight years (1405–33) that eventually covered thirty-three countries from the South China Sea across to eastern Africa. This unprecedented and highly successful massive undertaking would have required the strongest and most capable CEO or commander in any comparable situation.

Professor Hum has provided a detailed account of Zheng He's management skills and exploits within the context they were carried out to illustrate his business management approach based on Collaboration. The seven historic voyages were motivated by peace, harmony and goodwill by the then superpower and the smaller states in what was referred to as the 'Western Ocean'. This was made absolutely clear from the several imperial edicts that were issued to Zheng He and his fellow top commanding officers that were never military or aggressive in nature. Instead they bore gifts of goodwill, provided assistance against pirates, brokered peace between feuding states, healed the sick, shared agricultural and other needed technologies, imparted culture including spreading the Islamic faith to peoples in the Indonesian archipelago. In turn, the voyagers benefited from knowledge of local medicine, natural products, and they undertook trade with Arab, Persian and Indian merchants from regions beyond. This was truly a mission of Collaboration and mutual benefit through a grand mission of international peace and mutual respect."

Dr Chia Lin Sien
Co-editor, The Zheng He Epic

"*Zheng He's Art of Collaboration* makes for a fresh and fascinating read for business leaders and students alike. The author has meticulously researched and systematically presents an alternative management and leadership model from the great fifteenth-century explorer as a modern-day CEO and business leader. Understanding and drawing from *Zheng He's Art of Collaboration* will equip us to operate more effectively and achieve win-win results in a 'new normal' borderless multi-polar business world where no one has monopoly on information and resources."

Dr Steven Choo
CEO, Real Estate Developers' Association
of Singapore (REDAS)

"With many companies or states facing difficulties in the present-day economic situation, collaboration may be the best solution. The publication of this book is indeed timely as it is an excellent guide for business executives as well as politicians in the area of collaborative efforts."

Setyono Djuandi Darmono
President Director, PT Jababeka TbK

"In a world where human machinations abound as people try to outdo one another, I find *Zheng He's Art of Collaboration* a fascinating and refreshing read. The book is a drop of dew in the parched spiritual landscape of business and politics as its principles and practices are grounded in collaboration rather than conflict thus tapping on man's benevolence rather than his combative spirit. In his well-researched book, Professor Hum delves into the annals of ancient China depicting the life of Zheng He and his epic voyages and draws from them detailed practical lessons in leadership, teamwork and management which are relevant business models for today's world.

Now, more than ever, we need leaders with the right motives and attitudes, because after all the competition and beating others down, if people become watchful and aggressive as a result and the world becomes a worse place for all — what good is that? This is why I am thrilled to have Zheng He's alternative to Sun Zi's Art of War."

Dr Rosemary Khoo
President, NUS Senior Alumni;
Immediate Past President, University Women of Asia;
Founding President, University Women's Association Singapore

"This is a fascinating study of Admiral Zheng He's seven historic voyages to the West. Professor Hum has very creatively extracted from Zheng He's voyages certain principles and best practices, which are applicable to business and to life."

Professor Tommy Koh
Ambassador-at-Large, Ministry of Foreign Affairs, Singapore

"*Zheng He's Art of Collaboration* (AoC) is a uniquely crafted perspective which puts forward a less assertive and combative posturing in business. Professor Hum has succinctly articulated salient points on collaboration in businesses and how this perspective differs from the art of war. In essence, it provides another angle in looking at maintaining the balance of power and sustainability. The Art of War (AoW) through Sun Zi contained many tactics and manoeuvres used primarily to overwhelm, confuse, obfuscate and distract the opponents.

Professor Hum's book is a worthy read for an alternative perspective in the Art of Collaboration and it is particularly relevant in today's context of value management with peers and competitors."

David Leong
Managing Director, PeopleWorldWide Consulting

"Professor Hum Sin Hoon's excellent book *Zheng He's Art of Collaboration* provides an interesting alternative perspective for business people to consider when managing their businesses. Unlike the traditional model of running a business employing Sun Zi's Art of War tactics, this book provides an insight to a highly credible business model that I believe will be more applicable as collaborative efforts are becoming the cornerstone of developed societies. Indeed this book conveys a less combative approach to business that is much more suited to the current social climate as the development of information technology has encouraged a deeper sense of sharing and cooperation. Professor Hum has provided an effective and coherent argument that would go hand-in-hand with the other Sun Zi proponents for an all-rounded business approach."

Andy Lim
Chairman, Tembusu Partners

"Political and economic events of recent years have ushered in a new paradigm shift in the way we do business and conduct relationships. Just like the advent of the Industrial Revolution, the dawn of this new era has brought about exciting opportunities, uncertainly and increased volatility in both these arenas. Zheng He's Art of Collaboration teaches us the values of cooperative competition and mutual respect. It is a timely beacon of light in today's challenging times."

Roger Lim
CEO and Co-Founder, Webvisions

"An interesting read. It is a freshing presentation of an aspect of Zheng He's life that we know little of. The Art of Collaboration is a shift from what most of us were taught in business schools. It is an old ancient truth and it is based on a simple principle, i.e. developing strategies for all to win. Very readable. I recommend it to all who lead a team and/or are involved in developing strategies."

Ng Yong Hwee
President & CEO, City Gas and CEO, SingSpring

"Successful collaboration between stakeholders in supply chains is key to ensure that they prevail and grow. It helps to have some guidepost on the art and acts of collaboration. Professor Hum's elucidation of management principles from the highly successful Zheng He and his collaborative approach, gives a fresh perspective of his adventures. Understanding how Zheng He overcame the challenges as he conquered the high seas would help us navigate our supply chains through the competitive oceans."

Quek Keng Liang
Chairman, Singapore Logistics Association

"Rivalry is inherent in our fiercely competitive business world. While competition would undoubtedly provide the necessary impetus for a company to improve its business acumen and viability, mutual respect and peaceful coexistence are the very essence of our continued survival. Collaboration therefore plays an important role in enhancing a company's relationship with its competitors, one that would create mutually beneficial and the much vaunted 'win-win' relationships.

The maritime exploits of Zheng He as contained in his seven voyages provide the quintessence of this collaboration principle and epitomizes an approach that places an unflagging emphasis on diplomacy rather than on hostilities.

The strategies contained in Sun Zi's *Art of War* are premised on military principles. They might enable some initial gain for the victors, but with the passage of time, the vanquished would learn and counter with similar if not more virulent strategies. This could only mean the ultimate demise of dominant players like what had happened in the electronics industry.

Unlike the electronics industry, the aircraft industry with its multitude of supply chain players is collaboration in motion.

Professor Hum has illustrated well the principle that collaboration in any form would allow all companies to grow and prosper. It would allow each company to develop at its own pace and to fill a particular niche based on its forte and specialism. The axiom that the sum of parts will be greater than the whole is never more apparent in a collaborative strategy.

The Art of Collaboration would be a timeless virtue for all to emulate."

Seah Choo Meng
Director, Davis Langdon & Seah

"As an alternative, if not an updated version of Sun Zi's *Art of War*, Zheng He's Art of Collaboration is probably more relevant in today's context where commerce and social interaction have become borderless.

The collective power of the man in the street had become real and formidable because of the advent of instant and viral communication channels now known as the new media. Another term to describe Zheng He's 'win-win' approach is perhaps an 'inclusive' approach. While some may argue that this is not possible all the time, it must be attempted each and every time in the decision and policy-making process so that no one can claim or prove that he or she was sidelined. The uprising in the Middle East and 'Occupy Wall Street' protests bear testimony to the fact the voice of the people do matter.

To businesses which enjoy monopolistic advantages, the 'all-win' approach may sound too radical. However, if we were to consider both the tangible and intangible gains, Zheng He's collaboration approach can never go wrong. After all, a long-term customer can only last as long as the economic cycle we are in and that in itself had become shorter and shorter over the years."

Ricky Sim
CEO, Suntec Investment

"A factual and extensively researched book which provides valuable insights into the accomplishments of Zheng He and offers practical lessons in leadership principles and business collaboration. It reminds us that competitors need not necessarily be enemies and businesses can in fact gain more by forming allies and sharing more generously.

The author has produced a much needed and timely piece of work which will greatly enhance our understanding of the art of building collaboration and assist the modern-day CEOs in achieving better and more sustainable results."

Johnny Tan
President, National University of Singapore Society (NUSS)

"Winning in business in the twenty-first century takes more than just strategy and technology. It takes knowledge of how to work well with all stakeholders from investors, management, employees, partners and customers. In *Zheng He's Art of Collaboration*, Sin Hoon shares with us the need and know-how of achieving a 'win-win' strategy in business through collaborating well with all stakeholders."

James Tay
Director, National University of Singapore Extension

"Many business people all over the world are interested to know the reasons for China's economic success. The current Chinese leadership is applying a lot of Zheng He's philosophy as they invest all over the world to generate goodwill and win-win business propositions. I attribute part of China's economic success to its adoption of Zheng He's philosophy of the 'Art of Collaboration'. Therefore, this book is most timely and a 'must read' for all business people."

Dr Michael Teng
Best-selling author and Managing Director,
Corporate Turnaround Center; and
President, MBA Alumni-NUS

"Sin Hoon has eloquently presented the usefulness of Zheng He's Art of Collaboration. I find Zheng He and his voyages fascinating. If the history books are correct, China did not repeat his feat, destroyed his fleet and closed its doors for several centuries, thereafter. Why that happened, puzzles me."

Professor Tsui Kai Chong
Provost, SIM University

"This book presents an excellent analysis of the approach adopted by Zheng He. The insights presented in the book will certainly be of great value to many who are searching for new ways of co-creating solutions and approaches that engender ownership whilst achieving desired results and outcomes.

Zheng He's Art of Collaboration gives us a glimpse of man's wisdom, leadership principles and practices for winning, whether in life, business or in international relations. This book is a must-read for all strategic planners, entrepreneurs and CEOs who believe in 'All Win' as a way for the modern world to succeed, in contrast to 'Aggression', 'Competition', 'Confrontation' and 'Conflict'. It is also a book about how we as the community organizers can build Social Capital within a community and across communities, through generous sharing, giving and collaboration among the partners in the public, private and people sectors. Professor Hum pays a lot of attention to the details on how Zheng He did it. He has offered us an alternative approach, and a softer and more sustainable solution to an organization's success and growth."

Yam Ah Mee
CEO, People's Association

"Admiral Zheng He has long been touted and admired for his maritime skills and geographical explorations. For such success to be attained especially during the fifteenth century, much has to be attributed to Admiral Zheng He's leadership, management and motivational skills.

There are many lessons to be learnt from the wise and foresighted Admiral. His successes in explorations to new geographical territories, as a Muslim leading a fleet of Chinese vessels and representing the Chinese Emperor as an eminent envoy, provide insights into collaborating skills involving cross-cultural and religious issues. This non-threatening, non-aggressive style that Admiral Zheng He used sets the platform for the 'Art of Collaboration'. These skills and techniques in collaboration are necessary and especially relevant in today's complex and competitive environment. Business leaders (and political leaders) have much to benefit from this much needed publication.

I must commend Professor Hum for sharing the insights gleaned from the archives of Admiral Zheng He and organizing them systematically for today's students of management."

Yeo Keng Joon
Founding President, NUS Business School Alumni Association
and Past President, MBA Alumni-NUS

INTERNATIONAL ZHENG HE SOCIETY

Admiral Zheng He (or Cheng Ho) was the 15th century Ming China's great mariner. His seven historic voyages across the Southeast Asian and Indian oceans from 1405–1433 was a ground-breaking achievement. His contributions changed the face of the region for a more peaceful and prosperous world. The International Zheng He Society (Singapore) was formed in 2003 to undertake scholarly research on Zheng He's enduring contribution to peace, good will, and ethnic and cross-cultural understanding among nations.

The Society's aims are: (1) to promote research on Zheng He expeditions focussing on his exploits and contributions beyond China; (2) to study the social, economic, political and cultural influence of Zheng He's legacies in the pre-Colonial and modern world; and (3) to share research findings from Zheng He studies through publications and international fora and visits.

INSTITUTE OF SOUTHEAST ASIAN STUDIES

The Institute of Southeast Asian Studies (ISEAS) was established as an autonomous organization in 1968. It is a regional centre dedicated to the study of socio-political, security and economic trends and developments in Southeast Asia and its wider geostrategic and economic environment. The Institute's research programmes are the Regional Economic Studies (RES, including ASEAN and APEC), Regional Strategic and Political Studies (RSPS), and Regional Social and Cultural Studies (RSCS).

ISEAS Publishing, an established academic press, has issued more than 2,000 books and journals. It is the largest scholarly publisher of research about Southeast Asia from within the region. ISEAS Publishing works with many other academic and trade publishers and distributors to disseminate important research and analyses from and about Southeast Asia to the rest of the world.

郑

ZHENG HE'S ART OF COLLABORATION

Understanding the Legendary Chinese Admiral
from a Management Perspective

HUM SIN HOON

 国际郑和学会
INTERNATIONAL ZHENG HE SOCIETY

ISEAS
INSTITUTE OF SOUTHEAST ASIAN STUDIES
SINGAPORE

First published in Singapore in 2012 by ISEAS Publishing
Institute of Southeast Asian Studies
30 Heng Mui Keng Terrace
Pasir Panjang
Singapore 119614

E-mail: publish@iseas.edu.sg
Website: <http://bookshop.iseas.edu.sg>

The responsibility for facts and opinions in this publication rests exclusively with the author and his interpretations do not necessarily reflect the views or the policy of the publisher or its supporters.

ISEAS Library Cataloguing-in-Publication Data

Hum, Sin Hoon.
Zheng He's art of collaboration : understanding the legendary Chinese admiral from a management perspective.
1. Zheng, He, 1371–1435.
2. Admirals—China.
3. Voyages and travels.
4. Management.
5. Organizational effectiveness.
I. Title.
DS753.6 C48H91   2012

ISBN 978-981-4379-66-3 (soft cover)
ISBN 978-981-4379-70-0 (hard cover)
ISBN 978-981-4379-67-0 (E-book PDF)

Typeset by Superskill Graphics Pte Ltd
Printed in Singapore by Mainland Press Pte Ltd

CONTENTS

FOREWORD

The last decade of the twentieth century and the first decade of the twenty-first century have enjoyed peace and yet the world has been full of the smoke of gunpowder, conflicts and endless suicidal bomb explosions. One wonders what has gone wrong with our civilization that leads to the world becoming so chaotic, with countless ordinary people being destitute and dying.

Of course, one of the reasons is the ideological differences that lead to the struggle and clash of interests among the major powers. Former President of the United States, George W. Bush, maintained the policy of U.S. domination, unilateralism and forestalling of others who do not identify with the American position. Such behaviour has drawn the United States into deep trouble ever since.

Three years ago, President Barack Obama was well aware that George W. Bush's policy would drag the U.S. into an abyss. So he rode on the electoral slogans of "Change" and "Anti-war" and ascended to the U.S. Presidency, for which he was awarded the Nobel Peace Prize. Unfortunately, under the pressure of the hawkish faction, he promptly dispatched thirty thousand soldiers to Afghanistan. The recent surge of the "Arab Spring" and "Occupy Wall Street" movements highlight the discontent against the current political system. Does this mean that there is no other substitute system in mankind's 5,000 years of civilization?

In 1988, seventy-five Nobel Laureates assembled in Paris and issued a joint declaration: "Mankind in the 21st century requires learning from Confucian Wisdom prevailing 2,500 years ago in order to survive."

What is Confucian Wisdom? Generally speaking, it means Confucian thought. Confucian orthodoxy is the way "to ordain conscience for Heaven and Earth, to strive for people's life, to follow the Sage and spread his teachings, to create eternal peace for future generations"; "to care for the common people and to assume responsibility to serve the world". This orthodoxy seeks to secure good life and fortune for the people, dedicate oneself to the people and be patriotic. Guided by the principle of people first, society second and monarch less important, Confucian mandarins implemented governance of benevolence, humanity and virtue to realize an ideal and perfect society. This ideology that emphasizes the importance of the collective group, society and state is very different from the western ideology that places emphasis on individual freedom and democracy.

President Obama, after assuming office, has also realized the inadequacy of over-emphasizing western freedom and democracy. Hence, according to the *Wall Street Observer*, Obama has been inclined to use Zheng He's policy of projecting culture (soft power), something that Zheng He did 600 years ago. Then, Zheng He had commanded the world's most powerful naval fleet. He did not bring to the countries he visited bloody wars of aggression nor did he embark on any form of colonization. Instead, through the use of diplomacy of trade and good-neighbourliness, he promoted the benign image of Ming China and disseminated Chinese culture (soft power). President Obama therefore emphasize the policy of trade and humanistic assistance to spread American soft power so as to serve the national interest of the United States better.

In fact, the mission completed by Zheng He's voyages to the western ocean consisted of the following:

1. Politically, expanding Ming China's sphere of political influence. He promoted Ming China as a mighty nation but without bullying the weak in spite of his military and technical might. Instead, he actively helped the smaller states against foreign invasion. For example, he dissuaded Siam from attacking Malacca, and prevented Malacca from attacking Srivijaya.
2. Diplomatically, adhering to the notion of "China and native states are one family". He established friendly and fraternal ties, not wars, with native states, valuing peace and harmony above territorial gain. Rulers and envoys of foreign states were invited to visit the Ming Court.
3. Economically, he developed the East-West international trade in the framework of tributary trade. Through consultation and cooperation, he achieved the goal of an all-win situation and valuing justice above material gains. He stood firm against piracy. The notorious pirate in the Straits of Malacca, Chen Zuyi, was wiped out by him.
4. Culturally, emphasizing protocol and etiquette. In diplomatic exchange, the Ming Court adopted a principle of benevolence and conciliation and thus returned those native states offering tribute of local products with generous gifts. The Chinese were more concerned with disseminating Chinese culture.
5. Religious tolerance and broad-mindedness. All religions were respected.

The above-mentioned behavioural mode is what we call the "Zheng He spirit". Actually, it is an extension of Confucian philosophy. I think this would be the meaning of "Confucian Wisdom" as declared by the Nobel Laureates. If only the present political elites of the world would adopt this wisdom to rule the states, the world would be less chaotic and more peaceful for everyone.

History never repeats itself perfectly but it mirrors the similarities of the many historical events. In the thirteenth and fourteenth centuries, the Mongol Empire dominated the world, its vast territories stretching from Asia to Europe. Due to this enormous territory and very diverse culture, religion and race of the population under its rule, the whole empire eventually collapsed. China being the centre of the empire was captured by the founder of the Ming Dynasty, Zhu Yuanzhang in 1368 and the Han culture of benevolent governance through Confucian orthodoxy prevailed again. Twentieth-century America apparently dominates the world as a sole superpower and rules the world by hegemony, and to a certain extent, reflecting the similar ambition of the Mongol Empire in the thirteenth and fourteenth centuries. Historians have labelled the nineteenth century as the British century and the twentieth century as the American century. Some American scholars are predicting that America is on the decline and it will soon be replaced by China in the twenty-first century. However, in this so-called "China century", China has vouched repeatedly that she will never be a hegemony. Whether China will adopt the spirit of Zheng He and bring peace to the world is yet to be seen. We earnestly hope to see the revival of the Zheng He spirit in the twenty-first century.

Professor Hum Sin Hoon is the first scholar to apply the Zheng He spirit in business affairs. This deserves our admiration and support. He aptly extends Zheng He's spirit of good faith and cooperation to develop a concept of the Art of Collaboration (AoC) in contrast to Sun Zi's Art of War (AoW). The Art of Collaboration is a "strategy" and is the best standard of behaviour in business. Numerous successful entrepreneurs have applied this spirit of good faith and cooperation to achieve an all-win objective through mutual care and impartial collaboration. If every partner employs Sun Zi's Art of War for his own selfish material gain, then he will lose his business partners and the opportunity to succeed and grow. We consider Sun Zi's Art of War to be unsuitable to serve as the entrepreneurs' business strategy, but only as a tactic at best, in the attempt to reach greater strategic heights.

I hope that the elites in every profession and business can fully use the essence of Zheng He's AoC to yield twice the results with half the effort to achieve the goal of business success.

Dr Tan Ta Sen
President, International Zheng He Society

MESSAGE

What should be the relevant management philosophy and strategies for today's twenty-first century world?

Currently, one of the most popular management concepts is that based on "Sun Zi Bing Fa" or "Sun Zi's Art of War". Sun Zi was a brilliant Chinese military strategist and he developed his war strategies some 2,600 years ago (in the sixth century BC). Many books have since been written about his war strategies and how they can be effectively applied to modern business. Indeed, many business empires have been built based on the philosophy of Sun Zi's Art of War.

Under this doctrine, "business is a battlefield" where winners take all. It is either "kill or be killed" and usually, only the strongest prevail. It underlines the belief that "Big Fish Eat Small Fish and Small Fish Eat Shrimp". In short, it is either you eat or gobble up your opponent or you yourself will be eaten up.

While this management concept holds true for many people and for a very long period of time, recent events have shown otherwise. With the advent of the Internet, and after 911, and the current prevalence of mobile technologies and devices, the world has changed.

911 demonstrated that "shrimps" also have the abilities to fight back quite effectively. Computer hackers working alone in their bedrooms have caused havoc to the world's computer systems.

Suicide bombers are other examples of "shrimps" fighting back. The collective strength of the common people is being confirmed even in the most current uprising in the Middle East.

Today's technologies have transformed and created a huge paradigm shift in business strategies. With "business knowledge" and "information" easily available to all, should we still continue to adopt and practise "Sun Zi Bing Fa" or Sun Zi's Art of War which was developed some 2,600 years ago before the computer, Internet and today's wireless technologies?

My personal view is that we should review our dependence on "Sun Zi Bing Fa". But do we have any alternative? Again we can turn to history to give us an answer. More than 600 years ago, Zheng He made seven famous expeditions to Asia including Malacca, India, the Middle East and even Africa. With more than 200 ships and 27,000 soldiers/sailors, his armada was the largest the world had ever seen. He could have easily conquered whatever land he wanted, destroyed all resistance and be the mighty conqueror. But he did not.

Instead, he worked with the locals to earn their trust. He shared with them the finer art of weaving, fishing and agriculture. Friendship and mutual respect were the keys, though China then was the centre of civilization. As a result, Zheng He was widely respected by the people in all the countries he visited. He was the symbol of peace and harmony, regardless of race and religion.

So what new business model should we adopt or practise in this fast changing world to ensure a "win-win" business environment? Can we learn and adopt Zheng He's philosophy and practices? I believe we can and I am confident that a change in mindset from "Sun Zi Bing Fa" to "Zheng He" will be the key to harmony and respect for all humanity. It will help develop trust which is so lacking today.

Professor Hum Sin Hoon's *Zheng He's Art of Collaboration* is certainly a very timely and appropriate response to our continual search for the business model that will help to improve business negotiations and relationships among companies and among trading nations. Professor Hum has investigated and researched extensively the "value-add" of Zheng He from a management perspective. I believe this is the first attempt to view Zheng He as a Management Guru and Professor Hum has carefully extracted the historical and cultural writings on Zheng He to give us a fresh and substantive understanding of Zheng He from this management angle.

Professor Hum has also aptly positioned Zheng He's Art of Collaboration as an alternative model to Sun Zi's Art of War. In this way, he draws our attention to the possibilities of this alternate, collaborative, and all-win paradigm that is in Zheng He, and wisely guiding us away from the present, prevalent, competitive and combative win-lose mindset.

Is this model practical and workable in the current turbulent business world? We all agree that "history always repeats itself". The fact that this model worked well some 600 years ago without the support of modern technologies gives us the confidence that it can be successful in today's world. A classic example of the application of Zheng He's collaborative model is the agreement between Singapore and Malaysia on the massive "Iskandar" project. Another relevant example is the collaborative arrangement between China and Singapore on the "Suzhou Industrial Park". The Batam Industrial Park and Bintan are other collaborative examples that demonstrate the possibilities of this management approach.

Many businessmen in Asia are already adopting and practising this "collaborative" business model and I am sure they will be very happy to know that their business approach is the right one in this turbulent times, as exemplified by Zheng He long ago.

This book is a must-read for business students and businessmen. They can gain the wisdom of the alternative collaborative model provided by Zheng He to help them to be successful in their business relationships and collaborations in today's world. They can also learn from Zheng He in his various practices as a leader and manager.

Wong Ah Long
Chairman, Utraco Green Tech;
Deputy Chairman, Board of Trustees,
Institute of Southeast Asian Studies;
Former CEO, Suntec City Development

PREFACE

Just before the Lunar New Year in 2010, I met up with a group of Chinese businessmen led by Mr Wong Ah Long. These gentlemen explained quite quickly and seriously that they would like me to help in doing research on the legendary Admiral Zheng He.

I was actually quite surprised by the request. Prior to this, I had only vaguely remembered that I did study Zheng He in my secondary school history classes. I asked if they had made a mistake in "selecting the professor" since this is not the usual kind of research that I do as an academic. My training and work have been in operations and supply chain management, and even there, my usual mode of research is based largely on theoretical mathematical modelling, although in some instances, I do adopt an empirical approach in studying specific operations issues.

They ignored my "protest" and went on to explain that they have been impressed by Zheng He's contribution in spreading peace and goodwill through his seven imperial voyages carried out during the early part of the fifteenth century. They felt that Zheng He and his basic message of peace and goodwill should be introduced to the larger world, especially when the world today seems to be filled with conflicts and stresses of all kinds.

This group of businessmen included Dr Tan Ta Sen. Apart from his business background, Dr Tan was also introduced to me as the President of the International Zheng He Society. These men were clearly very earnest and genuine in their desire to propagate the Zheng He message. I was honestly quite inspired by their humility and determination, though I was not clear then as to what would constitute Zheng He's basic message.

I promised the businessmen that I would read about Zheng He over that Lunar New Year break, and would think about what I could or could not do in terms of research on this legendary Chinese character. As it turned out, my reading led to curiosity, which led to the desire to want to know more, and quite quickly, I concluded that the existing literature did not quite look at Zheng He from a management or business perspective. Also, as a professor of operations and supply chain management, I was especially intrigued by how Zheng He could have moved his huge crew and fleet across the open seas from China to Africa in the early fifteenth century without today's wireless and satellite communications technologies. So I told Mr Wong and Dr Tan that I would indeed do some research and see what I could contribute. These two gentlemen have since been my mentors on this new journey that I started with Admiral Zheng He.

With the help of a number of my NUS Business School undergraduate students, I proceeded on the first wave of my research on Zheng He. This involved our search on the existing Zheng He literature that was published in English. My students and I did not do an exhaustive search; our intention was to initially read and learn from the most readily available English sources on Zheng He. The approach that we adopted was to stand on the shoulders of these earlier experts and researchers on Zheng He by quoting from their writings when we saw relevance to our focus on understanding Zheng He from a management perspective. In other words, the approach we adopted involved culling from the existing literature anything that we read and interpreted as related to Zheng He's management practices; we then "connected these dots" of discovery of the managerial Zheng He by presenting them as a coherent whole in what we would refer to as a specific model of Zheng He's management practices in a particular area of management.

Because of this approach, the reader will see that the writing in this book is heavily endnoted. Every point that I make on Zheng He is based on what my students and I have read, interpreted, and cited from the existing literature. The endnotes point the reader to the specific pages in the writings that were cited, and in this way, explicit recognition and credits are given to these earlier experts and researchers on Zheng He. This is also an indication that my work in this book did not add any new historical, cultural, diplomatic or maritime facts on Zheng He. To facilitate easy reading, and flow of contents, I have decided not to use the usual quotation marks in quoting from the literature (there would be too many quotation marks, otherwise). In any case, I have largely paraphrased most of these cited references, though I do borrow some words from some references. I do resort to using quotation marks when it is helpful in making a point, as in putting forth a specific quotation from Sun Zi's *Art of War*, for example. Similarly, for the purpose of emphasis, I have used text indentation to present some specific quotes, as in the presentation of the imperial edicts. In all references, I have given the full reference information in the chapter endnotes when I first cited from that source within the chapter; subsequent citations from the same source are simplified with reference only to the title of the publication. In every reference or citation, however, I point to specific pages in the source. I do the same with the references to Chinese literature. Here, when I cite the reference fully in the first instance within a chapter, I also provide an English translation of its publication title and the publisher. This is to give the non-Chinese reader a basic sense of the Chinese references cited.

Together with a few of my students who can read Chinese readily, I have already embarked on the second wave of our research on Zheng He by searching through the literature written in Chinese. This explains why I have included some of such Chinese references in the writing in this book.

I started the research in March 2010. By July of that year, with encouragement from both Dr Tan and Mr Wong, my student Grace Chew and I co-authored a paper which we presented at the International Conference on Zheng He and the Afro-Asian World held in Malacca. We presented in that paper the first version of what we referred to as Zheng He's Art of Collaboration. To my surprise, the paper was quite well received by several of the conference participants who encouraged us to do more work in this area.

Following the conference, I therefore decided to press on with the research and put together this book to introduce the legendary Chinese Admiral Zheng He from the management perspective. By now, I have come to appreciate the "big message" that Zheng He seemed to represent, namely the message of peace and goodwill for all, through the cultivation of win-win collaboration amongst all people. I have therefore adopted the general mainstream perspective of Zheng He's grand voyages as a peaceful means for conveying Ming China's splendour and glory, and spreading goodwill and promoting economic trade, though I am also quite aware of alternative views on this. In this book, and as in the earlier conference paper, I have referred to this overall message as Zheng He's Art of Collaboration. At the same time, I have also come to appreciate Zheng He in his many apparent management and leadership practices which I believe should be introduced to today's managers and leaders.

This book therefore comprises two parts. The first part includes chapters 1 through 4, and it introduces what I now see as Zheng He's major contribution: the Zheng He Art of Collaboration. Chapter 1 first introduces Zheng He by putting forth some reasons why we may all want to pay attention to this fifteenth-century Chinese eunuch admiral. It then provides a broad sketch on the admiral from the management perspective, pointing out many questions on what his management practices were and how we could perhaps learn from them for application in today's environment.

Chapter 2 then introduces Zheng He's Art of Collaboration (AoC). It presents this as Zheng He's alternative model to the well-known Sun Zi's Art of War (AoW). Chapter 2 therefore represents Zheng He's central message of building collaboration with all people so as to help spread goodwill, peace and prosperity for the benefit of all people. It introduces the 4Cs model of Zheng He's strategies in building collaboration, and collectively, these 4Cs strategies represent Zheng He's Art of Collaboration.

Within Zheng He's AoC, Chapter 2 also briefly describes what is now referred to as Zheng He's 5Acts of Collaboration. Chapter 3 therefore follows with an elaboration on these Acts of Collaboration by providing more examples of them from the literature on Zheng He.

To conclude this first part of the book, Chapter 4 provides a comparison of Zheng He's AoC with Sun Zi's AoW. The intention here is to provide a better understanding of the AoC by comparing it directly with the well-known AoW. This chapter provides an examination of the fundamental philosophies, assumptions and contexts of both the Zheng He's and Sun Zi's strategies in their respective AoC and AoW.

Part 2 of the book, which comprises chapters 5 through 8, introduces Zheng He from the management perspective in the different specific functional areas of management. Here, the basic objective is to learn from Zheng He through his apparent management and leadership practices. Chapter 5 first introduces the Admiral Zheng He in terms of his leadership principles and practices. Here, the chapter presents Zheng He's ABCDE Model of Leadership that highlights what he apparently considered to be most important in his work of leadership, namely his Allegiance to Authority, his Band of Brothers, his Care for Crew, his Doing Due Diligence and his Embrace of the Eternal.

Chapter 6 then considers learning from Zheng He in his Human Resource Management (HRM) practices. It introduces Zheng He's Role Model of HRM where the highlight is on Zheng He in his three roles as a Strategic HR Planner, a Clever HR Organizer and a Wise HR Manager.

Chapter 7 introduces Zheng He's Supply Chain Management practices by presenting Zheng He's 7S Model of Importance in managing supply chains. Here, the highlight is on what Zheng He apparently considered to be important in his supply chain management work, namely the importance of: Strategic Intent and Clarity; Supply Ecosystem; Specialists Recruitment; Sights and Sound of Navigation; Selection of Regional Bases; Supply Chain Growth and Development; and Storage and *Guanchang*.

Finally Chapter 8 considers Zheng He and his faith practices. Here it introduces Zheng He and his Islamic faith heritage as well as his apparent faith practices through Zheng He's PC Model for managing religious beliefs and faith practices: to Zheng He, it was apparent that Personal Faith can be a Significant Plus for his sea-faring enterprise, while Corporate Inclusiveness is an Important Must for his mission success.

In summary, I have essentially drawn upon existing writings on Zheng He and considered them from the management perspective. In so doing, I have attempted to "connect the dots" in the ongoing discovery of a managerial Zheng He. This book therefore introduces Zheng He from the management perspective. In particular, it offers Zheng He's Art of Collaboration as a possible alternative model to the managerial mindset contained in Sun Zi's Art of War. At the same time, this book also offers Zheng He's apparent management and leadership practices as possible inspiration for today's managers and leaders.

Hum Sin Hoon
NUS Business School

ACKNOWLEDGEMENTS

I want to express my sincere thanks to Mr Wong Ah Long and Dr Tan Ta Sen for introducing me to Zheng He. Their request for me to do "some research on Zheng He" has allowed me to start my journey into a new area of work that is quite unlike what I usually do in mathematical modelling research. More importantly, their belief in me in doing this research has been most encouraging; never once did they waver in their confidence in me, even when I expressed to them on several occasions that this is not the usual type of research that I do and that I am too busy as an administrator in my NUS Business School to spend enough time on this project. Ah Long and Ta Sen: thank you for your belief in me and for constantly urging me on. And Ta Sen, thank you for giving me access to your personal library of materials on Zheng He.

I also want to acknowledge my friend Lee Junior for his time and efforts in travelling to Malacca just to listen to me make my first presentation on Zheng He in July 2010. Lee has been most passionate about my work on Zheng He's Art of Collaboration and he has shared many of his creative ideas to help propagate this message. Lee has also provided the original inspiration for the cover design for this book. Lee: thank you for your creativity, energy and belief in the Zheng He message of collaboration; thanks also for your confidence in my work.

Laurie Er and James Tay of NEX (NUS Extension) have also been most supportive of my work. They also travelled to Malacca specially to listen to me. Also, they created the platform through NEX to allow me to make my first public presentation on Zheng He in Singapore back in March 2011. They believed in my work even though it was still work-in-progress then. Laurie and James: thanks for your support for me and your confidence in the Zheng He message as presented in this book.

I must also acknowledge the tremendous help my NUS Business School undergraduate students have granted me in this Zheng He project. They include Chew Lusheng Grace, Yuan Yi, Chong Liyue, David Ng, Fong Ying Ying, Muhammad Aziz Bin Salim, Leong Li Ting, Cui Chunhao, Alvin Lim and Macey Tan. Grace in particular has helped me in the original version of Zheng He's Art of Collaboration; that version was presented at the Malacca conference and has been revised and expanded in the current version in Chapter 2. Yuan Yi has contributed largely and significantly in the Acts of Collaboration and the comparison between Zheng He's AoC and Sun Zi's AoW. Her contributions show up in Chapters 3 and 4. Yuan Yi has also been a major help in much of the translation work and access to Chinese literature. David interacted with me over Zheng He's leadership; Ying Ying challenged me in thinking about Zheng He's HRM; and Aziz helped me to appreciate Zheng He's faith practices. All my students' literature search, interpretation and discussion with me have been most helpful and enjoyable. Grace, David, Ying Ying and Aziz have since graduated; I am still privileged to be engaged in ongoing work with the rest. To my student team: a big thank you to each one of you; you have been my joy and will always be my pride.

I also want to acknowledge the help of Dr Sim Chuin Peng, Principal Librarian at the NUS Chinese Library, and a continuing

Ming Scholar himself in terms of his ongoing research. Dr Sim has helped my students and I in getting access to Chinese literature on Zheng He. He has also been most supportive of my work and has personally sent me specific references to Chinese literature on Zheng He in the area of HRM practices. Chuin Peng: thank you for your kind help; we must find the opportunity to work together on Zheng He.

I want to thank my two sons Samuel and Daniel who have grown up to be two fabulous young men whom any father would be proud of. They have experienced a reduced interaction with me during this period of work on this book. But I know they understand my passion in this. I want also to thank my dear wife Eunice who has quietly and patiently supported me in all my work over all these years; and this Zheng He project is no exception. She must have also experienced my tangible absence as I spend many minutes and hours in the evenings and nights to write this book on the home computer. Sam, Dan and Eunice: thank you for being my family, and this book is as much yours as it is mine.

Finally, like Zheng He, I "embrace the eternal" and am deeply thankful to my God for helping me to press on with joy and hope in all my work. Lord Jesus: thank you for your daily presence with me.

Hum Sin Hoon
NUS Business School

PART I

ZHENG HE AND HIS MESSAGE

Chapter 1

INTRODUCING ZHENG HE FROM THE MANAGEMENT PERSPECTIVE
Why Pay Attention to this Fifteenth-Century Chinese Eunuch?

INTRODUCTION

With the rise of Asia and China economically, much interest has been put on learning about doing business and practising management in this part of the world. And while much writing have focused on the current realities and issues that businesses are grappling with, there is also significant attention paid to learning about these realities through the writings of ancient wisdom, especially when such wisdom may be embedded in lesser known texts and sages from the Far East.

In this context, learning about doing business from the classic Chinese writings of Sun Zi and Confucius have been most popular. The classic *Art of War* as articulated by fourth-century-BC Sun Zi, for example, has long been translated into English and expounded by a whole host of modern-day authors seeking to draw inspiration and applications from it for modern-day business practices.[1] More recently, Yu Dan's 10-million-copy bestseller *Confucius from the Heart* has been translated into English to make the wisdom of sixth-century-BC Confucius even more widely available.[2]

In this book, we follow this trend by introducing to the modern world the fifteen-century-AD-Chinese-eunuch-Muslim-admiral *Zheng He*, also variously known as Cheng Ho or Ma He. But who is this person and why should we pay attention to him? Sure, he is no ancient-early-century-BC eastern sage of the order of Sun Zi or Confucius; he had also not penned his thoughts and practices for the benefit of posterity; writings about him in English have been limited; and outside of China, he is hardly known. Surprisingly, in Southeast Asia (especially in Malacca), South Asia (India and Sri Lanka), the Middle East (Saudi Arabia and the surrounding Muslim states), and Eastern Africa (Somalia and Kenya), Zheng He's legacy exists even today. Within China itself, Zheng He is now being regarded as a national hero and is held up as the trailblazer of the modern open-door policies that have brought China to today's world stage.[3] In the mass media, Zheng He's emperor-decreed early-fifteen-century-AD exploits in his seven grand voyages across the uncharted waters from China to Africa have been dramatized as an epic forty-episode TV drama serial that has gained a wide popular following throughout this region.[4]

While the writings in English on Zheng He have been limited, there is much literature on him in the Chinese language, including some original official materials from the days of the Ming Court which Zheng He served as a warrior and ambassador. Most, if not all of such writings about Zheng He, has been from the historical, maritime, diplomatic and cultural perspectives. Accordingly, Zheng He has been referred to as a great navigator, a global explorer, a diplomat, a warrior, an East-West trading network builder, a cultural disseminator, an adventurer and a Muslim eunuch in the Ming Court.[5]

Little has been explored and written about Zheng He from the management perspective. Yet Zheng He, in leading the world's largest ocean-going fleet in the early fifteen century, surpassing his western counterparts in terms of distance and duration of voyages, size and number of ships, and number of crew members, had clearly demonstrated much capability in the realm of effective management and leadership that can be relevant to today's business managers and leaders.

With the increasingly competitive business environment, effective management can provide businesses with a source of sustained competitive advantage. Accordingly, this chapter draws on historical sources on Zheng He's background and introduces him from a management perspective. The analysis of his management and leadership practices can be translated as insights to effective management for the benefit of all.

This chapter is organized as follows. The next section will provide an introduction of the young Ma He, followed by an introduction of the adult Zheng He. We will then present a brief historical background of China during the Song, Yuan and Ming dynasties; in particular, we will highlight Zheng He's emperor-decreed mission and the associated maritime voyages to the West. We will then explicitly highlight Zheng He's prominence and claim to fame, and explain therefore why he deserves our attention. In the last section of the chapter, we will focus specifically on Zheng He from a management perspective, highlighting what we can expect to learn from this legendary maritime person for today's business practices, management and leadership.

THE YOUNG MA HE

Zheng He was born into a noble Muslim family in 1371 during the fourth year of Emperor Hongwu's reign, at Hedai village of Kunyang in the Jinning district of Yunnan Province.[6] Zheng He's family name was "Ma", the Chinese version of "Mohammed",[7] and he was originally called "Ma He" from birth.[8]

The young Ma He commanded a huge presence; he was described as follows:

> seven feet tall... His cheeks and forehead were high but his nose was small. He had glaring eyes, teeth as white and well-shaped as shells, and a voice as loud as a huge bell. He knew a great deal about warfare and was well accustomed to battle.[9]

Ma He's ancestors were noblemen who came from the Western Region, the border between Uzbek and Xinjiang, and had migrated to China in 1070 during the Song Dynasty.[10] Ma He's father, Milijin, was the great-great-grandson of Sayyid Ajall Shamsuddin, a reknown political figure of the Yuan Dynasty with the inherited title of Dianyang Marquis; his grandfather Chaermidena also carried the honorific title of Dianyang Marquis.[11]

Ma He was brought up in a devout Muslim family, with strong Islamic faith and an awareness of Islam's heritage; both his grandfather and father had made pilgrimages to Mecca, and they were revered as "Haji".[12] Ma He's father, Haji Ma, was described as being tall-built, broad-minded, and benevolent, with a strong sense of righteousness.[13] Haji Ma was highly respected by the local community for his selflessness as evidenced by his acts of kindness and generosity; he was always ready to offer help and protection to the poor, weak and needy.[14] Ma He's mother, whose maiden name was "Wen", was described as a gracious lady[15] full of wifely values. Ma He had an elder brother, Ma Wen Ming, and four sisters.[16]

According to the Ma Haji Epitaph, Ma He was ambitious from young, intelligent and had a good memory.[17] He enjoyed reading classic books — the works of Confucius and Mencius,[18] and practised martial arts.[19] As a child, Ma He often asked his father and grandfather about their adventures to Mecca. Those long and adventurous journeys across the Indian Ocean, their many struggles against nature, having to fight plague and encounter strange customs of the people in foreign lands,[20] were fascinating for a boy who lived in a land-locked state like Yunnan.[21] When Ma He was young, he used to hang out at the lake near his house, Lake Dianchi, with his siblings and friends where they observed how fishermen built fishing boats, and returned home to build models of these boats from memory. When he grew older, he learned useful skills such as how to swim, row boats, control sails and the art of building boats. Back then, Kunyang was the largest fishing region by the Southwestern bank of the Dianchi Lake. It had flourishing fishing and shipping activities, and a well-developed shipbuilding industry. Standing at the jetty and observing shipping and trading activities, the young Ma He picked up his first valuable lessons in sailing and shipping.[22]

When the young Ma He was born, Yunnan was still under the Yuan Dynasty rule. Yunnan Province was under the control of Basalawarmi, Prince of Liang, a Mongol prince and a descendant of Khubilai, who had conquered Yunnan in the 1250s, before his succession as emperor and his conquest of Song China. Majority of the people in Yunnan were from non-Chinese ethnic groups who wanted the continuation of the Mongol rule over the Chinese conquest.[23] In 1374, founder of the Ming Dynasty Zhu Yuanzhang (Ming Taizu) dispatched an envoy to Yunnan, to advise the Mongol prince Basalawarmi to accept Ming rule. However, it did not work out; instead, the rebellious killing of the envoy by the Mongols brought subsequent diplomatic efforts to an end. Thus, with growing impatience, in 1381, Emperor Zhu Yuanzhang sent 300,000 army troops led by one of his most capable generals, Fu Youde, to invade the remaining Mongol forces in Yunnan, in an attempt to unify China. By 1382, Yunnan was defeated and China was unified.[24] The war resulted in widespread destruction and a massive loss of lives. Ma He's father, a faithful follower of the Liang Prince, was killed during the war. He was thirty-nine years of age then. Ma He was among the many young boys who were captured, castrated and sent back to the Ming Court to serve as eunuch slaves.[25] Ma He who was described as hardworking, courteous, alert and quick-witted, was soon given basic military training and was trained to fight in several battles.[26]

THE ADULT ZHENG HE

Due to the restructuring of the Ming army, Fu Youde's army came under the control of Emperor Zhu Yuanzhang's fourth son, Prince Yan, who was known as Zhu Di, in Beijing. In this process, Ma He was transferred to serve Zhu Di.[27] Growing up under the close watch of Zhu Di, the prince was convinced that Ma He was a man of high caliber.[28] Faithful, sincere and intelligent, Ma He won the confidence of Zhu Di over the years.[29] Zhu Di appointed Ma He as his trusted bodyguard,[30] groomed and entrusted him with important responsibilities. Since the attack on Yunnan, Ma He accompanied the Prince of Yan on all his military battles, learning the art of war, and fighting alongside with his master. He played a remarkably important role as a trusted bodyguard in the 1390s battle against the Mongols, where he served and protected Zhu Di at close range.[31]

Following the death of Emperor Zhu Yuanzhang in 1398, the throne was succeeded by his eldest grandson, as his eldest son had passed away. As this succession resulted in tension and grievances among the princes, the new emperor, Emperor Hui (Jianwen), heeded the advice of Defence Minister Qi Tai, and promptly reduced the princes' powers. Prince Yan (Zhu Di) thus used the imperial directive left by Zhu Yuanzhang before his death, which stated that the princes could rise to revolt against the court's unscrupulous officials, to stage a court revolt in 1399, the Battle of Jingnan.[32] As Zhu Guozhen in his *Huangming dazhengji* stated, Ma He was one of the most capable and intelligent eunuchs supporting the Yan Prince in his Jingnan Battle.[33] He was described to have fought fiercely beside Zhu Di and given him critical support in the mopping-up campaign. Emperor Jianwen was believed to have died or fled the country. In 1402, Zhu Di entered Nanjing and declared himself the third emperor of the Ming Dynasty, taking on the title of Ming Chengzhu or Emperor Yongle.[34]

As the *Ming Shi* (vol. 304) describes, "initially [Ma He] served in the mansion of Yan Prince. Later, he achieved merits in battles and was eventually promoted to become Grand Eunuch."[35] While the rank of Grand Director (*taijian*) was not high (corresponding to a prefect or mid-level administrator in the civil service),[36] it was the top position a eunuch could be promoted to; it held the upper grade of the fourth rank (4a for short) in the system of nine ranks that defined positions for Ming military officers and the civil officers.[37] In addition, regular and direct contact with the emperor accorded Ma He an importance beyond his formal position.[38] For his meritorious deeds, Emperor Yongle conferred him the family name "Cheng" (or "Zheng"). Ma He was thus known as Zheng He.[39]

Zhu Di also appointed Zheng He as the principal envoy and commander-in-chief to lead the grand voyages to the West. It was the first time in Chinese history that a eunuch had been given such an important military position. In addition, the emperor had utmost trust in Zheng He and presented him with blank scrolls stamped with his seal, so that Zheng He could issue imperial orders at sea.[40]

Zheng He's nickname Sanbao refers to the Buddhist "Three Treasures" or *Triratna*, which comprised of the Buddha, the Buddhist law (*dharma*), and the community (*sangha*) of Buddhist monks. While Zheng He was brought up in a devout Muslim family, he practised Buddhism and even adopted a Buddhist name. He also was a strong believer of Sea Goddess Tianfei, as evidenced by his inscriptions of 1431 at Liujiagang and Changle. Such was the eclectic nature of Zheng He's faith and religious beliefs.[41]

CHINA DURING THE SONG, YUAN AND MING DYNASTIES

Prior to the Ming Dynasty (and Emperor Yongle and Zheng He), the rulers of the Song and Yuan dynasties had already adopted an open-door policy to encourage foreign trade in China. For example, the Song Government set up offices of the Commissioners of Foreign Trade in various parts of China like Guangzhou and Mingzhou; they also sent envoys to foreign countries; and, for their people, they offered incentives to attract foreign ships to do business in China. The Yuan Court also pursued extensive measures to encourage foreign trade. Its trade relationships with Vietnam were described as close and cordial.[42]

However, during the Yuan Dynasty, there was a period of aggressive, military-based, territorial expansion which Emperor Ming Taizu (Zhu Yuanzhang) felt led to the downfall of the Yuan Dynasty. Thus, when he came into office, he opposed the use of force and adopted a friendly and peaceful foreign policy instead. To ensure that this was implemented, he went to the extent of issuing an imperial edict to warn his descendants that they should not invade foreign states:

> I fear that my descendants with no good reasons would go to war to show off China's wealth and strength, and cause loss of lives. [Therefore, I issue this non-invasion edict so that] you all must remember not to do that.[43]

In other words, peace and prosperity for China was the Ming Dynasty's vision as opposed to loss of lives and destruction in war. Emperor Ming Taizu even clearly designated fifteen states that were not to be invaded. They included Japan, Korea, Annam (Vietnam), Zhancheng (Champa in Central Vietnam), Zhenla (Cambodia), Siam (Thailand), Java, Sri Vijava (Palembang), Pahang, Samudra (Sumatra), Boni (Brunei) and others.[44]

During the Ming Dynasty, China was the richest and most advanced country in the world,[45] surpassing that of the Tang and Han dynasties.[46] Then, China was known as the "Middle Kingdom". Especially in the South where Zheng He lived, the economy was thriving because over the years of growth and development under the different dynasties, the maritime silk route began from there. Historically, businesses from the North moved South due to the prevalence of social unrest in the North. Ceramic and silk manufacturing and shipbuilding activities were key drivers of the economy and porcelain was China's major export commodity due to its durability. Additionally, there was a high demand for Arabic and Southeast Asian spices from the ruling classes of China;[47] thus trade was desirable in those days.

ZHENG HE'S MISSION[48]

After Emperor Yongle (Zhu Di) usurped the throne in 1403,[49] he continued to pursue Emperor Taizu's friendly and peaceful foreign policy. Emperor Yongle was very proactive in implementing his policy. Instead of waiting for foreign countries to send tribute missions to China, he actively dispatched Ming envoys to visit these countries. The mission of these envoys was to inform these foreign states of a new emperor in office and that the Ming Court would continue to pursue the friendly and peaceful foreign policy of its predecessor.[50]

In this context, Emperor Yongle also appointed Zheng He to lead grand voyages to the West to make manifest the wealth and power of the Middle Kingdom.[51] Zheng He was to spread the Chinese culture, maintain peace and forge friendly ties between China and countries in Southeast Asia and beyond. Zheng He's voyages were therefore a substantive representation of Emperor Yongle's foreign policy.[52]

For every voyage that Zheng He embarked on, the emperor would issue an imperial decree. The imperial decree would clearly state the mission of the voyage, the states that will be visited, and that gifts will be presented to the local rulers and chiefs. An example of the Imperial Decree (issued by Emperor Xuande for the seventh voyage) on Zheng He's Mission in the *Ming Shi Lu* is described as follows:

Imperial Decree on Zheng He's Mission in Ming Shi Lu[53]

On the 9th day of the 6th month in the 5th year of Xuande (1430), Zheng He was dispatched to visit foreign native states. The decree is as follows: I obeyed the decree of Heaven and inherited the throne from Emperors Taizu, Taizong and Renzong. Being the emperor of the universe with a reign title of Xuande, I fear that foreign native states located far away are not aware of it. Hence, I specially dispatch Eunuch Zheng He, Wang Jinghong etc. to notify them and urge them to rule in accordance with the ways of heaven, care for the people and share happiness. The mission will visit Hormuz, Ceylon, Calicut, Malacca, Cochin, Brava, Mogadishu, Lambri, Samudra, Lasa, Maldives, Aru, Ganbali, Aden, Dhofar, Juba, Kayal, 20 other states and the Palembang Commissioner of Pacification, and bestow gifts on their rulers and chiefs.

Another example of the Imperial Decree (as interpreted by a Singaporean playwright) is as follows:

Imperial Decree for Chief Eunuch Zheng He[54]

Now that the Ming Dynasty has firmly entrenched its majestic authority with heavenly blessings, with peace and prosperity prevailing upon the entire Zhong Hua nation, our attention should now turn to the coastal regions and our farther neighbours...It is therefore now my explicit wish that the power, prestige and splendour of the Imperial Court be extended once more to the farther shores. To expedite this historic mission, I appoint Grand Eunuch Zheng He Commander-in-Chief of the Imperial Expeditions. Details of the mission are herein listed: Go in power, authority and peace. Do justice to the grandeur and splendour of my Dynasty.

ZHENG HE'S PROMINENCE

From 1405–33, Zheng He led the world's largest ocean-going fleet in seven such epic and grand voyages to the West; six of these were during the reign of Emperor Yongle, while the seventh voyage was made at the decree of Emperor Xuande.

Zheng He's prominence today lies primarily in his leadership of these seven voyages. The voyages were epic in terms of their unprecedented fleet and crew sizes, as well as the long distances travelled; they were grand because of the sheer size of the so-called "treasure" ships that carried on board much of the royal gifts of the emperor that were to be bestowed upon the rulers of the different places he visited.

For every voyage, Zheng He mobilized over 100 (sometimes even more than 300) ships, including approximately 60 large ships to form the main body of the fleet, and over 20,000 crew members.[55] In his maiden voyage, for example, Zheng He had a crew of more than 27,000 men and a fleet of 317 ships.[56] His largest ships measured about 480ft by 194ft while the medium-sized ones measured about 399ft by 162ft.[57] Such vessels were considered colossal, and they reflected the advanced shipbuilding capabilities in China in the fifteenth century.[58]

Zheng He led the voyages through the vast ocean space and his fleet "with sails flying high like clouds, with a speed like stars shooting across the sky, cut through the rampaging waves as if they were strolling on a broad street".[59] Over the seven voyages, Zheng He made calls at more than thirty countries and territories, including present-day Vietnam, Thailand, Pahang, Kelantan, Java, Sumatra, Sri Lanka, India, Dhufar (Arabian Peninsular), Hormuz (Persian Gulf), Yemen, Mecca and Mogadishu in East Africa.[60] These voyages covered a total mileage of over 300,000 kilometres.[61]

Zheng He's prominence becomes even more obvious when we compare his voyages with those of the more renowned western navigators like Christopher Columbus, Vasco da Gama and Ferdinand Magellan. We pieced together Table 1.1 using data from the *Zheng He Epic*:[62]

TABLE 1.1

Zheng He's Voyages: Key Characteristics

Navigator	Number of Ships	Number of Crew	Tonnage
Zheng He (1405–33)	More than 100 (up to 317)	28,000	7000–8000 tons
Columbus (1492)	3 (Subsequent: 4–17)	88 (150–300)	100
Da Gama (1497)	4	170	120
Magellan (1519)	5	265	120

It is clear that in terms of timing, Zheng He's maiden voyage (in 1405) was made some eighty-seven years earlier than Christopher Columbus' arrival in America (in 1492). Similarly, Vasco da Gama sailed round the Cape of Good Hope to reach India some ninety-two years later than Zheng He's first voyage. And Ferdinand Magellan sailed round the world some 100 years after Zheng He's sixth voyage.

In terms of scale, Zheng He's fleet and crew sizes easily overwhelmed that of the later navigators. His ship sizes and tonnage also easily dwarfed those of the western navigators.

Evidently, Zheng He's prominence and success in these unprecedented epic grand voyages would suggest that we should pay attention to him. At the least, he should be made known to the larger world as much as the world today knows of the western navigators, who came onto the maritime scene only much later, and on a much smaller scale, than Zheng He did.

ZHENG HE FROM A MANAGEMENT PERSPECTIVE

Apart from the awe and grandeur attributed to Zheng He's fleet, a fundamental, puzzling question on Zheng He's seven voyages to the West remains: How were these voyages undertaken? How did Zheng He manage to move and feed his 27,000 plus men spread over 200–300 ships of unprecedented sizes seven times across the long and wide stretches of oceans that were in many places fraught with dangers and infested with pirates, and over long durations of 1.5 to 2 years, back in the early fifteenth century, without the help of modern-day communications and satellite technologies?

Evidently, Zheng He's success in leading these voyages would suggest that he had much capability in the realm of leadership and management; after all, it is obvious that these grand voyages were representative of careful and strategic planning, organization, coordination and control. In this regard, Zheng He had surely demonstrated much leadership and management capabilities than can be of relevance to today's businesses, leaders and managers.

Leadership

Studying Zheng He from a management perspective can therefore be fruitful and worthwhile. For example, what can we learn from Zheng He's background and growing up years that may have contributed to his subsequent work and apparent successes? After all, at the tender age of ten, Zheng He lost his father to the invading Ming imperial troops while he himself was among the thousands of young boys who were captured, castrated and sent to serve the Ming Court as eunuch slaves. By then, his life was no longer his own; he lived only because his masters allowed him to live; he had no idea of where he was going and what he would eventually grow up to be.[63] How did he end up serving as the emperor's commander-in-chief to lead the seven epic grand voyages? Surely there is inspiration and learning we can draw from this for the benefit of today's leaders.

By the same logic, how did Zheng He manage his relationship with his patron, the Emperor Yongle, who apparently trusted him enough to give him blank scrolls stamped with his imperial seal, so that Zheng He could issue imperial orders while at sea?[64] This has rich implications for today's managers in learning to manage their relationships with their immediate superiors.

Zheng He had been a land-based warrior and commander in the army; he knew a great deal about fighting on land and was well accustomed to battles. He fought alongside Zhu Di (the Emperor Yongle) on all his military missions, playing a major role in the 1390s fight against the Mongols.[65] Moving over to be commander-in-chief of an unprecedented fleet of hundreds of ships with tens of thousands of crew on the grand voyages down fairly uncharted maritime territories was therefore not a walk in the park for Zheng He. What did Zheng He do in managing such new assignments? How did he go about discharging his new mission? Again, Zheng He's acceptance and apparent successes in meeting this new challenge should tell us much about his leadership, management and command capabilities; we must therefore explore this further to draw lessons for businesses and leaders of today.

Human Resource Management

Further, as an army man rather than being a maritime commander, Zheng He must have known that without access to a wide pool of highly skilled maritime-oriented human capital, it would not have been possible for him to embark on his grand voyages and achieve notable success. Therefore Zheng He's access to places like Jiangnan, Taicang,[66] Changle[67] and Quanzhou,[68] offering highly skilled labour with the relevant expertise needed for the maritime expeditions, laid the foundation for recruiting his crew. In addition to selecting his crew, Zheng He also formed a team of close senior associates[69] to support him in achieving his mission. Zheng He's senior leadership team is akin to today's executive team that supports the modern-day CEO. What can we learn from Zheng He about his people skills and human resource management practices that can be of relevance to us today? How did he manage his team and crew to ensure that they stay together as a united whole while travelling to distant shores and peoples?

Logistics and Supply Chain Management

There is also much that we can learn from Zheng He in terms of the logistics and movement of people and materials. Preparing for and moving his massive fleet and crew over long distances and durations across the unknown oceans must have been a challenge, even for today's leaders and managers. How did Zheng He communicate and exercise command and control over his people during the actual movements across the open waters? As an example, we know that amongst the various ships on Zheng He's fleet, communications was made possible by an elaborate system of sound and sight signals.[70] But what relevance does this suggest for today's managers? Similarly, how did Zheng He ensure that his 27,000 plus men were well fed and kept healthy over the entire two-year duration of a given voyage? How did Zheng He store, protect and manage his supplies over each long voyage, including precious royal gifts and the large quantities of items used for trade? And where and how did Zheng He set up his supply and re-distribution centres along his itinerary route? Surely there must be rich lessons we can distill from the logistics and supply chain management practices of Zheng He for the benefit of today's supply chain managers.

Faith and Management

We have already introduced Zheng He as a Muslim Chinese, being born and brought up in a respectable Muslim family based in Yunnan and with the family name of "Ma". His father, Milijin, and his grandfather Chaermidena, both made pilgrimages to Mecca, and they were revered as "Haji".[71] Quite clearly, Zheng He was brought up in a devout Muslim family, with strong Islamic faith and awareness of Islam's religious heritage. How did this influence his fundamental mission in life? And how did this influence his relationship with his men throughout his many long voyages? How did Zheng He's faith practices contribute towards his mission success? What can we learn from Zheng He's practice of his religious faith?

The Bigger Message: Building Collaboration

Beyond all these specifics in the different areas of management and leadership practices, Zheng He apparently carried an even larger message for today's businesses and leaders through his management and discharge of his emperor-decreed mission.

We already know that Zheng He was charged by Emperor Yongle with the fundamental mission of pursuing a diplomacy of peace by spreading Chinese culture and forging friendly ties between China and countries in Asia and Africa.[72] Zheng He was to lead the voyages to the west to spread goodwill, help others progress, and in the process, network and build bridges for trade and collaboration, so that everyone would coexist peacefully and harmoniously as they were ruled in accordance with the ways of heaven,[73] and in this way, do justice to the grandeur and splendour of the Ming Imperial Court.[74]

This is in stark contrast to the European navigators such as Christopher Columbus and Vasco da Gama whose objectives were more commercial in nature and yet resulted in the colonization of new territories,[75] in many instances by force.[76] Their voyages opened up a new era of rising capitalism and colonial invasion of territories in Africa, expanding to South Asia and Southeast Asia.[77]

Zheng He's fulfillment of his emperor-decreed mission through his grand voyages therefore carried the much bigger message of pursuing peace, goodwill and collaboration for the benefit of all peoples. His fifteenth-century message and practices as demonstrated through his voyages represent what we consider in this book to be his fundamental contribution for the benefit of not only business leaders and managers, but for all mankind. We refer to this as Zheng He's *Art of Collaboration* and we introduce and present this in the next chapter as an alternative model to the very well-known and well studied Sun Zi's *Art of War*.

Perhaps Zheng He's message of goodwill and win-win in his *Art of Collaboration* may be especially relevant for our world of today that has been terrorized by fear since 9/11, fractured by wars since Afghanistan, threatened by the unknowns since SARS and the Avian Flu, and thrown into financial gloom and doom since the Lehman Brothers' collapse.

Endnotes

1. See, as examples: John Minford, *The Art of War* (U.S.: Penguin Books, 2002); C. H. Wee, *Sun Zi Bingfa: Selected Insights and Applications* (Singapore: Prentice Hall, 2005).

2. Yu Dan, *Professor Yu Dan Explains the Analects of Confucius* (Beijing: Zhonghua Book Company, 2006); translated and published as Esther Tyldesley, *Confucius from the Heart* (London: Pan Macmillan, 2009).

3. Tim Luard, "Swimming dragons", *BBC Radio*, 3 June 2005, <http://www.bbc.co.uk/radio4/history/swimming_dragons.shtml> (accessed 20 June 2010).

4. CCTV-8 TV Series, *Zheng He Xia Xiyang*, first aired in 2009; see <http://en.wikipedia.org/wiki/Zheng_He_Xia_Xiyang> (accessed 25 September 2011).

5. Tan Ta Sen, *Cheng Ho and Malacca* (Singapore: International Zheng He Society, 2005), p. 1.

6. Tan Ta Sen and Chia Lin Sien, eds., *The Zheng He Epic*, 1st edition in

Chinese edited by Zhou Wenlin et al. (Kunming, Yunnan, China: Yunnan's Publishing House, Yunnan Fine Arts Publishing House, Auora Publishing House, 2006), p. 48.

7. Kallie Szczepanski, "Zheng He, Ming China's Great Admiral", *About.com Asian History*, <http://asianhistory.about.com/od/china/p/zheng_he_bio.htm?p=1> (accessed 1 March 2011).

8. Edward L. Dreyer, *Zheng He: China and the Oceans in the Early Ming Dynasty, 1405–1433* (U.S.: Pearson Education, Inc., 2007), p. 11.

9. Louise E. Levathes, *When China Ruled the Seas* (U.S.: Oxford University Press, 1994), p. 64.

10. *Cheng Ho and Malacca*, p. 2.

11. *Zheng He Epic*, p. 48.

12. *Cheng Ho and Malacca*, p. 2.

13. *Cheng Ho and Malacca*, p. 2.

14. *When China Ruled the Seas*, p. 62.

15. *Zheng He Epic*, p. 48.

16. *When China Ruled the Seas*, p. 62.

17. *Zheng He Epic*, p. 55.

18. *When China Ruled the Seas*, p. 64.

19. *Zheng He Epic*, p. 55.

20. *Zheng He Epic*, pp. 55–57.

21. *Cheng Ho and Malacca*, p. 2.

22. *Zheng He Epic*, pp. 55–57.

23. *Zheng He: China and the Oceans in the Early Ming Dynasty*, p. 12.

24. *When China Ruled the Seas*, p. 57.

25. *Zheng He Epic*, p. 48.

26. *Cheng Ho and Malacca*, p. 3.

27. *Cheng Ho and Malacca*, p. 3.

28. *Zheng He Epic*, p. 68.

29. *Zheng He Epic*, p. 69.

30. *Cheng Ho and Malacca*, p. 3.

31. *When China Ruled the Seas*, p. 64.

32. *Cheng Ho and Malacca*, p. 3.

33. *Zheng He Epic*, p. 69.

34. *Cheng Ho and Malacca*, pp. 3–4.
35. *Zheng He Epic*, p. 68.
36. *Zheng He: China and the Oceans in the Early Ming Dynasty*, p. 22.
37. *Zheng He: China and the Oceans in the Early Ming Dynasty*, p. 5.
38. *Zheng He: China and the Oceans in the Early Ming Dynasty*, p. 22.
39. *Cheng Ho and Malacca*, p. 4; and *Zheng He: China and the Oceans in the Early Ming Dynasty*, p. 23.
40. *When China Ruled the Seas*, p. 87.
41. *Zheng He: China and the Oceans in the Early Ming Dynasty*, pp. 5 and 12.
42. *Zheng He Epic*, p. 8.
43. *Zheng He Epic*, p. 315.
44. *Zheng He Epic*, p. 315; and *Zheng He: China and the Oceans in the Early Ming Dynasty*, p. 16.
45. Tim Luard, "Swimming dragons", *BBC Radio*, 3 June 2005, <http://www.bbc.co.uk/radio4/history/swimming_dragons.shtml> (accessed 20 June 2010).
46. *Zheng He Epic: Mazu Temple in Changle*, p. 12.
47. *Zheng He Epic*, p. 8.
48. We follow in this book the general mainstream perspective of Zheng He's grand voyages as a peaceful means of portraying Ming China's splendour and glory, and spreading goodwill and promoting economic trade. We are aware that there are different views on this in the existing literature.
49. Chiu Ling-yeong, "Zheng He: Navigator, Discoverer and Diplomat", *Wu Teh Yao Memorial Lectures 2000* (Singapore: Unipress, Center for the Arts, National University of Singapore, 2001), p. 8.
50. *Zheng He Epic*, p. 316.
51. Zheng He's biography in *Mingshi 304.2b–4b*, as translated in Edward L. Dreyer, *Zheng He: China and the Oceans in the Early Ming Dynasty, 1405–1433* (U.S.: Pearson Education, Inc., 2007), p. 187.
52. *Zheng He Epic*, pp. 8–10.
53. *Zheng He Epic*, p. 316 (side bar).
54. From Kuo Pao Kun (playwright of "Descendants of the Eunuch Admiral"), as quoted in Paul Rozario, *Zheng He and the Treasure*

Fleet, 1405–1433 (Singapore: SNP International Publishing, 2005), p. 49.

55. *Zheng He Epic*, p. 352.
56. *When China Ruled the Seas*, p. 87.
57. *Zheng He Epic*, p. 352.
58. *Zheng He Epic*, p. 86.
59. *Zheng He Epic*, Preface.
60. *Cheng Ho and Malacca*, pp. 16–17.
61. *Zheng He Epic*, Preface.
62. *Zheng He Epic*, p. 352.
63. *Cheng Ho and Malacca*, pp. 2–3.
64. *When China Ruled the Seas*, p. 87.
65. *When China Ruled the Seas*, p. 64.
66. *Zheng He Epic*, p. 128.
67. *Zheng He Epic*, p. 159.
68. *Zheng He Epic*, p. 185.
69. *Zheng He: Navigator, Discoverer and Diplomat*, pp. 14–15.
70. *When China Ruled the Seas*, p. 83.
71. *Cheng Ho and Malacca*, p. 2.
72. *Zheng He Epic*, p. 318.
73. *Zheng He Epic*, p. 316 (side bar; decree of Emperor Xuande).
74. *Zheng He and the Treasure Fleet*, p. 49.
75. The Applied History Research Group, *The Sea-Route to India & Vasco da Gama*, The University of Calgary, 2007, <http://www.ucalgary.ca/applied_history/tutor/eurvoya/vasco.html> (accessed 22 June 2010).
76. *Zheng He Epic*, p. 318.
77. Ma Chaoqun, Professor of History, Yunnan Normal University, as quoted in *Zheng He Epic*, p. 352.

References

CCTV-8 TV Series. *Zheng He Xia Xiyang*. First aired in 2009. <http://en.wikipedia.org/wiki/Zheng_He_Xia_Xiyang > (accessed 25 September 2011.

Chiu Ling-yeong. "Zheng He: Navigator, Discoverer and Diplomat".

Wu Teh Yao Memorial Lectures 2000. Singapore: Unipress, Center for the Arts, National University of Singapore, 2001.

Dreyer, Edward L. *Zheng He: China and the Oceans in the Early Ming Dynasty, 1405–1433*. U.S.: Pearson Education, Inc., 2007.

Levathes, Louise E. *When China Ruled the Seas: The Treasure Fleet of the Dragon Throne, 1405–1433*. U.S.: Oxford University Press, 1994.

Luard, Tim. "Swimming dragons". *BBC Radio*, 3 June 2005, <http://www.bbc.co.uk/radio4/history/swimming_dragons.shtml> (accessed 20 June 2010).

Minford, John. *The Art of War*. U.S.: Penguin Books, 2002.

Rozario, Paul. *Zheng He and the Treasure Fleet, 1405–1433*. Singapore: SNP International Publishing, 2005.

Szczepanski, Kallie. "Zheng He, Ming China's Great Admiral". *About.com Asian History*. <http://asianhistory.about.com/od/china/p/zheng_he_bio.htm?p=1> (accessed 1 March 2011).

Tan Ta Sen. *Cheng Ho and Malacca*. Singapore: International Zheng He Society, 2005.

Tan Ta Sen and Chia Lin Sien, eds. *The Zheng He Epic*. 1st edition in Chinese edited by Zhou Wenlin et al. Kunming, Yunnan, China: Yunnan People's Publishing House, Yunnan Fine Arts Publishing House, Auora Publishing House, 2006.

Wee, C. H. *Sun Zi Bingfa: Selected Insights and Applications*. Singapore: Prentice Hall, 2005.

Yu Dan. *Professor Yu Dan Explains the Analects of Confucius*. Beijing: Zhonghua Book Company, 2006. Translated and published as Esther Tyldesley. *Confucius from the Heart*. London: Pan Macmillan, 2009.

Chapter 2

ZHENG HE'S ART OF COLLABORATION (AoC)
An Alternative Model to Sun Zi's Art of War (AoW)

INTRODUCTION

Much has been written on the grand voyages of Admiral Zheng He from the historical, diplomatic, cultural and maritime perspectives. We have therefore come to understand and appreciate Zheng He's body of work and contributions along these dimensions. Yet clearly, in planning, organizing, directing and controlling these voyages through uncharted geographic waters in the early fifteenth century, Zheng He demonstrated much capability in the realm of management and leadership that can be translated for the benefit of today's managers and leaders. However, little has been written from this management perspective about Zheng He.

In this chapter,[1] we draw from existing literature to provide a version of what we refer to as Zheng He's *Art of Collaboration* (AoC). We present this as Zheng He's alternative to the Art of War (AoW) of Sun Zi.

Because much has been written on Sun Zi's AoW, today's managers and leaders have come to learn from this Chinese classic by viewing business as warfare. One of Sun Zi's most popular strategies is "If you know the enemy and know yourself, you need not fear the result of a hundred battles".[2] It can be deduced from this quote that one should approach doing business like fighting a war, and that one should treat competitors like enemies.

While this can be helpful, we present here an alternative model in Zheng He's AoC that can perhaps be even more relevant in today's world. In the recent years, more emphasis has been placed on creating peace and stability in the world. For instance, in 2009, U.S. President Barack Obama was awarded the Nobel Peace Prize for "his extraordinary efforts to strengthen international diplomacy and co-operation between peoples".[3] This captured the attention of many who recognize that adopting a peaceful approach towards collaboration is a more sustainable solution than aggression, antagonism and colonization.

This notion of creating peace and stability to benefit mankind is manifested in Zheng He's grand voyages. We have sketched out some of Zheng He's practices and apparent strategies, and have categorized them into the 4Cs — Capability-building, Coordination, Communication and Continuity. Together, these 4C strategies demonstrate Zheng He's Art of building the much needed Collaboration for the benefit of governments, businesses and the man on the street.

This chapter is therefore organized as follows. In the next section, we provide a brief on the historical context for Zheng He's grand voyages. Here, we focus especially on his mission as dictated by the Emperor Yongle whom he served. We interpret this mission as that of building peaceful collaboration amongst peoples and nations. In the following section, we will then present the apparent 4C strategies that Zheng He adopted in fulfilling the mission given to him. Together, they represent Zheng He's *Art of Collaboration*. We then conclude the chapter by highlighting some implications of Zheng He's collaboration model by relating to present-day examples.

HISTORICAL CONTEXT FOR ZHENG HE'S VOYAGES

We have earlier described in chapter 1 that prior to Ming China, the rulers of the two preceding dynasties of Song and Yuan had already adopted open-door policies to encourage and support trade activities with foreign countries. The Song Government, for example, had set up offices in places like Guangzhou, Mingzhou, Quanzhou and Mizhou Banqiao to facilitate foreign trade; they had also purposely sent envoys to the foreign countries. Song China even specifically offered rewards to their people to attract foreign ships to do business in China. At that time, the foreigners who were based in China were also given many privileges. Similarly, the Yuan Court also supported foreign trade.[4]

When Emperor Zhu Yuanzhang came into office under the Ming banner at the end of Yuan China, he adopted a friendly and peaceful foreign policy. Emperor Zhu Yuanzhang had held the conclusion that the fall of the Yuan Dynasty was largely due to its territorial military aggression. He therefore wanted a China that seeks peace and prosperity rather than loss of lives and destruction through war. To ensure that his vision for peace was implemented, he even issued an imperial edict to warn his descendents that they should not invade foreign states.[5]

When Emperor Yongle came to the throne in 1403,[6] he continued to pursue Emperor Zhu Yuanzhang's friendly and peaceful foreign policy. Emperor Yongle actively dispatched Ming envoys to visit the foreign countries. He also appointed Zheng

He to lead grand voyages to the West to spread Chinese culture and forge friendly ties between China and countries in Southeast Asia, South Asia and Africa. Zheng He's voyages were therefore carried out as part of the overall representation of Emperor Yongle's peaceful foreign policy.[7] Also, by the time of Zheng He's grand voyages, Ming China was the richest and most advanced country in the world,[8] surpassing that of the Tang and Han dynasty.[9] China therefore had much to offer the world then.

ZHENG HE'S MISSION

It is clear from the context described above that Zheng He's fundamental mission was to pursue a diplomacy of peace by spreading Chinese culture[10] and forging friendly ties between China and countries in Asia and Africa.[11] Zheng He was to go out to help others progress, spread goodwill and in the long run, network and build bridges for collaboration, so that everyone would coexist peacefully and harmoniously. This is in stark contrast to navigators such as Christopher Columbus and Vasco da Gama whose objectives were more commercial in nature and yet resulted in the colonization of new territories.[12]

In fact, every time Zheng He embarked on an expedition, an imperial decree would be issued by the emperor where the objectives of the voyage and countries to be visited would be stated clearly on it. The imperial decrees also stated that gifts would be bestowed on the local rulers and chiefs. Evidence of the imperial decrees can be found in Nanjing's Mazu Temple.

An example of an imperial decree is as follows:

Imperial Decree (by Emperor Xuande)
on Zheng He's Mission in Ming Shi Lu[13]

On the 9th day of the 6th month in the 5th year of Xuande (1430), Zheng He was dispatched to visit foreign native states. The decree is as follows: I obeyed the decree of Heaven and inherited the throne from Emperors Taizu, Taizong and Renzong. Being the emperor of the universe with a reign title of Xuande, I fear that foreign native states located far away are not aware of it. Hence, I specially dispatch Eunuch Zheng He, Wang Jinghong etc. to notify them and urge them to rule in accordance with the ways of heaven, care for the people and share happiness. The mission will visit Hormuz, Ceylon, Calicut, Malacca, Cochin, Brava, Mogadishu, Lambri, Samudra, Lasa, Maldives, Aru, Ganbali, Aden, Dhofar, Juba, Kayal, 20 other states and the Palembang Commissioner of Pacification, and bestow gifts on their rulers and chiefs.

An abbreviated and slightly differently translated version of the above edict is as follows:[14]

The new reign of Xuande has commenced, and everything shall begin anew. [But] distant lands beyond the seas have not yet been informed. I send eunuchs Zheng He and Wang Jinghong with this imperial order to instruct these countries to follow the way of Heaven with reverence and to watch over their people so that all might enjoy the good fortune of lasting peace.

Another example of an Imperial Decree:

Imperial Decree by Emperor Yongle
(Issued to Zheng He before his Third Voyage in 1409)[15]

I, the emperor, send my words to the kings and chieftains of foreign states in the far west, that I follow heaven's order to rule the world, to execute heaven's will to grant blessings and virtues. It is my wish that in all lands covered with sunshine and showered with moonlight, and moistened by frost and dew, its people, regardless of age, may be granted a stable livelihood, and a safe shelter. Today, I send Zheng He to spread my message. All must obey heaven's will and follow my words, and know your limits. Do not bully the minority. Do not attack the weak. All should share in the prosperity of peaceful times. If you wish to pay tribute to my court, you will be bestowed with gifts of goodwill. I send my edict to let you know my message.

It is clear from these examples that Zheng He's emperor-decreed mission was to spread goodwill and peace so that people everywhere could share in the prosperity of peaceful times.

ZHENG HE'S ART OF COLLABORATION

To discharge his mission of bringing goodwill and peace to all so that collaboration may be built and trade may prevail, Zheng He's practices and strategies in his many voyages can be categorized into the 4Cs — Capability-building, Coordination, Communication and Continuity. We refer to this as Zheng He's 4C strategies that collectively define his *Art of Collaboration*.

The first two C strategies of Capability-building and Coordination may be understood as Zheng He's Preparation for Collaboration. The third C strategy of Communication may be seen as Zheng He's actual Acts of Collaboration on the ground, and it comprises the 5 specific Acts of Articulating Intent, Practising Generosity, Building Win-Win, Ensuring Sustainability and Cultivating Trust. And the final C strategy of Continuity refers to Zheng He's long view of patience and consistency within his *Art of Collaboration*.

CAPABILITY-BUILDING

This refers to Zheng He's art of building collaboration from a position of strength. This position of strength is developed from having both human and technological capabilities. This first strategy therefore refers primarily to the building of capabilities needed to bring Zheng He and China towards the table of collaboration. It may therefore be understood as part of Zheng He's attempt to prepare for collaboration. (Ming China already had much that may be placed on the collaboration table itself; in Southeast Asia, for example, Chinese ceramics had become a symbol of wealth among the local people. Zheng He recognized this and brought Chinese ceramics as gifts.)[16]

In Zheng He's voyages, he evidently attached much importance to this strategy of Capability-building as part of his art of building collaboration. We can see Zheng He's Capability-building in two dimensions: building human capital (leadership, specialist knowledge and ground knowledge), and building technological capital (ships, ports and navigational technologies). While such capabilities are essential to help Zheng He build pathways towards collaboration with other countries, such capabilities in themselves are also very attractive. With brilliant, knowledgeable leaders and crew members, and advanced state-of-the-art technologies and resources, others can be attracted to want to participate in collaboration.

Human Capital

Securing Continuing Corporate Sponsorship

Zheng He had the strong corporate sponsorship of Zhu Di, the Emperor Yongle. While the emperor himself was evidently a very capable leader with a clear vision for building peaceful ties with neighbouring countries and engaging them in trade,[17] Zheng He ensured that he had the continuing support of the emperor by maintaining close and frequent linkages with the latter. In fact, often times during his voyages, he would defer important decisions to the emperor, as in the sentencing of pirate Chen Zuyi,[18] the Ceylonese King Alagakkonara (also referred to as Alakeswara),[19] and the rebel Sekander.[20] Zheng He after all was in control of a 27,000-strong army, and thousands of miles away from the emperor; he could have proceeded to execute them. Hence, by capturing the aggressors alive and leaving the final say to the emperor, Zheng He established himself as one who respects the emperor, and thus, won his trust to continue leading one expedition after another. Such strong emperor sponsorship is an important element that helped in Zheng He's discharge of his mission of building collaboration.

Selecting the Right Person to Lead the Mission

Zhu Di knew Zheng He very well and was fully convinced that he was a man of high caliber. As a young eunuch slave serving in Prince Yan's residence, Zheng He grew up under the close watch of Zhu Di. He was apparently faithful, sincere and intelligent and won the confidence of Zhu Di over the years.[21] In fact, Zheng He accompanied the Prince of Yan on all his military battles, learning the art of war, fighting side by side with his master, and playing a significant role against the Mongols in the 1390s.[22]

Zheng He was also described as ambitious from young, intelligent and had a good memory.[23] He liked to read classic books and had read Confucius and Mencius.[24] On a Ma Haji Epitaph, it was recorded that Zheng He had often asked his father and grandfather about their adventures to Mecca. When he was young, Zheng He apparently used to hang out at the jetty area and watch all the shipping and trading activities. It was in Kunyang that he picked up his early lessons in sailing and shipping.[25]

It is clear that Emperor Yongle made the right choice in appointing Zheng He to lead the grand voyages. This is an important element in human capital selection and development that is crucial in Zheng He's overall art of building collaboration.

Supporting the Leader with a Team of Senior Associates

Zheng He's success in his grand voyages can also be attributed to his team of close senior associates, the equivalent of today's senior leadership team that supports the CEO. Apart from Zheng He himself, the literature records a team of senior eunuchs who accompanied Zheng He to the western seas: Wang Jinghong, Hou Xian, Li Xing, Zhu Liang, Zhou Meng, Hong Bao, Yang Chen, Zhang Da and Wu Zhong. These men were either experienced sailors or "old hands" in dealing with affairs of foreign countries. Of these men, Wang Jinghong and Hou Xian were particularly important to Zheng He because of their diplomatic linkages to several of the countries in the western seas then.[26]

Enlisting People with Specialist Skills for the Mission

Beyond the leader and his team of close senior associates, the Zheng He's *Art of Collaboration* also placed importance in building a specialist team that provides expertise in various specific areas to support the mission.

For example, in the first of the seven grand voyages, the *Zheng He Jiapu* recorded these specialists as including: 7 imperial eunuchs serving as envoys; 10 proctors serving as deputy envoys; 10 junior eunuchs; 53 eunuch-chamberlains; 2 regional military commissioners; 93 guard commanders; 104 battalion commanders; 403 company commanders; 1 director from the Ministry of Revenue; 2 officers from the Court of State Ceremonial; 2 drafters; 1 instructor; 1 Yingyang officer and 4 assistants; 108 medical officers and medical assistants; and 26,803 military officers, chosen officers, strong men, soldiers, cooks, interpreters and clerks.[27]

On interpreters and knowledge of foreign languages in particular, Emperor Yongle saw the need for capability in proper communication. He therefore had a *Siyi Guan* set up in Nanjing to train people to be proficient in foreign languages. Zheng He appointed well-known interpreters including Ma Huan and Feixin to be part of his fleet.[28]

To look after the health of his approximately 27,000 crew members, Zheng He carefully put together a specialized medical team where on average, it was one medical officer for 150 crew members. Some of these specialists came from the palace's elite medical institution and some were famous local medical practitioners. The medical team also conducted studies of local diseases and their cures in order to help them take the necessary precautions to safeguard the health of the crew. Such a well-organized medical team with the requisite knowledge and medical facilities on board was unprecedented in maritime history then. During the voyages, the team also collected local medicinal herbs and learned of local medical treatment methods. They also helped promote the exchange of medicine between China and the Afro-Asian countries by opening the door to import foreign herbs to China.[29]

In Quanzhou, Zheng He also specifically recruited technicians with knowledge of the sea routes and skilled navigators and shipbuilders.[30]

Building up a Repository of Ground Knowledge
Even as Zheng He embarked on his grand voyages, his fleet was conducting "market surveys" in the various places he visited. They collected data on local methods of trading, local products, local currencies and the demand for their Chinese products. In this way, much first-hand ground data on the desirability of China's products in Southeast Asian, Indian, Persian and East African markets were gathered. Such information showed that China's products have much potential in these overseas markets. Zheng He thus continued to build ground knowledge and capabilities

pertaining to each city or country he visited. This was clearly aimed at facilitating the opening up of new markets and extending China's influences. He was preparing Ming China for the long-term development of peaceful foreign trade,[31] an outcome from his *Art of Collaboration*.

Culturally, Zheng He sought to build the capability of being adaptable and he ensured that his fleet respected local customs. Wherever they travelled, they would approach the local people as friendly neighbours, respecting customs and traditions and treating them as equals. While spreading Chinese culture, Zheng He and his fleet also sought to learn from the cultural practices of the local people. In this way, they established friendly ties with the people they visited and prepared the way for peaceful collaboration.[32]

Technological Capital

Building the Largest and State-of-the-Art Fleet
Apart from human capital, Zheng He also paid close attention to building technological capital (ships, ports and navigational technologies). Such capabilities not only helped to pave the pathways that led Zheng He and his crew to the countries in the "western sea", but they are also attractive in themselves and that helped to draw others into collaboration, trade and peaceful coexistence.

To complete his many expeditions to the West, Zheng He had to first manage the construction of the world's largest and state-of-the-art fleet then. For every voyage, Zheng He mobilized more than 100 ships of various types, with more than 60 large and medium-sized treasure ships forming the main body of the fleet. The first expedition was reportedly the grandest with 208 ships.[33]

Some of Zheng He's ships were built in Fujian; many of them were also built in the Treasure Ship Shipyard in Nanjing which was a well-known ancient shipyard in China. A large ship measured some 444 *chi* (12.5 inches in a *chi*) long and 180 *chi* wide while a medium-sized ship was 370 *chi* long and 150 *chi* wide. Such vessels were considered colossal then, and they reflected China's very advanced shipbuilding technology.[34]

A large four-claw iron anchor was excavated in 1981 in Quanzhou Bay. It was referred to by Zheng He as the "heavenly stabilizing needle" weighing some 758 kg. It was used by a ship that weighed some 400 tons. Evidently, it was part of the technology that was built to endure the worst of storms along the long journeys of Zheng He's expeditions.[35]

Port Selection and Development

As a crucial part of Zheng He's preparation for his grand voyages, he must select and develop an ideal port as an assembly point because of the magnitude and duration of the expeditions, the considerable manpower to be mobilized and the large amounts of provisions to be acquired. The Emperor Yongle and Zheng He made the wise choice of Taicang because of its political, economic and cultural strengths, and also its excellent port facilities.[36]

Liujiagang in Taicang had a natural deep water harbour with wide and spacious berths to cater to Zheng He's fleet both before they set sail and also when they returned. Because of the massive amount of provisions (food and daily necessities) required to feed the 27,000 crew and the cargo (silver and gold coins, ceramics, spices, tools etc.) to be used as gifts and for trade with other countries, Zheng He must select a viable collection and distribution centre of these provisions and cargo. Quite readily, Taicang fitted the bill.[37]

In addition, Zheng He selected Taicang because it was able to offer skilled manpower and expertise in navigation and it also allowed him to keep close contact between the Ming Court and the fleet as it took just a day's voyage to reach Nanjing from Taicang (which was 696 *li* by road and 712 *li* by sea from Nanjing).[38]

Navigational Technology

Zheng He's expeditions also built capabilities in the realm of navigational technologies. "With full sails flying high, the fleet sailed day and night. Despite storms, the fleet sailed like walking along the road." This was clearly guided by the application of navigational technologies, including the use of knowledge relating to characteristics of the monsoon winds and seasons.[39]

Some of the navigational technologies developed and used by Zheng He included: the Water Floating Compass, the Landmark Piloting Method in conjunction with the Zheng He Navigational Map, Astronomical Navigation (the "Star Observation Across Oceans" technique), and the use of "Geng" and a "Sand Hour-Glass" to measure the depth of water, speed and time.[40]

Zheng He's Navigational Map in particular reflected China's high level of technological development in the sphere of maritime navigation.[41] Zheng He's fleet had applied the most advanced navigational technologies of the day to guide ships to sail safely through the waters from Asia to Africa. Such technological capital helped to engender awe and marvel amongst the local peoples in the visited countries, thereby helping Zheng He in fulfilling his mission by drawing them into collaboration and peaceful trade with China.

COORDINATION

This refers to Zheng He's art of building collaboration by pulling resources to work together as an integrated whole. This second strategy is therefore aimed at Coordination: the careful, strategic and operational coordination of Zheng He's massive fleet and crew so that they may work collectively towards facilitating trade and collaboration with the locals in the countries that they visited. This Coordination strategy can be seen as an extension of the first strategy of Capability-building since Coordination is in itself the building of Organization Capital that serves as the means that brings people together in achieving a common end. It may therefore also be understood as part of Zheng He's attempt to prepare for collaboration.

Coordinating to Deal with External Factors

For a fleet of some 200 ships and a crew of some 27,000 men, the most suitable time to gather and set sail together called for careful coordination. This is especially so since the navigation waters are subject to external winds and storms.

From experience, the Chinese people knew the characteristics of the monsoons and Zheng He's fleet made full use of seasonal monsoons in coordinating their voyages. The monsoons change in the fourth to fifth month and reverse in the tenth month each year. Zheng He's fleet therefore set sail to the West in winter using the northeast monsoon while returning to China by the southwest monsoon.[42]

Zhu Yunming's *Qianwenji* which recorded Zheng He's seventh voyage to the West provided important data on how the fleet made use of the monsoons to travel: 19 January 1431 — Zheng He and his companions set sail from Long Wan; 8 April 1431 — Reached Changle River; 12 January 1432 — Reached Wuhumen and left for Champa. From this log, it is clear that from Long Wan to Wuhumen, Zheng He had to coordinate his fleet to wait patiently for about one year before they set sail for Champa;

they had to stay in the Fujian waters because of the winter monsoon.[43] And he carefully coordinated his fleet to take refuge in Changle's Taiping port since it had the least chance of being hit by typhoons.[44]

Coordinating to Harness Internal Capabilities

Zheng He designed and used different ships to help him coordinate the different functions that needed to be performed by these ships. The ships therefore come under several categories according to their function and use: treasure ships, battle ships, grain ships, water ships and horse ships. Each ship was given a formal name (such as "Qinghe", "Huikang", "Changnin", "Anji") and each name was followed by a number.[45] These no doubt helped in the entire coordination process.

Zheng He also apparently coordinated his seven grand voyages in two phases. The first phase comprised the first three expeditions; in his first expedition, the main destinations he visited were Champa, Java, Sumatra, Ceylon, Calicut and Palembang. Gradually, he increased the main destinations over subsequent voyages to include visits to Malacca, Siam, Brunei, Quilon, Cochin, Kayal, etc. Only in the second phase from the fourth expedition onwards did he lead his fleet to venture out towards places like Hormuz, Mogadishu, Aden, and Malindi on the African coast.[46] This also shows that Zheng He built his internal capabilities gradually and made sure that his crew succeeded in their less demanding challenges before taking on more difficult ones.

On his various expeditions, as Zheng He himself could not visit all the countries, he had to coordinate his deputies to act on his behalf. To facilitate this, he explicitly created a structure comprising the main fleet led by himself which was called the *dazong* and those led by his deputies which were called the *fenzong* (branch fleets). The latter would leave the former in cities like Champa, Sumatra, Ceylon, Calicut and Quilon and sail to their assigned countries. Then as part of the overall coordination, all the *fenzong* and the *dazong* would assemble in Malacca after accomplishing their respective missions. Zheng He had set up his depot in Malacca which was therefore significantly fortified; and while they awaited the summer monsoon for their homeward journey, various treasures and materials, including important documents, were kept away safely there.[47]

Ma Huan (Zheng He's interpreter) provided some details on this systematizing process instituted by Zheng He at the Malaccan depot, as recorded in Ma Huan's book (the *Yingya Shenglan*):

> Whenever the treasure ships of the Middle Kingdom arrived there, they at once erected a line of stockading, like a city-wall, and set up towers for the watch-drums at four gates; at night they had patrols of guards carrying bells; inside, again, they erected a second stockade, like a small city-wall, [within which] they constructed warehouses and granaries; [and] all the money and provisions were stored in them. The ships which had gone to various countries returned to this place and assembled; they repaired [their vessels] and marshalled the local goods and loaded them in the ships; [then] waited till the south wind was perfectly favourable.[48]

Because of the massive size of his fleet and crew that were spread out over the vast expanse of the navigational waters, Zheng He had to consciously coordinate them in order to effectively discharge his fundamental mission of building collaboration with and spreading goodwill amongst the locals. In Zheng He's *Art of Collaboration*, this strategy of Coordination is therefore crucial in constructing the organizational glue that rallies the ships and crew together in achieving the overall mission.

COMMUNICATION

This third strategy of Communication may be seen as Zheng He's actual Acts of Collaboration on the ground. It involves communication in words as well as in actions, and refers to Zheng He's conscious and active efforts in building collaboration with others. It comprises the 5 specific Acts of Articulating Intent, Practising Generosity, Building Win-Win, Ensuring Sustainability and Cultivating Trust.

Act of Articulating Intent

This refers to Zheng He's act of building collaboration through consciously articulating his mission and values to others, making his purpose and objectives transparent to all, and communicating in words his intent and desire for collaboration. This is in contrast to Sun Zi's mindset that "all warfare is based on deception".[49]

Upon arrival at each destination on his voyages, Zheng He therefore communicated his emperor-decreed mission to others and sought to reassure the locals and rulers in *words* by having the imperial decree read out in public. The imperial decree was an in-principle guarantee of the purpose of his visits to their countries. By announcing the Ming Court's vision of peace and stability and his maritime mission undertaken to achieve that vision, Zheng He was able to give the locals the peace of mind that his large fleet's visit was not a threat. Oftentimes, Zheng He would also read out the imperial decree on the imperial appointments which represented the emperor's endorsement and respect for the authority of the local rulers.[50]

Indeed, Emperor Yongle had great foresight and saw the need to maintain China's ties with other countries in order to create peace and stability. His vision was that if there were peace and friendly ties amongst nations, trade would prosper and all peoples would benefit. To support Zheng He in his mission, Emperor Yongle sent out groups of envoys to vassal states to notify them that a new emperor was on the throne and that the Ming Court was committed to maintaining the friendly and peaceful foreign policy of the previous emperor.[51]

However, the emperor's decree in words can only be worth as much as Zheng He's *actions* on the ground. We therefore see Zheng He engaged in 4 other specific Acts of Collaboration on the ground.

Act of Practising Generosity

This refers to Zheng He's practice on the ground of developing collaboration by being generous towards others. This generosity takes the form of gift-giving as well as sharing of resources, knowledge and technology, thereby generating goodwill which lays the foundation for collaboration.

While a large part of gift-giving gestures was diplomatic formality, often instructed by the emperor according to the rites of the Ming Court, there was no strings attached to these gifts and there was no expectation of a fair return. In fact, to demonstrate the generosity of China, Zheng He practised *"Hou Wang Bo Lai* [give more than receive]",[52] which was strongly advocated by Emperor Hongwu.[53]

Zheng He did not stop building goodwill at the government and official level. After presenting the emperor's edict and official gifts to the local rulers and chieftains, he often spent time interacting with the locals, extending the gift-giving gesture into sharing of China's resources and knowledge, and hence enhanced collaborative relations with the civilians of these foreign lands.

For example, he presented Chinese almanacs to neighbouring countries such as Champa and Ryukyu to help local people there enhance the quality of life as well as to help them understand the Chinese custom.[54] In 1417, after the envoys of Pahang, Calicut and Java visited China together, Zheng He sent the envoys home on board his treasure ships during his fifth voyage, showing his willingness to share what he had with others.[55]

Act of Building Win-Win

This refers to Zheng He's act of building win-win collaboration by facilitating trade with the peoples and countries he visited. This specific act of collaboration may be seen as Zheng He's attempt at ensuring sustainability of the collaborative relationship as no collaboration will last if it is only one party giving generously while the other merely receives without offering anything in return.

Apparently, the Emperor Yongle supported Zheng He in this by allowing private trade, lifting earlier restrictions on pepper and gold.[56] And while he issued his imperial orders for materials to be gathered for building Zheng He's treasure fleet, provinces were also instructed to supply these ships with goods that were in demand for trading abroad. These included silk and cotton cloth, as well as large quantities of iron, salt, hemp, tea wine, oil, and candles.[57]

On the other hand, import data from records in *Minghui Dian*, *Ming Shi*, and *Yingya Shenglan* showed that foreign goods imported into China during the period of Zheng He's voyages were of as many as 191 different types, including metal goods, medical herbs, precious gems, food items, fabric, spices, household items, wood, flora and fauna, and various raw materials.[58] In fact, the import of more than 160 different types of goods was directly linked with Zheng He's voyages. Among these goods, pepper was found to be the highest in terms of import quantity.[59] Amongst all these imports, apparently only twenty-three types were of precious gems and other luxurious items meant for the imperial family. The majority were still daily necessities that eventually flowed to the open market.

Apart from official trade transactions between Zheng He's fleet and the foreign government, crew members of the fleet also engaged extensively in business activities with the people of these countries.[60] The *Yingya Shenglan* recorded that in Siam, crew members used small boats to trade with the natives.[61] Zheng He's fleet was also especially welcomed in Dhofar. It was recorded that after Zheng He had presented the imperial edict and gifts, the King of Dhofar sent his men to inform all the natives to come and trade with Zheng He.[62] Quite clearly, both the crew and the natives had gained materially and directly from Zheng He's voyages.

By building and facilitating such win-win trading relations, both China and the countries Zheng He visited enjoyed greater material benefits and prospered together. Such trade collaborations also translated into a greater interdependence that binded China closer to these foreign states.

Act of Ensuring Sustainability

This refers to Zheng He's act of securing an external environment that would facilitate peaceful diplomatic and mutually-beneficial trade activities. This would then ensure the sustainability of the overall collaborative environment and relationship.

To help create peace that facilitated trade, Zheng He went out to capture the criminals who were preventing social stability. For instance, in 1407, Zheng He obeyed the instructions of the Ming Emperor to go to Palembang to apprehend bandits and pirates who were posing a threat to the Straits of Malacca. Zheng He thus captured chief pirate Chen Zuyi and brought him back to Nanjing where he was executed under the emperor's order.[63]

Another example was that relating to the capture of Alagakkonara. Although he was not a pirate himself, he was a contributor to the piracy problem rampant in Ceylon at that time. As recorded in *Ming Taizong Shilu*, Alagakkonara bore evil intentions. As a ruler, he oppressed his people, bullied his neighbour[64] and robbed foreign envoys visiting or passing through Ceylon.[65] Besides, his oppression forced his people to become pirates to earn a living. Hence, the piracy problem was serious in that region.[66] All neighbouring states suffered as a result.[67] After Zheng He had captured Alagakkonara and a new ruler was installed, the piracy problem was mitigated and this benefited the countries and traders in the region as it became much safer for them to sail and carry out their trade activities.

Act of Cultivating Trust

This refers to Zheng He's conscious act on the ground of always seeking to build trust with all the countries and peoples he visited through both economic and non-economic activities and interactions.

Thus, even as Zheng He carried out Emperor Yongle's policy of foreign diplomacy (articulating the intent of spreading peace and goodwill for all), treated the local rulers and their peoples respectfully and generously (practising generosity), forged friendly ties and initiated trade with the countries he visited (building win-win collaboration with all), secured an external environment that was stable, peaceful and pirates-safe (ensuring a sustainable collaborative environment), Zheng He was at the same time cultivating and earning trust for the long term through all these "acts of collaboration".

What was equally important in cultivating trust lies also in what Zheng He did not do. In all of his voyages and visits, Zheng He carried himself as a man of integrity. He did not engage in any conquests, killing, looting or destruction.[68] Although there were some 27,000 crew and 200 ships involved in the expeditions, none of his expeditions resulted in the occupation of a single inch of territory.[69] Such non-antagonistic, non-aggressive and non-colonization behaviours and actions on the ground clearly helped to engender trust and goodwill amongst the peoples he visited.[70]

Zheng He also went the extra mile and showed that he cared for the peoples. At ports of call, Zheng He directed the 150 medical officers designated to treat the crew to also treat local patients.[71] This showed that he had compassion for the sick. This touched the hearts of the locals and helped Zheng He to establish trust and credibility with them.

Zheng He also sought to establish other means of connection with the locals. As an example, before his fourth voyage, Zheng He made the long journey to Xi'an in Shaanxi to personally invite Hasan, the spiritual leader of the Qingjing Mosque, to join the expedition as a translator and adviser.[72] This was clearly a conscious effort on Zheng He's part to have Hasan help him in linking with the locals more effectively. Similarly, in his second visit to Ceylon, Zheng He erected an unusual trilingual stone tablet. The Chinese portion of the tablet praised Buddha and recorded the gifts and offerings that Zheng He made in honour of the Lord Buddha; the Tamil portion of the tablet offered similar praise to the Hindu god Tenavarai-Nayanar; and the Persian inscription on the tablet praised the glory of Allah and the saints of Islam. Zheng He also ensured that the offerings made to each god was in equal amounts so that none was seen to be more favoured.[73] This showed Zheng He's conscious efforts to connect with the people of Ceylon of all religious and cultural backgrounds. Such efforts of connection also demonstrated his act of seeking to cultivate and earn the trust of the locals.

Through this third strategy of Communication in words and actions on the ground — paying visits to rulers of neighbouring countries personally to explicitly articulate the intent to collaborate, giving gifts and sharing resources generously, facilitating win-win trade, ensuring a peaceful collaborative external environment, and cultivating and earning trust from the peoples, Zheng He gained the respect of the locals and helped them understand China's mission and vision. By making highly visible investments in his 5Acts of Collaboration, Zheng He not only demonstrated his commitment to collaboration but also helped in the implementation of the friendly and peaceful foreign policy of Ming China. This in turn showed that China was a credible contender for collaboration.

This is the fundamental strategy in Zheng He's *Art of Collaboration* as practised on the ground: businesses must communicate its mission and values relating to win-win collaboration upfront; they then need to patiently build a reputation in faithfully discharging and fulfilling their mission so that their potential collaborators may identify with the stated goals and be motivated to work collaboratively towards achieving them. In this way, a credible platform is set up for continued, sustainable collaboration in the long run.

CONTINUITY

This refers to Zheng He's art of building collaboration through patience in continuity of purpose and actions. This fourth strategy that supports Zheng He's *Art of Collaboration* is therefore one that is focused on the long term; it holds the fundamental tenet that collaboration cannot be built overnight.

This strategy is obvious in Zheng He's voyages across the vast body of waters linking China to Southeast Asia, India, the Middle East and Africa. Zheng He knew that making one voyage alone was not adequate in spreading goodwill and building trust in order to sustain long-term collaboration and peaceful trade. In his first voyage, he could not visit all the countries that he may have originally intended. He therefore had to make additional expeditions. And in all his seven grand voyages over a period of twenty-eight years between 1405 and 1433, Zheng He's fleet would faithfully visit and revisit a total of some thirty different cities and countries.

Looking at the historical timeline for Zheng He's seven grand voyages, the first six were made almost consecutively, one after the other, with hardly a break in terms of time: 1405–07, Voyage 1; 1407–09, Voyage 2; 1409–11, Voyage 3; 1412–15, Voyage 4; 1416–19, Voyage 5; 1421–22, Voyage 6; and 1430–33, Voyage 7.[74] Only for the last expedition (Voyage 7) was there a significant break of some eight years, and this was because of the death of Emperor Yongle (in 1425), the patron of Zheng He's expeditions. After Emperor Yongle's death, his successor and son, Emperor Renzong was not supportive of such maritime voyages and he therefore appointed Zheng He to be the Grand Commandant at Nanjing. When Emperor Renzong died the following year, his successor Emperor Xuanzong followed his father's policy initially. However, he soon (in the sixth month of 1430) found out that foreign countries had not paid tribute and he therefore issued the decree for Zheng He to lead the seventh grand expedition.[75] And in the immediate years following the seventh voyage, the tribute trade was apparently successfully revived with the Indian Ocean countries.[76]

Therefore, in Zheng He's art of building collaboration, it is clear that collaboration requires patience and continuity in nurturing and building it.

It should also be noted that Zheng He maintained relationships that his predecessors already created. During the period of the Three Kingdoms (in 230), Sun Quan of the Wu kingdom sent a fleet of some 10,000 soldiers to Yizhou (today's Taiwan). Since that time, the subsequent dynastic governments continued in their linkage with Taiwan. When Zheng He made his grand voyages, he did not forget the work already done by his predecessors; he sent a sub-fleet under the command of his deputy Wang Jinghong to visit Taiwan. There, they participated in the planting of ginger and digging of wells and also provided medical help for the local people.[77]

Following Zheng He's last voyage in 1433, large-scale expeditions came to a halt. The Ming Emperor issued an edict to ban all voyages and implemented an anti-foreign trade policy.[78] China closed its doors to the world, and this continued for approximately the next five hundred years. Zheng He's art of building collaboration therefore undoubtedly called for continuity in efforts and purpose; without such, the repercussion can be severe isolation.

IMPLICATIONS OF ZHENG HE'S ART OF COLLABORATION

Impact

The Zheng He's *Art of Collaboration* consequently did bear much fruit. By the end of his fleet's seven grand voyages, China had become an unrivaled maritime power respected for its massive ship-building capability and the use of advanced navigational techniques and technologies that were unrivalled by the West then.

Beyond this, it is apparent that the other greater legacy of Zheng He's *Art of Collaboration* was the peaceful coexistence of different religious and racial groups through his faithful fulfillment of his emperor-decreed mission of building the spirit of tolerance, openness, and inclusiveness through trade and cultural exchanges.[79]

An Alternative Model

It is therefore clear that Zheng He's *Art of Collaboration* provides an alternative model for the approach towards achieving a goal. Instead of using aggression, antagonism and colonization to help China prosper and rule the waves and hence the world, Zheng He used a softer approach and collaborated with other countries for mutual benefit. In contrast to the more well-known Sun Zi's Art of War which sees and seeks to overcome others as competitors and enemies, the lesser known Zheng He's *Art of Collaboration* sees and seeks to work with others as friendly neighbours and peaceful partners. This alternative worldview and mindset embodied in the Zheng He's *Art of Collaboration* is a major implication for our consideration and adoption in today's world.

China Re-embracing Zheng He's Model

Indeed, the end of Zheng He's expeditions ushered in some five hundred years of isolation for China. The late Deng Xiaoping had said that China's "long periods of closing its doors had made the country poor, backward, ignorant and naïve".[80] China itself has therefore returned to its practice in Zheng He's *Art of Collaboration* and Zheng He is now being regarded as a hero and held up as the trailblazer of the open-door policies that have brought China once again to the world stage.[81]

As a matter of fact, the phrase, "China's peaceful rise" (中国和平崛起), has been commonly used to describe China's approach to foreign policy in this century.[82] It seeks to characterize China's commitment towards improving relations with the world, emphasizing soft power, yet standing rooted in its path towards economic progress.

At the 2011 Singapore Global Dialogue, Mr Jusuf Wanandi of Indonesia's Center for Strategic and International Studies was reported as saying that in the past, "competition, confrontation and conflict" had characterized a rising power's clash with the power that was waning. While the main China representative at the dialogue, Major-General Yao Yunzhu, downplayed China's rise, she stressed that China was committed to being a responsible member of the international system.[83]

Chinese officials today therefore seem to see China as "a gentle giant with enduring goodwill" and uphold Zheng He as representing China's commitment to "good neighborliness, peaceful coexistence and scientific navigation".[84]

U.S. President Practising Zheng He's Art of Collaboration

As indicated earlier, U.S. President Barack Obama was awarded the 2009 Nobel Peace Prize for his efforts to strengthen international diplomacy and cooperation between peoples.[85] This is apparently in line with the Zheng He's *Art of Collaboration* described here. To see its full dimension however, the world will have to await history's subsequent evaluation of the president's further actions. After all, Zheng He's *Art of Collaboration* involves much work in capability-building (for collaboration), coordination (of execution), communication (in words and in actions), and continuity (in purpose and patience).

Nonetheless, the U.S. President does seem to be embarking on this Zheng He model. His new strategy is reportedly rooted in engagement and cooperation, rejecting the "Bush Doctrine" that emphasized unilateral American power and the right to wage pre-emptive war. President Obama stressed international engagement over Bush's "Cowboy Diplomacy". To President Obama: "the burdens of this century cannot fall on (American) soldiers alone, it also cannot fall on American shoulders alone".[86]

Similarly, anticipating the second U.S.-China Strategic and Economic Dialogue, analysts had described the previous year's talks as setting the new tone of mutual respect.[87] At the 2010 talks, U.S. Treasury Secretary Timothy Geithner was reported as using the trip to showcase a more relaxed side of himself — that of a "Chinese-proverb-quoting, basketball-playing, former exchange student".[88] This seems to suggest Zheng He's Coordination strategy being practised within the Obama administration; it also suggests the Zheng He model being adopted beyond President Obama himself.

Today's Businesses

Should modern-day businesses adopt Zheng He's model? This means moving over to building collaborative partnerships and networks based on mutual respect and trust, which was Zheng He's fundamental emperor-decreed mission. Is this the way businesses are already operating on?

Even when we consider today's business partnerships (as opposed to Sun Zi's mentality of others as competitors and enemies), one would argue that much of such are based on vested strategic interests. As such, MOUs are signed, joint ventures are structured and business alliances are formed because each party has its own vested interests that can be furthered by the other. The mere act of signing documents and writing contracts belie this self-oriented, self-guarded approach. As long as there is a reasonable balance in such mutual dependence, the partnership will work. But when the balance tilts in favour of one party, this is then seen as at the expense of the other. Termination of the relationship then becomes commonplace.

If businesses move on Zheng He's *Art of Collaboration*, it must seek the goodwill of others and build trust that will provide for peaceful coexistence and partnership. This will require ongoing capability-building to allow one to give and share generously and hence adds to the collaboration from a position of strength (not superiority); it will necessitate careful coordination of efforts and resources so that each contributes as an integrated whole; it will need constant communication of this collaborative vision and alignment of the value of trust through words and actions; and, it will call for perseverance and continuity in building the desired sustainable long-term collaborative relationship.

Perhaps, it is indeed better to give than to receive because the capacity to give is indicative of a position of real strength. As the famous proverb goes, "A candle loses no lighting by lighting another candle." Businesses can actually gain from giving and sharing generously as doing business together today may no longer be a zero-sum game.

Endnotes

1. An earlier version of the contents in this chapter was presented at the International Conference on Zheng He and the Afro-Asian World, Malacca, Malaysia, 5–7 July 2010; it is a shorter and simplified version of this chapter and will be included in the conference proceedings that is being put together. It has my student Grace Chew as co-author.

2. "Sun Tzu Quotes, The Art of War Quotes", <http://www.military-quotes.com/Sun-Tzu.htm> (accessed 20 June 2010).

3. "Obama wins 2009 Nobel Peace Prize", *BBC News*, 9 October 2009, <http://www.bbc.co.uk/2/hi/europe/8298580.stm> (accessed 21 June 2010).

4. Tan Ta Sen and Chia Lin Sien, eds., *The Zheng He Epic*, 1st edition in Chinese edited by Zhou Wenlin et al. (Kunming, Yunnan, China: Yunnan's Publishing House, Yunnan Fine Arts Publishing House, Auora Publishing House, 2006), p. 8.

5. *Zheng He Epic*, p. 315.

6. Chiu Ling-yeong, "Zheng He: Navigator, Discoverer and Diplomat", *Wu Teh Yao Memorial Lectures 2000* (Singapore: Unipress, Center for the Arts, National University of Singapore, 2001), p. 8.

7. *Zheng He Epic*, pp. 8–10.

8. Tim Luard, "Swimming dragons", *BBC Radio*, 3 June 2005, <http://www.bbc.co.uk/radio4/history/swimming_dragons.shtml> (accessed 20 June 2010).

9. *Zheng He Epic: Mazu Temple in Changle*, p. 12.

10. *Zheng He Epic*, p. 321.

11. *Zheng He Epic*, p. 318.

12. The Applied History Research Group, *The Sea-Route to India & Vasco da Gama*, The University of Calgary, 2007, <http://www.ucalgary.ca/applied_history/tutor/eurvoya/vasco.html> (accessed 22 June 2010).

13. *Zheng He Epic*, p. 316 (side bar).

14. Louise E. Levathes, *When China Ruled the Seas* (U.S.: Oxford University Press, 1994), p. 169.

15. 《郑和家谱 • 敕谕海外诸番条》，收录于《郑和下西洋资料汇编》上册，海洋出版社2005年增编本，531页。(Compilation of Records and Materials on Zheng He's Voyages to the West Seas, Ocean Publication) (own translation into English).

16. *Zheng He Epic*, p. 323.

17. *Zheng He Epic*, p. 66.

18. *Zheng He Epic*, p. 232.

19. *When China Ruled the Seas*, p. 115.

20. *When China Ruled the Seas*, p. 139.

21. *Zheng He Epic*, p. 69.

22. *When China Ruled the Seas*, p. 64.

23. *Zheng He Epic*, p. 55.

24. *When China Ruled the Seas*, p. 64.

25. *Zheng He Epic*, p. 57.

26. *Zheng He: Navigator, Discoverer and Diplomat*, pp. 14–15.

27. *Zheng He: Navigator, Discoverer and Diplomat*, p. 10.

28. *Zheng He Epic*, p. 96.

29. *Zheng He Epic*, p. 345.

30. *Zheng He Epic*, p. 185.

31. *Zheng He Epic*, p. 320.

32. *Zheng He Epic*, Preface by Bai Enpei.

33. *Zheng He Epic*, p. 212.

34. *Zheng He Epic*, pp. 84–86.

35. *Zheng He Epic*, p. 194.

36. *Zheng He Epic*, p. 121.

37. *Zheng He Epic*, p. 126.

38. *Zheng He Epic*, pp. 128, 130.

39. *Zheng He Epic*, p. 220.

40. *Zheng He Epic*, pp. 221–22.

41. *Zheng He Epic*, p. 225.

42. *Zheng He Epic*, p. 220.

43. *Zheng He: Navigator, Discoverer and Diplomat*, pp. 12–13.

44. *Zheng He Epic*, p. 150.

45. *Zheng He Epic*, pp. 212–16.

46. *Zheng He Epic*, pp. 226–29.

47. *Zheng He: Navigator, Discoverer and Diplomat*, pp. 13–14.

48. *Zheng He Epic*, p. 248.

49. "Sun Tzu Quotes, The Art of War Quotes", <http://www.military-quotes.com/Sun-Tzu.htm> (accessed 20 June 2010).

50. *Zheng He Epic*, p. 316.

51. *Zheng He Epic*, p. 316.

52. 傅海滨，《郑和对外交往的再认识》，收录于《郑和研究》1996年第三期，第51页。(Journal of Zheng He Research, Nanjing Zheng He Research Society).

53. 《明太祖实录》卷七十一，洪武五年壬子，国立北平图书馆藏红格，第1314页。(Ming Taizu Shilu: Factual Record of Ming Taizu's Reign, Peking Library Collection).

54. *Zheng He Epic*, p. 321.

55. *Zheng He Epic*, p. 248.

56. *When China Ruled the Seas*, p. 88.

57. *When China Ruled the Seas*, p. 84.

58. 鹿世明，《郑和下西洋与中国对外贸易》，载《走向海洋的中国人》，海潮出版社，1996年，第35页。(The Chinese on Their Path to the Oceans, Hai Chao Publishing).

59. 辛元欧，《郑和下西洋纵论》，刊登于《郑和研究》，1996年第3期第10页，中国南京郑和研究会。

60. *Zheng He Epic*, p. 8.

61. （明）马欢，《瀛涯胜览》，商务印书馆影印，第31页。(Yingya Shenglan, Corrmmercial Publishing).

62. （明）马欢，《瀛涯胜览》，商务印书馆影印，第69页。

63. *Zheng He Epic*, p. 232.

64. 《明太宗实录》卷84。

65. 《明太宗实录》卷77。

66. 孔远志，郑一钧，《东南亚考察论郑和》，北京大学出版社，2008年，第74页。(Southeast Asian Study on Zheng He, Peking University Publication).

67. （清）张廷玉，《明史》，卷三百二十六，列传第二百十五，外国八，锡兰山传；《明太宗实录》卷77，载于：<http://www.guoxue.com/shibu/24shi/mingshi/ms_326.htm>.

68. *Zheng He Epic*, p. 315.

69. *Zheng He Epic*, pp. 8–9.

70. Evidence can be found in the Padmanabhapura Palace in India, where paintings of the bloody battle between the king's troops and the Portuguese are on display but there are only ornamental Chinese porcelain pieces and no sign of Chinese weapons. This suggests that the Chinese voyagers like Zheng He maintained diplomacy

and friendship instead of antagonizing the countries they visited; *Zheng He Epic*, p. 284.

71. *Zheng He Epic*, p. 345.

72. *When China Ruled the Seas*, p. 138.

73. *When China Ruled the Seas*, p. 113.

74. *Zheng He Epic*, p. 226.

75. *Zheng He: Navigator, Discoverer and Diplomat*, p. 11.

76. *When China Ruled the Seas*, p. 173.

77. *Zheng He Epic*, p. 206.

78. *Zheng He Epic*, p. 10.

79. Leo Suryadinata, *Admiral Zheng He and Southeast Asia* (Singapore: Institute of Southeast Asian Studies and International Zheng He Society Publication, 2005), p. 119.

80. *Zheng He Epic*, p. 16.

81. Tim Luard, "Swimming dragons", *BBC Radio*, 3 June 2005, <http://www.bbc.co.uk/radio4/history/swimming_dragons.shtml> (accessed 20 June 2010).

82. Nicholas D. Kristof, "The rise of China", Council on Foreign Relations, 1993, <http://www.foreignaffairs.com/articles/49405/nicholas-d-kristof/the-rise-of-china> (accessed 15 June 2010).

83. "All eyes trained on China's posture: Panellists", *Straits Times*, 23 September 2011, p. A12.

84. Kahn J., "China celebrates Zheng He", The New York Times Company, 2005, <http://forums.yellowworld.org/showthread.php?t=25134> (accessed 15 June 2010).

85. "Obama wins 2009 Nobel Peace Prize", BBC News, 9 October 2009, <http://news.bbc.co.uk/2/hi/europe/8298580.stm> (accessed 21 June 2010).

86. "No More 'Cowboy Diplomacy' for US", *Straits Times*, 24 May 2010, p. A13.

87. "Softer Push for Stronger Yuan", *Straits Times*, 22 May 2010, p. C15.

88. R. Christie, "Can Geithner pull the right strings in Beijing?", *Bloomberg Businessweek*, 31 May–6 June 2010, p. 24.

References

"All eyes trained on China's posture: Panellists". *Straits Times*, 23 September 2011, p. A12.

BBC News. "Obama wins 2009 Nobel Peace Prize", 9 October 2009. <http://news.bbc.co.uk/2/hi/europe/8298580.stm> (accessed 21 June 2010).

Chiu Ling-yeong. "Zheng He: Navigator, Discoverer and Diplomat". *Wu Teh Yao Memorial Lectures 2000*. Singapore: Unipress, Center for the Arts, National University of Singapore, 2001.

Christie, R. "Can Geithner pull the right strings in Beijing?". *Bloomberg Businessweek*, 31 May–6 June 2010, p. 24.

Kahn J. "China celebrates Zheng He". The New York Times Company, 2005. <http://forums.yellowworld.org/showthread.php?t=25134> (accessed 15 June 2010).

Kristof, Nicholas D. "The rise of China". Council on Foreign Relations, 1993. <http://www.foreignaffairs.com/articles/49405/nicholas-d-kristof/the-rise-of-china> (accessed 15 June 2010).

Levathes, Louise E. *When China Ruled the Seas: The Treasure Fleet of the Dragon Throne, 1405–1433*. U.S.: Oxford University Press, 1994.

Luard, Tim. "Swimming dragons". *BBC Radio*, 3 June 2005. <http://www.bbc.co.uk/radio4/history/swimming_dragons.shtml> (accessed 20 June 2010).

"No More 'Cowboy Diplomacy' for US". *Straits Times*, 24 May 2010, p. A13.

"Softer Push for Stronger Yuan". *Straits Times*, 22 May 2010, p. C15.

"Sun Tzu Quotes, The Art of War Quotes". <http://www.military-quotes.com/Sun-Tzu.htm> (accessed 20 June 2010).

Suryadinata, Leo. *Admiral Zheng He and Southeast Asia*. Singapore: Institute of Southeast Asian Studies and International Zheng He Society Publication, 2005.

Tan Ta Sen and Chia Lin Sien, eds. *The Zheng He Epic*. 1st edition in Chinese edited by Zhou Wenlin et al. Kunming, Yunnan, China: Yunnan's Publishing House, Yunnan Fine Arts Publishing House, Auora Publishing House, 2006.

The Applied History Research Group, *The Sea-Route to India & Vasco da Gama*. The University of Calgary, 2007. <http://www.ucalgary. ca/applied_history/tutor/eurvoya/vasco.html> (accessed 22 June 2010).

《郑和家谱·敕谕海外诸番条》，收录于《郑和下西洋资料汇编》上册，海洋出版社2005年增编本. (Compilation of Records and Materials on Zheng He's Voyages to the West Seas, Ocean Publication).

傅海滨，《郑和对外交往的再认识》，收录于《郑和研究》1996年第三期. (Journal of Zheng He Research, Nanjing Zheng He Research Society).

《明太祖实录》卷七十一，洪武五年壬子，国立北平图书馆藏红格，第1314页。(Ming Taizu Shilu: Factual Record of Ming Taizu's Reign, Peking Library Collection).

鹿世明，《郑和下西洋与中国对外贸易》，载《走向海洋的中国人》，海潮出版社，1996年. (The Chinese on Their Path to the Oceans, Hai Chao Publishing).

辛元欧，《郑和下西洋纵论》，刊登于《郑和研究》，1996年第3期，中国南京郑和研究会.

（明）马欢，《瀛涯胜览》，商务印书馆影印. (Yingya Shenglan, Commercial Publishing).

孔远志，郑一钧，《东南亚考察论郑和》，北京大学出版社，2008年. (Southeast Asian Study on Zheng He, Peking University Publication).

（清）张廷玉，《明史》，卷三百二十六，列传第二百十五，外国八，锡兰山传；《明太宗实录》卷77，载于：<http://www.guoxue.com/shibu/24shi/mingshi/ms_326.htm>.

Chapter 3

ZHENG HE'S ACTS OF COLLABORATION
Zheng He's Mission and Art of Collaboration on the Ground

INTRODUCTION

In the previous chapter, we introduced Zheng He's *Art of Collaboration* (AoC) as comprising the 4C strategies of Capability-building (in preparation for collaboration), Coordination (of people and activities in moving towards collaboration), Communication (of intent in words and through actual actions of building collaboration), and Continuity (in collaborative purpose and patience over the longer term).

The first two strategies of Capability-building and Coordination may be understood as Zheng He's preparation for collaboration. The third strategy of Communication refers to his actual actions of building collaboration with others on the ground; and for this, we have also earlier introduced Zheng He's 5Acts of Collaboration. The final strategy of Continuity points to the need to be steadfast in collaborative purpose and actions over the long term.

In this chapter,[1] we elaborate on Zheng He's 5Acts of Collaboration: the Act of Articulating Intent, the Act of Practising Generosity, the Act of Building Win-Win, the Act of Ensuring Sustainability, and the Act of Cultivating Trust. Together, these 5Acts of Collaboration represent that part of Zheng He's *Art of Collaboration* as practised on the ground.

This chapter is therefore organized as follows. In the next section, we will first elaborate on Zheng He's mission and provide some insights on Zheng He's authority in making decisions. In particular, we will highlight the scope and flexibility that were apparently available to him in deciding on what to do on his grand voyages. We will then elaborate on Zheng He's 5Acts of Collaboration, giving more details on what he actually did on the ground through these acts. We will also highlight the implications of these 5Acts of Collaboration for today's businesses and suggest application possibilities and examples.

ZHENG HE'S MISSION AND AUTHORITY IN MAKING DECISIONS

In order to further understand the 4C strategies in Zheng He's *Art of Collaboration*, and his specific 5Acts of Collaboration, we need to first qualify Zheng He's authority and autonomy in deciding on these strategies and actions for the grand voyages that he led.

Traditionally, under the autocracy of feudalistic Ming China, all national-level strategic decisions were made or could only be authorized by the emperor himself. After all, "the will of the emperor may conquer all that's under the heavens, or lose all that's under the heavens".[2] So the decision to send envoys led by Zheng He to visit countries on the various grand voyages was made by Emperor Yongle himself. However, the intentions and motives of Emperor Yongle behind his bold decision to support maritime activities on such an unprecedented scale were not quite clear. Scholars have therefore proposed various possibilities.

First, Emperor Yongle had the intention to explore unchartered waters. This, however, is often readily ruled out based on two strong arguments: (1) the size and structure of the flat-bottomed treasure ships and the scale of the fleet were unsuitable for exploration purposes;[3] and (2) according to the itinerary recorded in the inscription on the Stone Tablet of the Heavenly Princess[4] erected by Zheng He at Liujiagang in 1431, the first three voyages were made on the same routes to the same destinations, which were not foreign to Chinese traders even before Zheng He's time. So Zheng He's emperor-decreed mission was not exploratory in terms of objectives or goals.

Second, in the *Ming Shi*,[5] the official history of the Ming Dynasty written by Qing Dynasty scholar Zhang Tingyu, it was stated that the purpose of the voyages was to trace and remove Emperor Yongle's nephew and predecessor, the Emperor Jianwen, whose whereabouts had become a mystery after the military revolt led by his uncle. However, this is again an unlikely intention of Emperor Yongle as it is unlikely that repeated voyages of such scale were solely devoted to locating a likely powerless rival who could have already died or who could never be found. Furthermore, for the search to be effective, one would also reasonably expect it to be carried out in a low profile manner rather than through the deployment of a grand fleet of more than 200 ships.

It is more likely that the motive behind Emperor Yongle's decision was complex with multiple objectives. While these objectives could include exploration and locating Emperor Jianwen, they were not likely to be the main purpose. The grandeur of the fleet was more likely a display of China's power and prosperity, and the voyages therefore an expression of Emperor Yongle's political ideology to create a China-centred feudal system under which all states could coexist peacefully and prosper together.[6] This would be what Dreyer concluded as the main purpose of the voyages, namely, that of power projection by Ming China.[7] Dreyer is not wrong in his claim; however, he may have missed the essence of peace in Emperor Yongle's political ideology, which was greatly influenced by the Chinese concept of *Tianxia*, referring to all under heaven, often including lands outside China, that the Chinese emperor owes a responsibility to, and which he already "owns". As Levathes puts it: if one already owned everything, why should one use force to conquer? Peace and prosperity can yield greater loyalty than forceful capture through fighting.[8]

The founding emperor of Ming Dynasty, Emperor Hongwu, who is also the father of Emperor Yongle, was recorded in *Ming Shi* to have advocated that China should maintain a harmonious relationship with states from afar and share the prosperity and blessings of a peaceful time.[9] In *Ming Taizu Shilu*, which provides a historical record of the Ming emperors' life, Emperor Hongwu was also recorded as having said that the foreign states outside China were only expected to send tribute once each generation, as a show of respect,[10] and that no war should be waged against those that did not constitute a threat to China.[11] Emperor Yongle's political ideology was likely to be influenced by his father, and was clearly expressed in the edict he issued to Zheng He before his third voyage in 1409:

> I, the emperor, send my words to the kings and chieftains of foreign states in the far west, that I follow heaven's order to rule the world, to execute heaven's will to grant blessings and

virtues. It is my wish that in all lands covered with sunshine and showered with moonlight, and moistened by frost and dew, its people, regardless of age, may be granted a stable livelihood, and a safe shelter. Today, I send Zheng He to spread my message. All must obey heaven's will and follow my words, and know your limits. Do not bully the minority. Do not attack the weak. All should share in the prosperity of peaceful times. If you wish to pay tribute to my court, you will be bestowed with gifts of goodwill. I send my edict to let you know my message.[12]

Here we can see that Emperor Yongle's intentions were to obtain respect and recognition of his legitimacy and authority, and to convey the message of his willingness to establish goodwill.

For these, he was sending Zheng He to spread his message, which was really a rather vague instruction for Zheng He to establish good relations with foreign states. There was therefore much room for Zheng He to interpret and translate this mission into more specific actions at his own discretion.

Some scholars have also inferred that Emperor Yongle's intention was to mitigate threat to the coastal security of China from the south and west seas,[13] since Ming China at that time was haunted by piracy and the Ming Court was fearful of the possible collusion between foreign powers and Ming rebels in exile.[14]

While such a motive was not explicitly stated in Emperor Yongle's decree, it could be a possible interpretation made by Zheng He himself. Many scholars had referenced in their papers a dialogue between Zheng He and Emperor Renzong, son of Emperor Yongle, where Zheng He was supposedly trying to persuade Emperor Renzong to relaunch the grand voyages. This apparent dialogue was quoted in the preface of *Les Chinois De La Diaspora*, a book about Chinese in foreign countries, written by French journalist and researcher Debre Francois. According to this quote, Zheng He had said:

> To build a strong and prosperous nation, we can't neglect the
> oceans. Our wealth comes from the sea, so does our threat...once
> rulers of other nations gain control over south sea, China would
> be in danger. With our invincible fleet, we can expand trade,
> and deter other nations from coveting the south sea...[15]

The problem with this popular piece of evidence is that no
equivalent had been found in Chinese records. Also, efforts to
trace it to reliable primary sources had been fruitless.[16]

Nonetheless, judging from the experience Zheng He had gained
during his first six voyages before Emperor Renzong's reign, it is not
unlikely that he had gained such a strategic vision about China.
And assuming Debre Francois' quote is credible, Zheng He would
then appear to be more than a mere follower of Emperor Yongle's
instructions. He would have established his own vision to protect
the interest of China through building collaborative relationships
with oversea countries in trade and marine security.

Quite apart from this quoted dialogue, judging from Zheng
He's management of his fleet and what he had done on his grand
voyages, it can be seen that as the commander-in-chief, Zheng He
did not just "do the job" in following Emperor Yongle's decree;
instead, he had to first interpret the emperor's decree and define
for himself the job that he needs to get done. As we will see in
more details later, these would include his 5Acts of Collaboration
that gave rise to extensive trading and economic activities with
the foreign countries he visited.

Other diplomats such as Hou Xian, who had in twenty-
five years led envoys to Tibet and fifteen other Southeast Asian
countries,[17] did not engage in significant economic activities like
Zheng He did. This suggests that Zheng He had exercised much of
his own discretion and had substantial authority in planning and
executing his seven voyages. In fact, for the convenience of Zheng
He, Emperor Yongle even gave him blank scrolls pre-stamped

with his imperial seal so that Zheng He could issue authorized imperial orders on a timely basis during his voyages.[18]

ZHENG HE'S 5ACTS OF COLLABORATION

It is quite clear from our preceding discussion that while Emperor Yongle may have had multiple intentions and motives, Zheng He's emperor-decreed mission was nonetheless fundamentally aimed at showing and sharing Ming China's glory and splendour through the establishment of collaborative relationships with the *xiyang* countries so that *Tianxia* (all under heaven) may progress and prosper together harmoniously. Zheng He was therefore apparently very clear of his mission throughout all his seven voyages as we see him working hard at announcing his mission's intention, sharing goodwill, facilitating trade, protecting mutual interest, and building trust through his specific acts and actions at every place he visited.

We have earlier referred to such conscious and active efforts of Zheng He in building collaboration with others as Zheng He's actual Acts of Collaboration on the ground. These include the five specific Acts of Articulating Intent, Practising Generosity, Building Win-Win, Ensuring Sustainability and Cultivating Trust. We elaborate further on these as follows.

Act of Articulating Intent

This refers to Zheng He's act of building collaboration through consciously articulating his mission and values to others, making his purpose and objectives transparent to all, and communicating in words his intent and desire for collaboration. As indicated earlier, this stance is in contrast to Sun Zi's mindset that "all warfare is based on deception".[19]

Zheng He visited more than thirty countries in his *Xia Xiyang* (Travels to the Western Seas) voyages. Whenever he arrived at a country, Zheng He would communicate his emperor-decreed mission to others and sought to reassure the locals and rulers in *words* by having the imperial decree read out in public; oftentimes, this would also include the reading of the imperial appointments which represented the emperor's endorsement and respect for the authority of the local rulers.[20]

An example of the imperial decree is that highlighted earlier in this chapter (issued by the Emperor Yongle before Zheng He's third voyage in 1409):

> I, the emperor, send my words to the kings and chieftains of foreign states in the far west, that I follow heaven's order to rule the world, to execute heaven's will to grant blessings and virtues. It is my wish that in all lands covered with sunshine and showered with moonlight, and moistened by frost and dew, its people, regardless of age, may be granted a stable livelihood, and a safe shelter. Today, I send Zheng He to spread my message. All must obey heaven's will and follow my words, and know your limits. Do not bully the minority. Do not attack the weak. All should share in the prosperity of peaceful times. If you wish to pay tribute to my court, you will be bestowed with gifts of goodwill. I send my edict to let you know my message.[21]

When Zheng He shared such an imperial decree with the locals, there was a clear articulation of the intent to share blessings and goodwill, and that all peoples should live in peace and be able to have a stable livelihood. There was also a call for all to follow heaven's will, and therefore Ming China's way, and not to bully or attack others, especially the weak.

The imperial decree was therefore an in-principle guarantee of the purpose of Zheng He's visits to the various countries. By announcing the Ming Court's vision of peace and stability and his maritime mission undertaken to achieve that vision, Zheng He was able to give the locals the peace of mind that his large fleet's visit was not a threat.

Indeed, Emperor Yongle had great foresight and saw the need to maintain China's ties with other countries in order to create peace and stability. His vision was that if there were peace and friendly ties amongst nations, trade would prosper and all peoples would benefit. The Emperor Yongle therefore proactively sent out groups of envoys to vassal states to notify them that a new emperor was on the throne and that the Ming Court was committed to maintaining the friendly and peaceful foreign policy of the previous emperor.[22] In this way, Zheng He's voyages were a further manifestation of Ming China's intention to pursue peace and goodwill for all. Zheng He therefore engaged himself in the conscious Act of Articulating (this) Intent at every place he visited.

However, the emperor's decree in words would only be worth as much as Zheng He's *actions* on the ground. We therefore see Zheng He also engaged in 4 other specific Acts of Collaboration on the ground.

Act of Practising Generosity

This is Zheng He's practice on the ground of developing collaboration by being generous towards others. This generosity took the form of gift-giving as well as sharing of resources, knowledge and technology, thereby generating goodwill which then laid the foundation for collaboration.

While a large part of gift-giving gestures was diplomatic formality, often instructed by the emperor according to the rites of the Ming Court, there were no strings attached to these gifts. *Ming Taizong Shilu* recorded that on the first epic grand voyage, Zheng He carried with him imperial letters and gifts to the kings of the countries of the Western Ocean; these gifts included gold brocade, patterned silks, and coloured silk gauze, and they were given according to the status of these kings.[23] Silk products were often the most valued gifts to foreign rulers as at that time China was the only source of silk.[24]

Some have argued that such gift giving is a less explicit form of export.[25] However, trade was unlikely the intention of the Ming Court. The gifts were given with no expectation of a fair return. In fact, to demonstrate the generosity of China, Zheng He practised "*Hou Wang Bo Lai* [give more than receive]",[26] which was strongly advocated by Emperor Hongwu.[27]

Zheng He did not stop his generosity and the building of goodwill at the government and official level. After presenting the emperor's edict and official gifts to the local rulers and chieftains, he often spent time interacting with the locals, extending the gift-giving gesture into sharing of China's resources and knowledge, and thereby enhancing the collaborative relationships with the peoples of these foreign lands.

For example, he presented Chinese almanacs to neighbouring countries such as Champa and Ryukyu to help local people there enhance the quality of life as well as to help them understand the Chinese custom.[28] In 1417, after the envoys of Pahang, Calicut and Java visited China together, Zheng He sent the envoys home on board his treasure ships during his fifth voyage, showing his willingness to share what he had with others.[29] In fact, as early as on his first voyage, Zheng He already helped in sending the Malaccan envoys back on board his treasure fleet in 1406.[30]

Another example of Zheng He's act of generosity was the giving of free medicine to treat local patients. In *Haiguo Jianwen Lu* written in the Qing Dynasty, Cheng Lunjiong described the incident in which Zheng He dispensed medicine to the people of Siam; there were apparently so many locals who were approaching Zheng He for medical help that he had to pour medicine into a stream so that more of these people can be treated by showering with the stream water.[31] In Indonesia, there are also folk stories of how Zheng He taught them to treat plague by consuming durian fruits.[32]

In fact, Zheng He's fleet was equipped with a team of 150 highly specialized medical officers and pharmacologists; some of these specialists came from the palace's elite medical institution and some were famous local medical practitioners.[33] In *Jiaxing Fuzhi*,[34] a highly reputable medical officer called Chen Yicheng was recorded to have worked in *Taiyi Yuan* [imperial medical hall] and was deployed to serve on Zheng He's fleet.[35] Such a well-staffed medical team was more than what would be necessary to take care of the health needs of Zheng He's crew during the voyages. In fact, the recruitment of the medical team was intended by Zheng He to serve greater medical needs. The medical officers on board also had research responsibilities to record and find cures for common diseases in the foreign countries they visited.[36] This often led to treating of local patients and studying of local herbs. Therefore, Zheng He did not merely give free medical treatment to the local people; he also broadened and shared knowledge in medicine, pharmacology and nutrition with the local people as well.

In addition, the crew of Zheng He also shared agriculture and fishing techniques that were commonly used in China with others. Agricultural techniques, for example, had helped to mitigate food shortages in East Africa. In fact, Chinese plows were used for farming by people of the Kalimantan Islands in Borneo till the nineteenth century.[37] Zheng He also gave Chinese calendars to foreign countries and city-states, which informed them of important times for agricultural activities.[38] In Cochin, fishermen use fishnets with an attached lever system, which they call "Chinese fishnet".[39] These fishnets were similar to those used by fishermen in the coastal regions of Yunnan, China; and such a fishing method was learned from crew members from Yunnan on Zheng He's fleet when they made a stopover in Quilon and Cochin.[40]

In the Maldives, locally produced lacquerware bears significant resemblance to those produced in Fujian. It is believed that the local people learned to make lacquerware from the Fuzhou crew members on Zheng He's fleet.[41] In Champa, there were popular folk stories of Zheng He teaching the native people agriculture and construction techniques; recent research seemed to support this point that Zheng He had indeed shared agricultural technology with the locals when he was in Champa.[42]

Zheng He's generosity in sharing resources, knowledge and technology with the foreign countries he visited was not without rewards. Apart from local specialty goods received by Zheng He as gifts, Zheng He's medical officers found new herbs and learned from local prescriptions to cure diseases. They had also learned by directly helping to treat local patients. This had benefited China greatly during the early Ming period when the Chinese population increased dramatically and when there were frequent outbreaks of infectious diseases, including measles and smallpox.[43] Also, the Arabic medicine and therapies learned on the voyages gained popularity in China, especially after the publication of the pharmaceutical prescriptions of Muslims in the *Hui Yao Fang*.[44] Even the architectural design of Dabao'en Temple, which was built under Zheng He's charge, was greatly influenced by Angkor Wat architecture.[45] This was likely a result of Zheng He's experience in Southeast Asia.

Zheng He's act of generosity in the sharing of resources, knowledge and technology therefore benefited both China and the foreign countries that Zheng He had visited. Beyond this, Zheng He also explicitly facilitated trade that led to explicit win-win collaborative relationships.

Act of Building Win-Win

This refers to Zheng He's act of building win-win collaboration by facilitating trade with the peoples and countries he visited. This specific act of collaboration may be seen as Zheng He's attempt at ensuring sustainability of the collaborative relationship as no collaboration will last if it is only one party giving generously while the other merely receives without offering anything in return.

Zheng He's Initiative rather than the Ming Emperors'

This act of building win-win collaboration through trade was more likely Zheng He's own expression and extension of his emperor-decreed mission than a direct instruction from the emperor himself.

Historical records showed that early Ming emperors were not positive about maritime trade. Emperor Hongwu was actually suspicious of such overseas trade; he allowed trade only through official channels; and he disallowed private trade with foreigners.[46] He implemented the policy of *Haijin*, prohibiting private vessels from sailing out to sea.[47] And during Emperor Hongwu's reign, strict laws were also instituted to control smuggling.[48] While the strict laws against overseas trade were relaxed slightly during the short reign of Emperor Jianwen, Emperor Yongle apparently resumed tight control over trade after he came into power.[49] Records on the ascendance of Emperor Yongle to the throne (即位诏书) showed the following:

> Military personnel and civilians of the costal region were found to have illegally left the country and colluded with foreign countries. From now on, this is banned. The rules and punishments shall follow those enforced in the Hongwu reign.[50]

Also, in 1403 when foreign envoys engaged in illegal private trade while paying tribute to the Ming Court, the Emperor Yongle neither charged them tax[51] nor punished them,[52] in his desire to show the graciousness of his Ming Court. His basic rationale in establishing relationships with foreign countries was apparently more political than economic. When he rejected the suggestion to tax the foreign envoys, the Emperor Yongle stated that the purpose of the commercial tax was really to discourage people from pursuing trade for a living; he was not looking to such tax as a means for generating income for the country.[53]

The trading activities carried out by Zheng He's fleet during his seven voyages were therefore unlikely to be dictated by the Ming emperors.

Yet Zheng He, who probably had recognized the importance of trade to China, and the entrepots in Southeast Asia, India and the Arab world, was apparently serious and strategic in establishing trade relations with the countries he had visited. During the Yuan Dynasty, maritime trade policies were very relaxed. Foreign envoys were allowed to trade freely in China, and Chinese traders frequented the south and west seas.[54] In fact, Yuan emperors encouraged trade so as to increase tax revenue.[55] Hence, foreign countries including Java, which was rising in influence in the south seas, established close trading relations with the Yuan Court. When Ming came into power, the restrictive Ming trading policies affected China's relation with these foreign countries and led to much unhappiness.[56] While the Ming emperors remained conservative over maritime trade, Zheng He apparently recognized the importance of trade as an incentive in resuming collaborative relationships with such countries that were previously involved in much trade with China.

Further, before 1400, the inflows of foreign goods through tributes were never enough to satisfy the Chinese demand; the gap between supply and demand for foreign goods continued to prevail after 1400.[57] Such demand for foreign goods and resources, such as foreign herbs, spices and dyes, may also have spurred Zheng He to carry out large scale trading activities during his voyages.

Strategic Preparation and Execution

Zheng He prepared for and carried out his trade activities strategically and deliberately.

Even while imperial orders were issued for materials to be gathered for building Zheng He's treasure fleet, provinces were also instructed to supply these ships with goods that were in demand for trading abroad. These included silk and cotton cloth, as well as large quantities of iron, salt, hemp, tea, wine, oil, and candles.[58] The treasure ships were therefore built not just to carry supplies for the 27,000 crew members, but also a large amount of product items for trading purposes.

In terms of logistics, Zheng He also made careful and strategic plans to facilitate the transport and storage of trade items. Apparently, Zheng He set up four logistics/trade bases in the Southeast Asian and other major trading regions in the Indian Ocean; of these four bases, Champa and Sumatra belong to the Indo-China Peninsula and Malaya Peninsula region and they served as strategic locations for Zheng He's fleet to establish marine transport in the South China Sea and trade with the Southeast Asian nations; Sri Lanka and Calicut belong to the Indian subcontinent and they served as strategic locations for Zheng He's fleet to establish marine transport in the Indian Ocean and Arabic Seas, as well as develop trading relations with the Indian, Arabian and East African coastal countries.[59]

Beyond these bases, Zheng He had also built a government depot, called *Guanchang*, in Malacca.[60] Both the *Zheng He Navigation Map*[61] and the *Yingya Shenglan* provided evidence for the existence and location of *Guanchangs*. The *Yingya Shenglan* provided a vivid description of the *Guanchang* in Malacca:

> Whenever Chinese treasure ships arrived, stockades would be set up, like walls of a city. A four-gate Drum Tower was built. At night, officers will patrol to ensure security. Within the outer stockades, another layer of stockades was set up to create a small town of heavily guarded warehouses, in which all money and supplies were kept. Ships that returned from various countries would be re-organised. Foreign goods would be packed, and loaded into the ships. When the south monsoon starts in mid May, the fleet would depart for China.[62]

Further, to maximize coverage and efficiency, Zheng He's fleet was often separated into different squadrons at the bases and sent out in a fan formation to carry out independent trading activities.[63]

Some have argued that the motive for Zheng He's voyages was mainly political, and that the self-sufficient Chinese agricultural economy obviated the need for maritime trade.[64] Also, it has been suggested that Zheng He's main task was to purchase luxury and precious goods for the imperial family; as such, while there were trading activities, these were rare and infrequent.[65]

Quite to the contrary, and as highlighted above, we can see that the trading activities carried out by Zheng He were well organized, strategically planned, and systematically executed. Hence, while trade was not explicitly instructed by the emperor, it was clearly one of Zheng He's major acts of collaboration, not just a fringe activity.

Trade Items and Activities

In fact, trade items and activities were extensive. There were seven main kinds of export goods traded by Zheng He's fleet:

1. Food items, including tea and oranges;
2. Household items, including lacquerware, umbrella, silk and other fabrics;

3. Trade currencies, including silver, gold and copper coins;
4. Hardware, including tools and other metal products;
5. Porcelain;
6. Spices and fragrances, including camphor and musk; and
7. Construction materials, including roof tiles and glass tiles.[66]

Imports were even more extensive. Import data from records in *Minghui Dian*, *Ming Shi*, and *Yingya Shenglan* showed that foreign goods imported into China during the period of Zheng He's voyages were of as many as 191 different types, which can be classified into 11 categories, including 17 types of metal goods, 22 types of medical herbs, 23 types of precious goods, 6 types of food items, 51 types of fabric, 29 types of spices, 8 types of household items, 8 types of wood, 19 types of flora and fauna, and 6 types of other raw materials. In fact, the import of more than 160 different types of goods was directly linked with Zheng He's voyages.[67] Among these goods, pepper was found to be the highest in terms of import quantity.[68] Amongst all these imports, apparently only 23 types were of precious gems and other luxurious items meant for the imperial family. The majority were still daily necessities that eventually flowed to the open market.

In *Nandu Fanhui Tu*,[69] a Chinese scroll painting of the Ming era, the shops in Nanjing (the capital of Ming China at that time) were depicted as carrying hanging banners that read "Goods from both East and West Seas readily available". Hence, the imported goods from Zheng He's voyages had most likely flowed to private traders in the open market.

Win-Win Trade Benefits

Zheng He's act of win-win through trade generated much benefit for all. For example, the huge appetite of the Chinese market for foreign goods contributed to the economic development of the supplying countries and the entrepots visited by Zheng He's fleet.

Pepper plantations in Java and Sumatra, for example, expanded rapidly under the demand of the Chinese market and fuelled economic development in those regions. Pepper trade during that time also raised the status of Banten and Batavia (Jakarta) to become pepper-trading hubs.[70] Ports that were frequented by Zheng He's fleet also rose in importance. For example, with the establishment of an official depot (or *guanchang*) in Malacca, the latter soon overtook Palembang as the regional trade hub.[71] According to Debre Francois, during the period of Zheng He's voyages, the ports in India also began to enjoy great prosperity.[72] Zheng He's voyages also led to the rising status of Muslim traders in the region.[73]

Apart from the official trade transactions between Zheng He's fleet and the foreign governments, Zheng He's crew also engaged extensively in private business activities with the locals in these countries.[74] The *Yingya Shenglan* recorded that in Siam, crew members used small boats to trade with the natives.[75] Zheng He's fleet was also especially welcomed in Dhofar. It was recorded that after Zheng He had presented the imperial edict and gifts, the King of Dhofar sent his men to inform all the natives to come and trade with Zheng He.[76] Household items such as porcelain and fabrics were bartered for local spices. Both the type of goods traded and the way trade was conducted bore characteristics of private trade.[77] Quite clearly, both the crew and the local people had gained materially and directly from Zheng He's voyages.

The impact of Zheng He's trading activities on the Chinese economy was also significant. The external demand for Chinese silk and porcelain led to rapid expansion of these industries. For example, the rise of Jingde Zhen to become the most reputable porcelain production centre was due largely to the high demand for its specialty bluish-white porcelain products, after Zheng He introduced porcelain to Southeast Asia and the Arab world. In fact, its reputation as the Porcelain Town is still being recognized today. Apparently, the production of bluish-white porcelain only became mainstream after Zheng He began his voyages.[78] In fact, the increase in production was evident in the increase in the number of kilns in Jingde Zhen from twenty during Hongwu's reign to fifty-eight in the Xuande reign.[79]

Apart from bluish-white porcelain, other porcelain ware also gained a greater overseas market, such as the Cizhou, from northern China with painting or incised decoration under a clear glaze; the Dehua, from Fujian with a brownish glaze; and the pale green celadons. Iron works in Guangdong also expanded, making iron products such as nails, needles, pots and wires for export.[80]

Besides increase in the scale of production, porcelain craftsmanship was also refined and its associated artistic style expanded as a result of the greater overseas trade. Many Ming porcelain pieces unearthed in Southeast Asia, for example, bear Islamic motifs. The bluish-white porcelain bowl in the collection of the Jakarta Museum in Indonesia has Arabic inscription as part of its design. It was found to be part of a range of porcelain products customized for Muslim buyers.[81]

Another benefit of Zheng He's win-win trade was the exchange of resources that improved the life of both the Chinese and the natives of the countries visited. For example, some natives used porcelain bowls to eat instead of their usual palm leaves; Chinese silk expanded the choice of fabric and helped improve the comfort of clothing for the foreigners; Chinese tiles were used on the roofs in Malacca; and some Chinese plows were used by Kalimantan people till today.[82] The Chinese also brought brushes and paper to Champa, and passed on to the locals there paper, brush, and ink-making crafts.[83] For the Chinese, pepper became an essential ingredient for seasoning food,[84] and chaulmoogra-seed oil obtained from Siam was used in the treatment of leprosy.[85] As another example, Zheng He also imported materials *Suni* and

Boqing from Semudera and Kalimantan, which improved the firing techniques of bluish-white porcelains.[86]

By building and facilitating such win-win trade relationships, both China and the countries Zheng He visited enjoyed greater material benefits and prospered together. Such trade collaborations also translated into a greater interdependence that binded China closer to these foreign countries.

Major Criticism

Zheng He's voyages have been criticized by both modern-day scholars as well as Ming-era officials. Their major criticism relates to what they argued as the intensive consumption of resources by Zheng He's voyages. Many felt that Zheng He's voyages had cost huge financial losses for the Ming Court and had therefore weakened its financial position.[87] The voyages had also shifted the Court's focus from its basic purpose, wasted the country's resources, and allowed the eunuch to wield too much power.[88] In 1473, Ming official Liu Daxia instructed the burning of documents and records regarding Zheng He's voyages[89] and commented that Zheng He's voyages cost so much and consumed so much manpower that even if Zheng He had brought back some precious treasures, these did not benefit the country enough.[90]

While there could be losses caused by generosity in imperial gift-giving, extravagant purchase of luxury goods, and corruption related to welcoming of foreign envoys, Zheng He's detractors had likely disregarded the wealth that Zheng He had brought back as a consequence of the trade activities. As recorded in the *Shuyu Zhouzi Lu*,

> Since the beginning of the Yongle reign, envoys were sent to foreign countries all over the world to issue the emperor's edicts. As a result of the diplomatic activities, foreign tributes kept coming. The government warehouses were filled with rare goods and lavish treasures that were longed for in other

dynasties. Civilians under poverty bought large quantities of
foreign goods under government recommendation, and many
had become affluent as a result, and the government treasury
also enjoyed greater wealth.[91]

Apparently, after having observed the first three successful voyages
led by Zheng He, Emperor Yongle was confident enough with
the financial position of the Ming Court that he ordered the
construction of the Dabao'en Temple, including an extravagant
porcelain pagoda to be built in gratitude to his mother, Empress
Ma. The project was reported to have cost 2.5 million ounces of
silver and this was taken from the surplus revenues brought back
by Zheng He's treasure fleet.[92]

The eventual financial problems faced by the Ming Court
in the later part of Emperor Yongle's reign had other complex
causes. There were four major projects carried out under the
instruction of Emperor Yongle at that time, namely, the War
with Vietnam, Zheng He's voyages, the move of the capital from
Nanjing to Beijing, and the five Mongolian military campaigns
in the North.[93] Of these major projects, only Zheng He's voyages
actually brought in revenue. The military campaigns against
Vietnam and Mongolia were expensive and largely unsuccessful.
The building and shifting of the capital was a lavish imperial
expenditure. It may therefore be an unfair analysis to attribute
the eventual financial woes of the Ming Court solely to Zheng
He's voyages and ignore the many economic and non-economic
benefits the voyages had brought to the Ming Court and Ming
China.

It may therefore be more valid to say that Zheng He's Act
of Building Win-Win through trade collaboration was wise and
mutually beneficial for China and the countries Zheng He had
traded with.

Act of Ensuring Sustainability

This refers to Zheng He's act of securing an external environment that would facilitate peaceful diplomatic and mutually-beneficial trade activities. This would then ensure the sustainability of the overall collaborative environment and relationship.

At the time of Zheng He's voyages, the south and west seas were threatened by rampant pirate activities and political instability in the region. Therefore, Zheng He's act of ensuring sustainability was aimed at securing this external environment to help in the sustainability of peaceful diplomatic and trading activities.

Eradicate Piracy and Threats to Regional Security

As part of this act, Zheng He was involved in the three incidents where he had to invoke his military force to capture the culprits who were posing as threats to regional stability.

The first incident relates to the capture of pirate chief Chen Zuyi in 1407. The *Yingya Shenglan* recorded Chen Zuyi as a Cantonese renegade who escaped to Palembang with his family during the reign of Emperor Hongwu. He was self-appointed as the local chieftain and became an arrogant and fierce bandit who robbed ships passing by.[94] Even though he paid tribute to the Ming Court, the emperor was not pleased with his involvement in piracy.[95] Zheng He also personally came to know of Chen Zuyi's threat to emissaries and traders in the region on his first voyage. After his personal encounter with him on his return trip in 1407, Zheng He pursued and captured Chen Zuyi and brought him back to Nanjing where he was executed under the emperor's order.[96] Since then, travellers and traders need not worry about being robbed when sailing through Palembang and the Malacca straits.

The second incident was the capture of King Alagakkonara. Although he was not a pirate himself, he was a contributor to the piracy problem rampant in Ceylon at that time. As recorded in *Ming Taizong Shilu*, Alagakkonara bore evil intentions. As a ruler, he oppressed his people, bullied his neighbour[97] and robbed foreign envoys visiting or passing Ceylon.[98] Further, his oppression forced his people to become pirates to earn a living. Hence, the piracy problem was serious in that region.[99] All neighbouring states suffered as a result.[100] In fact, the problem Zheng He encountered with Alagakkonara deterred him from reaching Hormuz on the third voyage as was originally instructed in the edict by Emperor Yongle.[101] After Zheng He had captured Alagakkonara and a new ruler was installed, the piracy problem was much mitigated and the relationship between Ceylon and her neighbouring countries improved. Quite clearly, removing the threat of Alagakkonara and pirates in the region did not only benefit Zheng He and cleared his path to Hormuz, it also benefitted the countries and traders in the region, as it became much safer for them to sail and carry out their trade activities.

The third incident took place during the fourth voyage of Zheng He, out at Samudra (also known as Semudera) in north Sumatra. Here, Sekander, though not a pirate, was in a political conflict caused by his rebellion against Zain al-Abidin, the legitimate prince, and this had become a threat to the security of the region. Hence, by fighting and arresting Sekander, Zheng He helped to ensure a more peaceful and secure environment for traders and emissaries in the region.[102]

Traders from Ryukyu Islands, for example, had benefited greatly from this Zheng He Act of Ensuring Sustainability, and their trading activities flourished. With ships given to them as a gift by the Ming Court, Ryukyu traders sailed on the sea routes cleared by Zheng He and participated in the sino-centred trade network linking Japan, Korea, Malaysia, Indonesia and other south sea countries. Much of this trading network was established after the first voyage of Zheng He.[103]

Maintaining Power Balance in the Region

Another source of instability in the region during Zheng He's time was the rising power of Siam and Java. These two states often threatened and bullied neighbouring smaller city-states. Zheng He established strong relations with these smaller city-states and took them under Ming China's wings and in this way, maintained the power balance of the region and protected these smaller states and entrepots from constant disturbances.

In this context, the experience of Malacca served as evidence of such efforts by Zheng He. As recorded in the *Yingya Shenglan*, Malacca was originally a feudal state of Siam. Parameswara, alias Iskandar Shah, was the ruler of Malacca and he was instructed to pay 40 *Liang* (Chinese ounce) of gold as tribute to Siam. If Malacca failed to pay, Siam threatened to invade the city-state.[104] Feeling oppressed by Siam in this way, Iskandar Shah approached the Ming Court for help. On his first voyage, on behalf of Emperor Yongle, Zheng He delivered an imperial decree to appoint Iskandar Shah as the King of Malacca.[105] Stone tablets were also erected to canonize the status of Malacca[106] as a feudal state of China. With the support of the Ming Court behind Malacca, a direct invasion into Malacca was no longer an option for Siam, as that would damage its trading relationship with China.[107] However, Siam harassment of Malacca continued.

In 1419, Zheng He carried a letter of reprimand for the King of Siam from Emperor Yongle. The letter stated that the emperor had learned about the military harassment of Malacca by Siam and it carried the emperor's reprimand that "those who are fond of employing troops do not have virtuous hearts". The Emperor

Yongle went on to restate Malacca's status as a feudal state of China and reminded the King of Siam that the King of Malacca is a "minister of the (Ming) court". The Emperor Yongle gave the King of Siam "face" by suggesting that perhaps it was the King's ministers who had been using his name in this quarrel with Malacca.[108] The effort to protect Malacca was consistent; even on the seventh voyage, Zheng He sent another imperial edict to Siam to discourage them from harassing Malacca.[109]

Largely due to the support of the Ming emperors and the mediation efforts of Zheng He, there was no war between Ayutthaya (capital of Siam) and Malacca, until the mid-fifteenth century.[110] By then, large-scale imperial voyages had stopped, and Zheng He had already passed away, and so interaction and communication among Malacca, Siam and China dissipated; and, without China's presence, war broke out between Siam and Malacca in the mid-fifteenth century.

Apart from establishing a close relationship with Malacca to secure the influence of China over the south sea and hence maintain the fine power balance between Siam, China, and Java, Zheng He also had other allies in maintaining the political stability in the region. Champa, for example, was also protected by China from invasion by Annam, Vietnam. In return, Champa also sent troops to aid Chinese against Annam when a conflict broke out.[111] Zheng He also honoured Cochin to keep Calicut in check and to maintain stability on the Malabar Coast.[112] The Sultan of Aden also liaised with Zheng He in his attempt to have Ming China as an ally against the aggressive sultans of Egypt.[113]

With all the political allies of Ming China, Zheng He's efforts in this Act of Ensuring Sustainability of win-win trade relations had helped in the development of cosmopolitan trading ports all over the region.[114]

Act of Cultivating Trust

This refers to Zheng He's conscious act on the ground of always seeking to build trust with all the countries and peoples he visited through both economic and non-economic activities and interactions.

Thus, even as Zheng He carried out Emperor Yongle's policy of foreign diplomacy (articulating the intent of spreading peace and goodwill for all), treated the local rulers and their peoples respectfully and generously (practising generosity), forged friendly ties and initiated trade with the countries he visited (building win-win collaboration with all), secured an external environment that is stable, peaceful and pirates-safe (ensuring a sustainable collaborative environment), Zheng He was at the same time cultivating and earning trust for the long term through all these "Acts of Collaboration".

We highlight here three specific areas where Zheng He was apparently consciously cultivating trust with the foreign countries he visited: (1) Advocate for Fairness in Trade; (2) Use of Military Force for Defence; and (3) People, Cultural and Religious Connections.

Advocate for Fairness in Trade

Zheng He made a conscious effort to survey the markets in the places he visited, seeking to find out the respective currencies used, the methods of trade, the measurements used and their conversion, and other business customs and conventions. For example, in Champa, gold was used instead of silver to purchase Chinese porcelain and silk. In Java, Chinese copper coins could be used in trade. In Sri Lanka, Chinese goods were bartered with precious stones. In other places, even Chinese handicrafts could be used to barter for local products.[115] In general, Zheng He would follow the local business convention and ensure fairness, integrity, and credibility in all business transactions, and in the process, built business collaborations based on mutual respect and mutually beneficial exchanges.[116]

Zheng He was likely to have stayed in Calicut from December 1406 to April 1407 to barter and trade.[117] The *Yingya Shenglan* had a detailed description of how trade was carried out with traders in Calicut during this period:

> There were two Muslim chieftains authorized by the King to be in charge of government affairs in Calicut...whenever treasure ships arrive, they would be in charge of the trade transactions. Usually an Indian broker would be sent to fix a date with Ming official to discuss the price for Chinese goods. On that day, goods would be inspected and prices negotiated for each of the goods. The final prices agreed by both sides would be written in a contract, a copy of which was kept by each party. The Indian chieftain will join hands with the Chinese officials and seal the contract with a handclasp, after which no repudiation of price would be entertained even if the market condition had changed.[118]

From this, we can see that the trade agreements were taken very seriously and carried out in a transparent and fair manner. In fact, prices were negotiated vigorously and decided only after much calculation and haggling. Often, prices could not be fixed in one day, and they may eventually take 1 month to 2–3 months to decide.[119]

Zheng He would rigorously maintain his position of paying a fair share for the goods his fleet purchased. In Siam, for example, Zheng He discovered mahogany in the forest. It is an extremely hard wood that is suitable for making rudders, and it was clearly very important for Zheng He's fleet in the case of emergency replacement needs. Instead of just cutting them and taking them as free, Zheng He paid the Siamese in gold[120] for the wood that was cut. In this way, it was not surprising that the countries Zheng He had visited welcomed the treasure ships and were willing to trade with them, as the fleet has earned for itself the credibility as a trustworthy business partner.

Use of Military Force for Defence

What was equally important in cultivating trust lies also in what Zheng He did not do. In all of his voyages and visits, Zheng He carried himself as a man of integrity. He did not engage in any conquests, killing, looting or destruction.[121] Although there were some 27,000 crew and 200 ships involved in the expeditions, none of his expeditions resulted in the occupation of any stretch of territory.[122] Such non-antagonistic, non-aggressive and non-colonization behaviours and actions on the ground clearly helped to engender trust and goodwill amongst the peoples he visited.[123]

This is in spite of the fact that according to the *Zhenghe Jiapu*[124] (Zheng He's family record), the majority of Zheng He's 27,000 crew were military officers. Such a large army would therefore easily constitute a significant military threat to the foreign countries visited. As such, Zheng He was specially guarded in his use of military force, limiting it to only situations where self-defence was called for. And indeed, in all his seven epic grand voyages, there were only three occasions where Zheng He had to invoke the use of the army.

As we had described earlier, on the return leg of his first voyage in 1407, Zheng He used his troops against the pirate chief Chen Zuyi. Even then, it was after the latter had pretended to turn himself in, and then planned a sneak attack against Zheng He's fleet instead. Zheng He captured him alive and sent him back to the emperor for his judgment and decision. The *Yingya*

Shenglan, *Xingcha Shenglan* and *Ming Taizong Shilu* all had detailed records of this incident.

The second military action was against Alagakkonara of Ceylon on the third voyage of Zheng He. Alagakkonara was apparently not the legitimate ruler and he had flatly refused to pay tribute to the Chinese emperor or to erect the stone tablet.[125] According to *Ming Taizong Shilu*, he sent 50,000 men to attack and rob Zheng He's fleet.[126] His plan was to make a surprise attack on the fleet while Zheng He was cut off from direct communication with his ships.[127] Therefore Zheng He had to defend the fleet. With a troop of 2,000, Zheng He cut off the return route of Alagakkonara's army and caught him and his family alive.[128] Even so, Alagakkonara was forgiven by Emperor Yongle and sent back to Ceylon on a subsequent voyage. Unlike Chen Zuyi, who was executed for piracy, Alagakkonara was respected as the leader of Ceylon, and his armed attack was treated as an ignorant political decision.

The third armed conflict as described earlier was in Samudra (Semudera) on the fourth voyage of Zheng He in 1410. Sekander, a rebel of the prince in power was unhappy that Ming China pledged support for the Prince, brought gifts for him and traded with him. Hence Sekander led ten thousand men against Zheng He.[129] Zheng He retaliated in self-defence and pursued Sekander and finally caught him alive.[130] This event was recorded in Zheng He's biography in *Ming Shi*, *Yingya Shenglan* and *Shuyu Zhouzi Lu*. It was clear that Zheng He only used his troops as defence after Sekander took action.

It is noteworthy that pirate Chen Zuyi and rebel Sekander were treated as criminals, and hence executed after they were sent back to the Ming Court. Being a ruler, even if he may be illegitimate, Alagakkonara was mercifully released though he had actually launched his attack on Zheng He. We therefore see that the Ming Court and Zheng He had no intention to annex or to take control of the states in the south and west seas. Zheng He's army was therefore apparently not a threat to the states and countries he visited.

Zheng He also did not use his army for offensive purposes. In fact, in many instances, Zheng He tolerated or avoided animosity and hostility of the local people. On his first voyage, for example, according to record in *Ming Shi*, end of June 1407, Zheng He sailed to Java and found himself caught in the middle of the armed conflict between the East and West King of Java. When some of his crew members went to trade in the East King's territory, they met the West King's army; 170 of Zheng He's men were killed. Zheng He was furious about the incident. However, after the West King sent his men to make apologies, Zheng He gave up his plan to attack and revenge.[131] Zheng He's tolerance gained the respect of the West King, and since then Java had consistently sent envoys to China to pay respect and had maintained collaborative relations with China.[132]

Why then did Zheng He travel with such a large army when it can appear to be intimidating to others? We already know that the Ming Emperor wanted to share Ming China's glory and spendour with all under *Tianxia*; this is in agreement with the purpose of "power projection" as argued by Dreyer,[133] but there was also an underlying intention of spreading peace and goodwill. The large fleet of Zheng He would therefore do justice to Ming China's glory and splendour, while at the same time affording a sense of security for the politically troubled states seeking Ming China's protection and help.

Further, considering the amount of precious trade items and expensive imperial gifts carried on Zheng He's fleet, it may be understandable that a significant military force for self-defence and protection against pirates and bandits was called for.

As Zheng He acted to cultivate trust, many of the foreign rulers indeed came to trust Zheng He enough to sail back with him personally to visit the Ming Court. A good example of this is Borneo King Abdul Majid Hassan. He was recorded as having sailed with Zheng He and had brought his family and government officials along.[134] Without considerable assurance of security about his own safety, and trust in Zheng He, he was not likely to have made such a decision.

People, Cultural and Religious Connections

Zheng He also went the extra mile and showed that he cared for the peoples. At ports of call, Zheng He directed the 150 medical officers designated to treat the crew to also treat local patients.[135] This showed that he had compassion for the sick. This touched the hearts of the locals and helped Zheng He to establish trust and credibility with them.

Zheng He also sought to establish other means of connection with the locals. As an example, before his fourth voyage, Zheng He made the long journey to Xi'an in north China to personally invite Hasan, the spiritual leader of the Qingjing Mosque, to join the expedition as a translator and adviser.[136] This was clearly a conscious effort on Zheng He's part to have Hasan help him in linking with the locals more effectively.

Similarly, in his second visit to Ceylon, Zheng He erected an unusual trilingual stone tablet. The Chinese portion of the tablet praised Buddha and recorded the gifts and offerings that Zheng He made in honour of the Lord Buddha; the Tamil portion of the tablet offered similar praise to the Hindu god Tenavarai-Nayanar; and the Persian inscription on the tablet praised the glory of Allah and the saints of Islam. Zheng He also ensured that the offerings made to each god was in equal amounts so that none was seen to be more favoured.[137] This showed Zheng

He's conscious efforts to connect with the people of Ceylon of all religious and cultural backgrounds. Such efforts of connection also demonstrated his act of seeking to cultivate and earn the trust of the locals.

As another example, a stone tablet was erected in Calicut in 1407 to commemorate the friendship between Ming China and Calicut. This was recorded in the *Yingya Shenglan*, *Xiyang Fanguo Zhi*[138] and *Xiyang Chaogong Dianlu*.[139] Again, this gesture by Zheng He was aimed at establishing connections with the local people and hence to earn their trust and friendship.

Implications

We have provided more details and insights into Zheng He's 5Acts of Collaboration in this chapter. Once Zheng He arrived at his potential collaborator's location, he would apparently announce his intention for collaboration (the act of articulating intent), and then followed that by giving gifts and sharing resources, knowledge and technology (the act of practising generosity). Then, to ensure that this collaborative relationship can be sustained for the long term, Zheng He facilitated trade to generate benefits for all (his act of building win-win), while at the same time, he paid attention to the external environment to ensure that it remained secure and safe from pirates and bandits, and stable in terms of the political balance of power (the act of ensuring sustainability). Zheng He's fifth act of collaboration involved him working hard on ensuring fairness in trade, using his military force for good and connecting with people in all ways so as to earn their trust and confidence for long-term collaboration (his act of cultivating trust).

As a result of Zheng He's 5Acts of Collaboration as practised on the ground, Zheng He was able to create a stable political atmosphere, a secure trading environment, and a mutually beneficial social-economic network in the south and west seas. He carried the Ming flag high and upheld the respected authority of the Ming Court in the region. In this sense, Zheng He had executed his mission with finesse and had also achieved his own vision of protecting the interest of China through his maritime strategies. Indeed, we have referred to Zheng He's maritime strategies in this book as the overall Zheng He's *Art of Collaboration*.

What does this mean for today's managers and leaders?

Quite clearly, in the highly connected world of today, collaboration is an inevitable and unavoidable element of business. The formula to prosperity and growth is much more complex than that of a zero-sum game. To look at others doing business within the same industry as competitors and enemies, as in the mindset of Sun Zi's Art of War, may help us to win market share off them; but, looking at others as potential collaborators can yield the possibility of increasing the overall pie of business for all and hence move us all into the realm of win-win or positive-sum games.

Zheng He's *Art of Collaboration*, and his specific 5Acts of Collaboration on the ground, advocates more of a win-win relationship among businesses, as we recognize here that a friendly collaborative network generates much more synergy and results than a self-isolating aggressive entity can ever hope to achieve. Hence, there is much wisdom in Zheng He's *Art and Acts of Collaboration* that managers today should and can learn to use.

This is especially so for a large, established corporation doing business in a relatively fragmented industry, which is analogous to Zheng He's Ming China seeking to exercise its dominant position in the Asia-African region in the fifteenth century. It is important to defend this pole position while remaining active in collaborating with others to develop and grow the market as a whole. This would call for careful management of the delicate relationships with the smaller entities in the industry who would want to learn from you and yet fear you. This management of the collaborative relationships is indeed an art.

For managers and leaders in such a context, and for all others, practising this art of collaboration according to Zheng He's model will mean a need to:

(1) embrace and articulate the collaborative mindset (which means seeking out collaborators; embrace and share values of collaboration and mutual help; and, recognize and entrench collaborative behaviour within the organization);

(2) learn to be more generous in giving and sharing (which means managing goodwill; manage effective resource sharing; and build capabilities to facilitate sharing from a position of strength);

(3) search for ways to build win-win to grow the business pie (which means building on complementary assets and skills; and generating synergies and economies);

(4) keep an eye on environmental threats (which means managing external risks to ensure the sustainability of the collaborative relationship; tracking disruptive technologies; and monitoring game-changing practices); and

(5) find ways and means to connect with others (which means trust management; guarding of reputation; and growing reliability and dependability).

Hopefully this chapter, and this book, would have given today's managers and leaders the motivation and conceptual structure to stimulate inspirations for our own versions of collaborative strategies that will benefit our own businesses as well as the bigger business world.

Endnotes

1. My student Yuan Yi joined me at the International Conference on Zheng He and the Afro-Asian World in Malacca in July 2010. Since then, we have discussed about extending Zheng He's Art of Collaboration to specifically delineate Zheng He's actual acts of collaboration on the ground. Yuan Yi undertook an independent study module on this with me as the supervising professor. The contents in this chapter represent part of the outcome from that module of study.

2. 辛元欧，《郑和下西洋纵论》，载《郑和研究》，1996年第3期，中国南京郑和研究会，第13页。(*Journal of Zheng He Research*, Nanjing Zheng He Research Society).

3. Edward L. Dreyer, *Zheng He: China and the Oceans in the Early Ming Dynasty, 1405–1433* (U.S.: Pearson Education, Inc., 2007), Author's Preface.

4. 《天妃灵应之纪》碑文，收录于《郑和下西洋资料汇编》上册，海洋出版社2005年增编本，558页。(*Compilation of Records and Materials on Zheng He's Voyages to the West Seas,* Ocean Publication).

5. <http://www.guoxue.com/shibu/24shi/mingshi/ms_304.htm> (*Ming Shi-Official History of Ming Dynasty*).

6. 毛佩琦，《郑和的使命：天下共享太平之福》，载《郑和下西洋研究》，2005年第二期，北京郑和下西洋研究会，第225页。(*Journal of Research on Zheng He's Voyages to the West Seas*, published by Beijing Zheng He Research Society).

7. *Zheng He: China and the Oceans in the Early Ming Dynasty*, see Author's Preface.

8. Louise E. Levathes, *When China Ruled the Seas: The Treasure Fleet of the Dragon Throne, 1405–1433* (U.S.: Oxford University Press, 1994), p. 146.

9. 张廷玉［清］，《明史》，摘录于：何川芳，《文明视角下的郑和远航》，收录于《郑和远航与世界文明—纪念郑和下西洋600周年纪念论文集》，北京大学出版社，2005年，第3页。(*Zheng He's Voyage and World Civilization*, Peking University Publication).

10. 《明太祖实录》卷八十八，洪武七年三月癸巳，国立北平图书馆藏红格本，第1565页。(*Ming Taizu Shilu: Factual Record of Ming Taizu's Reign*, Peking Library Collection).

11. 《明太祖实录》卷六十八，洪武四年九月辛未，国立北平图书馆藏红格本，第1277页。

12. 《郑和家谱·敕谕海外诸番条》，收录于《郑和下西洋资料汇编》上册，海洋出版社2005年增编本，531页。(Compilation of Records and Materials on Zheng He's Voyages to the West Seas, Ocean Publication); own translation into English.

13. 孔远志，郑一钧，《东南亚考察论郑和》，北京大学出版社，2008年，第36页。(*Southeast Asian Study on Zheng He*, Peking University Publication).

14. 孔远志，郑一钧，《东南亚考察论郑和》，北京大学出版社，2008年，第382页。

15. （法）弗朗索瓦．德勃雷著，赵喜鹏译，《海外华人序言》，摘录于：《欲国家富强不可置海洋于不顾》，《郑和研究》，2001年第2期，中国南京郑和研究会，第15页。(*Chinese in Foreign Countries*, quoted in *Zheng He Research*).

16. 苏明阳，《法国的月亮比中国圆吗？评几篇有关郑和海权思想论文》，收录于《郑和研究与活动简讯》，第六期2002年8月30日。(*Zheng He Research and Activities Newsletter*).

17. 彭勇，《2009年郑和研究综述》，载《郑和研究》，2010年第1期第8页，江苏省郑和研究会与太仓市郑和研究会联合出版。(*Journal of Zheng He Research*, Jiangsu Zheng He Society and Tai Cang Zheng He Society Publication).

18. *When China Ruled the Seas*, p. 87.

19. "Sun Tzu Quotes, The Art of War Quotes", <http://www.military-quotes.com/Sun-Tzu.htm> (accessed 20 June 2010).

20. Tan Ta Sen and Chia Lin Sien, eds., *The Zheng He Epic*, 1st edition in

Chinese edited by Zhou Wenlin et al. (Kunming, Yunnan, China: Yunnan's Publishing House, Yunnan Fine Arts Publishing House, Auora Publishing House, 2006), p. 316.

21. 《郑和家谱•敕谕海外诸番条》，收录于《郑和下西洋资料汇编》上册，海洋出版社2005年增编本，531页; own translation into English.

22. *Zheng He Epic*, p. 316.

23. *Zheng He: China and the Oceans in the Early Ming Dynasty*, p. 51.

24. *Zheng He: China and the Oceans in the Early Ming Dynasty*, p. 37.

25. 王海洲，潘望，《郑和的时代：大航海时代的反思，东西方相互的认识》，第四章：1405纵横大洋的郑和船队，古吴轩出版社，第138页。(*The Zheng He Era: Reflections of a Era of Sea Voyages, and Mutual Understanding of the East and the West*, Gu Wu Xuan Publication).

26. 傅海滨，《郑和对外交往的再认识》，载《郑和研究》1996年第3期，中国南京郑和研究会，第51页。(*Journal of Zheng He Research*, Nanjing Zheng He Research Society).

27. 《明太祖实录》卷七十一，洪武五年壬子，国立北平图书馆藏红格，第1314页。

28. *Zheng He Epic*, p. 321.

29. *Zheng He Epic*, p. 248.

30. Tan Ta Sen, *Cheng Ho and Malacca* (Malacca: Cheng Ho Cultural Museum and International Zheng He Society, 2005), p. 41.

31. （清）陈伦炯，《海国见闻录南洋记》，摘录于：《郑和与东南亚》，新加坡郑和学会出版，第19页。(*Zheng He and Southeast Asia*, published by Singapore Zheng He Society).

32. 田连谟，《论徐福与郑和的民族精神》，载《郑和研究》，1996年第3期24页，中国南京郑和研究会。(*Journal of Zheng He Research*, Nanjing Zheng He Research Society).

33. *Zheng He Epic*, p. 345.

34. 《嘉兴府志》，四库全书存目丛书，史部，地理类，第179册，齐鲁书社。(*Record of Jian Xin Prefecture*, Qi Lu Publishing).

35. 王海洲，潘望，《郑和的时代：大航海时代的反思，东西方相互的认识》，第四章：1405纵横大洋的郑和船队，古吴轩出版社，第126页。

36. 王海洲，潘望，《郑和的时代：大航海时代的反思，东西方相互的认识》，第四章：1405纵横大洋的郑和船队，古吴轩出版社，第127页。

37. 肖忠生，《郑和、王景弘下西洋的历史功绩与现实意义》，载《郑和研
   究》，2010年第1期第25页，江苏省郑和研究会与太仓市郑和研究会联
   合出版。(*Journal of Zheng He Research*, published by Jiangsu Zheng
   He Research Society and Tai Cang Zheng He Research Society).

38. *When China Ruled the Seas*, pp. 186–87.

39. People's Republic of China, *Envoy of Peace from China: In
   Commemoration of the 600th Anniversary of Zheng He's Great Voyages*
   (Beijing: Ministry of Culture, 2005), p. 78.

40. *Zheng He Epic*, p. 281.

41. *Zheng He Epic*, p. 287.

42. 梁志明，《略论占城在郑和下西洋中的历史地位与作用》，收录于《郑
   和远航与世界文明—纪念郑和下西洋600周年纪念论文集》，北京大学出
   版社，2005年，第418页。

43. *When China Ruled the Seas*, p. 112.

44. *When China Ruled the Seas*, p. 171.

45. *Zheng He Epic*, p. 240.

46. *Zheng He: China and the Oceans in the Early Ming Dynasty*, p. 40.

47. （清）张廷玉，《明史》，卷二百五列传第九十三《硃纨传》，载于：
   <http://www.guoxue.com/shibu/24shi/mingshi/ms_205.htm>.

48. Roderich Ptak, "Ming Maritime Trade to Southeast Asia, 1368–1567:
   Visions of a 'System'", in *From the Mediterranean to the China Sea:
   Miscellaneous Notes*, edited by C. Guillot, D. Lombard, and R. Ptak
   (Germany, 1998), p. 159.

49. 郑克晟，《从郑和下西洋看明初海外贸易政策的转变》，收录于《郑和
   远航与世界文明—纪念郑和下西洋600周年纪念论文集》，北京大学出版
   社，2005年，第197页。

50. (明)吕毖撰，《明朝小史》卷四永乐纪，四库全书存目丛书，史部，
   第19册，北京出版社。(*A Short History of Ming Dynasty*, Beijing
   Publishing).

51. 《皇明世法录》，卷10《文皇帝宝训》，四库全书存目丛书，史部，
   第13册，北京出版社。(*Legal and Institutional Records of Ming Imperial
   Court*, Beijing Publishing).

52. 王海洲，潘望，《郑和的时代：大航海时代的反思，东西方相互的认
   识》，第三章：1402郑和下西洋的支持者和反对者，古吴轩出版社，
   第83页。

53. Wang Guangwu, "The Opening of Relations between China and Malacca, 1403–05", *Admiral Zheng He and Southeast Asia* (Singapore: Institute of Southeast Asian Studies, 2005), p. 8.

54. 郑永常，《郑和下西洋前南海形式：论明帝国与满者伯夷的角力》，收录于《郑和远航与世界文明—纪念郑和下西洋600周年纪念论文集》，北京大学出版社，2005年，第424页。

55. 李映发，《中国古代的远洋航行与沿海海运》，载《郑和研究》，2010第2期第19页，江苏省郑和研究会与太仓市郑和研究会联合出版。

56. 郑永常，《郑和下西洋前南海形式：论明帝国与满者伯夷的角力》，收录于《郑和远航与世界文明—纪念郑和下西洋600周年纪念论文集》，北京大学出版社，2005年，第424页。

57. Roderich Ptak, "Ming Maritime Trade to Southeast Asia, 1368–1567: Visions of a 'System'", in *From the Mediterranean to the China Sea: Miscellaneous Notes*, edited by C. Guillot, D. Lombard, and R. Ptak (Germany, 1998), p. 165.

58. *When China Ruled the Seas*, p. 84.

59. 郑一钧，《郑和下西洋对15世纪初期世界文明的发展》，收录于《郑和远航与世界文明—纪念郑和下西洋600周年纪念论文集》，北京大学出版社，2005年，第32页。While this reference mentioned four bases, our analysis and writing in chapter 7 based on other references suggest Zheng He established five bases.

60. 陈达生，《马六甲'官厂'遗址考》，收录于《郑和与东南亚》，新加坡郑和学会2005年出版，第97 – 105页; also in *Cheng He and Malacca*, p. 44.

61. （明）茅元仪，《武备志》卷二百四十，《郑和航海图》又名《茅坤图》，四库全书存目丛书，子部，第26册，北京出版社。(*Wu Bei Zhi*, Beijing Publishing).

62. （明）马欢，《瀛涯胜览》，商务印书馆影印，第36 – 37页。(*Yingya Shenglan*, Commercial Publishing); own translation into English; see another translation in *Cheng Ho and Malacca*, p. 46.

63. 郑一钧，《郑和下西洋对15世纪初期世界文明的发展》，收录于《郑和远航与世界文明—纪念郑和下西洋600周年纪念论文集》，北京大学出版社，2005年，第32页。

64. 毛佩琦，《郑和的使命：天下共享太平之福》，载《郑和下西洋研究》，2005年第二期，第224页，北京郑和下西洋研究会。

65. 林孟欣，《从明实录探索郑在明代朝廷的角色以及郑和下西洋的采买任务》，载《郑和研究与活动简讯》，24期合订本（上），第三期第11页。

66. 王海洲，潘望，《郑和的时代：大航海时代的反思，东西方相互的认识》，第四章：1405纵横大洋的郑和船队。

67. 鹿世明，《郑和下西洋与中国对外贸易》，载《走向海洋的中国人》，海潮出版社，1996年，第35页。(*The Chinese on Their Path to the Oceans*, Hai Chao Publishing).

68. 辛元欧，《郑和下西洋纵论》，载《郑和研究》，1996年第3期第10页，中国南京郑和研究。

69. 《南都繁会图》，中国国家博物馆藏。(*Chinese National Museum Collection*, accessible online at: <http://www.chnmuseum.cn/tabid/212/Default.aspx?AntiqueLanguageID=220#> (accessed 30 September 2011).

70. 辛元欧，《郑和下西洋纵论》，载《郑和研究》，1996年第3期第10页，中国南京郑和研究会。

71. *Zheng He: China and the Oceans in the Early Ming Dynasty*, p. 61.

72. （法）弗朗索瓦. 德勃雷著，赵喜鹏译，《海外华人-序言》，摘录于：《郑和下西洋纵论》，《郑和研究》，1996年第3期，第10页。

73. 陆芸，《从海南、泉州穆斯林的流动看中国与东南亚的伊斯兰联系》，载《西北民族学院学报》第四期。(*Journal of Northwest University for Nationalities*, Northwest University Publication).

74. *Zheng He Epic*, p. 8.

75. （明）马欢，《瀛涯胜览》，商务印书馆影印，第31页。

76. （明）马欢，《瀛涯胜览》，商务印书馆影印，第69页。

77. 孔远志，郑一钧，《东南亚考察论郑和》，北京大学出版社，2008年，第104页。

78. 万明，《从明代青花瓷崛起看郑和下西洋伟大功绩》，载《郑和下西洋研究》，北京郑和下西洋研究会，2007年第4期，第77页。

79. *When China Ruled the Seas*, p. 84.

80. *When China Ruled the Seas*, p. 84.

81. 韩胜宝，《郑和之路》，经贸篇，上海科学技术文献出版社，2005，第100页。(*Zheng He's Path*, Shanghai Science and Technology Publishing).

82. 肖忠生，《郑和、王景弘下西洋的历史功绩与现实意义》，载《郑和研究》，2010年第1期第25页，江苏省郑和研究会与太仓市郑和研究会联合出版。

83. 梁向明，《郑和下西洋对东南亚诸国的影响》，载《云南民族大学学报》，2005年第22卷第5期，第109页。(*A Preliminary Study of the Influence of Zheng He's Voyages to the West Seas on the South East Asian Countries*, Journal of Yunnan Nationalities University).

84. *Zheng He Epic*, p. 232.

85. *When China Ruled the Seas*, pp. 105–6.

86. 韩胜宝，《郑和之路》，经贸篇，上海科学技术文献出版社，2005，第100页。

87. 李映发，《中国古代的远洋航行于沿海海运》，载《郑和研究》，2010年第2期第19页，江苏省郑和研究会与太仓市郑和研究会联合出版。

88. Andrew R. Wilson, "Southern Trade and Northern Defence: The Ming Mission to Manila, 1603", in *Chinese Diaspora Since Admiral Zheng He with Special Reference to Maritime Asia*, edited by Leo Suryadinata (Singapore: Chinese Heritage Centre, 2007), p. 95.

89. Rivers, P. J., *'1421' Voyages: Fact & Fantasy* (Ipoh, Malaysia: Perak Academy, 2004), p. 24; also see *When China Ruled the Seas*, p. 179.

90. 王海洲，潘望，《郑和的时代：大航海时代的反思，东西方相互的认识》，第三章：1402郑和下西洋的支持者和反对者，古吴轩出版社，第90页。

91. （明）严从简，《殊域周咨录》，续修四库全书，史部，地理类，735－736册，北京图书馆藏本，齐鲁书社影印。(*Records on Foreign lands*, Qi Lu Publishing).

92. *When China Ruled the Seas*, p. 121.

93. *Zheng He: China and the Oceans in the Early Ming Dynasty*, p. 24.

94. （明）马欢，《瀛涯胜览》，商务印书馆影印，第26页。

95. *Zheng He: China and the Oceans in the Early Ming Dynasty*, p. 42.

96. *Zheng He Epic*, p. 232.

97. 《明太宗实录》卷84。

98. 《明太宗实录》卷77。

99. 孔远志，郑一钧，《东南亚考察论郑和》，北京大学出版社，2008年，第73–74页。

100. （清）张廷玉，《明史》，卷三百二十六，列传第二百十五，外国七，锡兰山传；《明太宗实录》卷77，载于：<http://www.guoxue.com/shibu/24shi/mingshi/ms_326.htm>.

101. 孔远志，郑一钧，《东南亚考察论郑和》，北京大学出版社，2008年，第75页；《郑和下西洋资料汇编》下册，第851页。

102. *Zheng He: China and the Oceans in the Early Ming Dynasty*, pp. 79–81.

103. 徐斌，《郑和下西洋对琉球贸易的影响》，载《郑和研究》，2002年第1期，中国南京郑和研究会第23页。

104. （明）马欢，《瀛涯胜览》，商务印书馆影印，第32页。

105. *Zheng He: China and the Oceans in the Early Ming Dynasty*, p. 42.

106. （明）马欢，《瀛涯胜览》，商务印书馆影印，第33页；see also *When China Ruled the Seas*, p. 109.

107. *When China Ruled the Seas*, p. 109.

108. Kasetsiri Charnvit, "Zheng He-Sam Po Kong: History and Myth in Thailand", in *Chinese Diaspora Since Admiral Zheng He With Special Reference to Maritime Asia*, edited by Leo Suryadinata (Singapore: Chinese Heritage Centre, 2007), p. 78.

109. *When China Ruled the Seas*, p. 169.

110. *Zheng He-Sam Po Kong: History and Myth in Thailand*, p. 78.

111. *Zheng He: China and the Oceans in the Early Ming Dynasty*, pp. 52–53, 59.

112. *When China Ruled the Seas*, p. 145.

113. *When China Ruled the Seas*, p. 149.

114. Johannes Widodo, "Zheng He's Voyages, Maritime Trades, and the Architecture of Cosmopolitan Port Cities in Southeast Asia", in *Chinese Diaspora Since Admiral Zheng He With Special Reference to Maritime Asia*, edited by Leo Suryadinata (Singapore: Chinese Heritage Centre, 2007), p. 63.

115. 韩胜宝，《郑和之路》，经贸篇，上海科学技术文献出版社，2005，第106页。

116. 田连谟，《论徐福与郑和的民族精神》，载《郑和研究》1996年第3期24页，中国南京郑和研究会。

117. *When China Ruled the Seas*, p. 100.

118. （明）马欢，《瀛涯胜览》，商务印书馆影印，第58–59页; see also *When China Ruled the Seas*, p. 101.

119. （明）马欢，《瀛涯胜览》，商务印书馆影印，第59页。

120. *When China Ruled the Seas*, pp. 111–12.

121. *Zheng He Epic*, p. 315.

122. *Zheng He Epic*, pp. 8–9.

123. Evidence can be found in the Padmanabhapura Palace in India, where paintings of the bloody battle between the king's troops and the Portuguese are on display but there are only ornamental Chinese porcelain pieces and no sign of Chinese weapons. This suggests that the Chinese voyagers like Zheng He maintained diplomacy and friendship instead of antagonizing the countries they visited; *Zheng He Epic*, p. 284.

124. 《郑和家谱-随使官军员名条》，摘录于《郑和下西洋资料汇编》上册，海洋出版社2005年增编本60页。

125. *When China Ruled the Seas*, pp. 114–16.

126. 《明太宗实录》卷116。

127. *Zheng He: China and the Oceans in the Early Ming Dynasty*, p. 70.

128. 《明太宗实录》卷116。

129 *When China Ruled the Seas*, p. 139.

130. （明）马欢，《瀛涯胜览》，商务印书馆影印，第39–40页。

131. 孔远志，郑一钧，《东南亚考察论郑和》，北京大学出版社，2008年，第65页。

132. （清）张廷玉，《明史》，卷三百二十四，列传第二百十二，外国五，爪哇传，载于：<http://www.guoxue.com/shibu/24shi/mingshi/ms_324.htm>.

133. *Zheng He: China and the Oceans in the Early Ming Dynasty*, Author's Preface.

134. 肖忠生，《郑和、王景弘下西洋的历史功绩与现实意义》，载《郑和研究》，2010年第1期第24页，江苏省郑和研究会与太仓市郑和研究会联合出版。

135. *Zheng He Epic*, p. 345.
136. *When China Ruled the Seas*, p. 138.
137. *When China Ruled the Seas*, p. 113.
138. （明）巩珍，《西洋番国志古里国》四库全书存目丛书，史部，地理类，第255册，北京图书馆藏本影印，齐鲁书社。(*Record of Countries of the West Seas — Calicut*, Qi Lu Publishing).
139. 《西洋朝贡典录》卷下《古里国》，四库全书存目丛书，史部，地理类，第255册，暨南大学图书馆藏本影印，齐鲁书社。(*Records of Tributes from the West Seas*, Qi Lu Publishing).

References

Charnvit, Kasetsiri. "Zheng He-Sam Po Kong: History and Myth in Thailand". In *Chinese Diaspora Since Admiral Zheng He With Special Reference to Maritime Asia*, edited by Leo Suryadinata. Singapore: Chinese Heritage Centre, 2007.

Dreyer, Edward L. *Zheng He: China and the Oceans in the Early Ming Dynasty, 1405–1433*. Singapore: Pearson Education Inc., 2007.

Guillot, C., Lombard, D. and Ptak, R., eds. *From the Mediterranean to the China Sea: Miscellaneous Notes*. Germany, 1998.

Levathes, Louise E. *When China Ruled the Seas: The Treasure Fleet of the Dragon Throne, 1405–1433*. New York: Oxford University Press, 1994.

People's Republic of China. *Envoy of Peace from China: In Commemoration of the 600th Anniversary of Zheng He's Great Voyages*. Beijing: Ministry of Culture, 2005.

Ptak, Roderich. "Ming Maritime Trade to Southeast Asia, 1368–1567: Visions of a 'System'". In *From the Mediterranean to the China Sea: Miscellaneous Notes*, edited by C. Guillot, D. Lombard, and R. Ptak. Germany, 1998.

Rivers, P. J. *'1421' Voyages: Fact & Fantasy*. Ipoh: Perak Academy, 2004.

"Sun Tzu Quotes, The Art of War Quotes". <http://www.military-quotes.com/Sun-Tzu.htm> (accessed 20 June 2010).

Suryadinata, Leo, ed. *Admiral Zheng He and Southeast Asia*. Singapore: Institute of Southeast Asian Studies, 2005.

———. *Chinese Diaspora: Since Admiral Zheng He With Special Reference to Maritime Asia*. Singapore: Chinese Heritage Centre, 2007.

Tan Ta Sen. *Cheng Ho and Malacca*. Malacca: Cheng Ho Cultural Museum and International Zheng He Society, 2005.

Tan Ta Sen and Chia Lin Sien, eds. *The Zheng He Epic*. 1st edition in Chinese edited by Zhou Wenlin et al. Kunming, Yunnan, China: Yunnan's Publishing House, Yunnan Fine Arts Publishing House, Auora Publishing House, 2006.

Wang Guangwu. "The Opening of Relations between China and Malacca, 1403–05". In *Admiral Zheng He and Southeast Asia*, edited by Leo Suryadinata. Singapore: Institute of Southeast Asian Studies, 2005.

Widodo, Johannes. "Zheng He's Voyages, Maritime Trades, and the Architecture of Cosmopolitan Port Cities in Southeast Asia". In *Chinese Diaspora Since Admiral Zheng He With Special Reference to Maritime Asia*, edited by Leo Suryadinata. Singapore: Chinese Heritage Centre, 2007.

Wilson, Andrew R. "Southern Trade and Northern Defence: The Ming Mission to Manila, 1603". In *Chinese Diaspora Since Admiral Zheng He with Special Reference to Maritime Asia*, edited by Leo Suryadinata. Singapore: Chinese Heritage Centre, 2007.

辛元欧，《郑和下西洋纵论》，载《郑和研究》，1996年第3期，中国南京郑和研究会 。(*Journal of Zheng He Research*, Nanjing Zheng He Research Society).

《郑和下西洋资料汇编》，海洋出版社，2005年增编本。(*Compilation of Records and Materials on Zheng He's Voyages to the West Seas,* Ocean Publication).

（清）张廷玉，《明史》，网上电子版：<http://www.guoxue.com/shibu/24shi/mingshi/lianshu.htm>，2011年9月浏览。(*Ming Shi — Official History of Ming Dynasty*).

毛佩琦，《郑和的使命：天下共享太平之福》，载《郑和下西洋研究》，2005年第2期，北京郑和下西洋研究会。(*Journal of Research on Zheng*

He's Voyages to the West Seas, published by Beijing Zheng He Research Society).

《郑和远航与世界文明—纪念郑和下西洋600周年纪念论文集》，北京大学出版社，2005出版。(*Zheng He's Voyage and World Civilization*, Peking University Publication).

《明实录》，国立北平图书馆藏红格本。(*Ming Shilu: Factual Record of Ming Reign*, Peking Library Collection).

孔远志，郑一钧，《东南亚考察论郑和》，北京大学出版社，2008年出版。(*Southeast Asian Study on Zheng He*, Peking University Publication).

王诗成，《欲国家富强不可置海洋于不顾》，载《郑和研究》，中国南京郑和研究会，2001年第2期。(*Journal of Zheng He Research*, Nanjing Zheng He Research Society).

苏明阳，《法国的月亮比中国圆吗？评几篇有关郑和海权思想论文》，载《郑和研究与活动简讯》，第六期，2002年8月30日。(*Zheng He Research and Activities Newsletter*).

彭勇，《2009年郑和研究综述》，载《郑和研究》，2010年第1期，江苏省郑和研究会与太仓市郑和研究会联合出版。(*Journal of Zheng He Research*, Jiangsu Zheng He Society and Tai Cang Zheng He Society Publication).

王海洲，潘望，《郑和的时代：大航海时代的反思，东西方相互的认识》，古吴轩出版社，2005年出版。(*The Zheng He Era: Reflections of a Era of Sea Voyages, and Mutual Understanding of the East and the West*, Gu Wu Xuan Publication).

傅海滨，《郑和对外交往的再认识》，载《郑和研究》，1996年第3期，中国南京郑和研究会。(*Journal of Zheng He Research*, Nanjing Zheng He Research Society).

廖建裕［编］，《郑和与东南亚》，新加坡郑和学会2005年出版。(*Zheng He and Southeast Asia*, published by Singapore Zheng He Society).

田连谟，《论徐福与郑和的民族精神》，载《郑和研究》，1996年第3期，中国南京郑和研究会。(*Journal of Zheng He Research*, Nanjing Zheng He Research Society).

《嘉兴府志》，四库全书存目丛书，史部，地理类，第179册，齐鲁书社。(*Record of Jian Xin Prefecture*, Qi Lu Publishing).

肖忠生，《郑和、王景弘下西洋的历史功绩与现实意义》，载《郑和研究》，2010年第1期，江苏省郑和研究会与太仓市郑和研究会联合出版。(*Journal of Zheng He Research*, published by Jiangsu Zheng He Research Society and Tai Cang Zheng He Research Society).

（明）吕毖撰，《明朝小史》卷四永乐纪，四库全书存目丛书，史部，第19册，北京出版社。(*A Short History of Ming Dynasty*, Beijing Publishing).

《皇明世法录》，卷10《文皇帝宝训》，四库全书存目丛书，史部，第13册，北京出版社。(*Legal and Institutional Records of Ming Imperial Court*, Beijing Publishing).

李映发，《中国古代的远洋航行与沿海海运》，载《郑和研究》，2010年第2期，江苏省郑和研究会与太仓市郑和研究会联合出版。(*Journal of Zheng He Research*, published by Jiangsu Zheng He Research Society and Tai Cang Zheng He Research Society).

（明）茅元仪，《武备志》卷二百四十，《郑和航海图》又名《茅坤图》，四库全书存目丛书，子部，第26册，北京出版社。(*Wu Bei Zhi*, Beijing Publishing).

（明）马欢，《瀛涯胜览》，商务印书馆影印。(*Yingya Shenglan*, Commercial Publishing).

林孟欣，《从明实录探索郑和在明代朝廷的角色以及郑和下西洋的采买任务》，载《郑和研究与活动简讯》，24期合订本（上），第3期。(*Zheng He Research and Activities Newsletter*).

鹿世明，《郑和下西洋与中国对外贸易》，载《走向海洋的中国人》，海潮出版社，1996年。(*The Chinese on Their Path to the Oceans*, Hai Chao Publishing).

《南都繁会图》，中国国家博物馆藏。(*Chinese National Museum Collection*, Accessible online at: <http://www.chnmuseum.cn/tabid/212/Default.aspx?AntiqueLanguageID=220#> (accessed 30 September 2011).

陆芸，《从海南、泉州穆斯林的流动看中国与东南亚的伊斯兰联系》，载《西北民族学院学报》第四期。(*Journal of Northwest University for Nationalities*, Northwest University Publication).

万明，《从明代青花瓷崛起看郑和下西洋伟大功绩》，载《郑和下西洋研究》，2007年第四期。(*Journal of Research on Zheng He's Voyages to the West Seas*, published by Beijing Zheng He Research Society).

韩胜宝，《郑和之路》，经贸篇，上海科学技术文献出版社，2005年出版。
(*Zheng He's Path*, Shanghai Science and Technology Publishing).

梁向明，《郑和下西洋对东南亚诸国的影响》，载《云南民族大学学报》，
2005年第22卷第5期。(*A Preliminary Study of the Influence of Zheng He's Voyages to the West Seas on the South East Asian Countries*, Journal of Yunnan Nationalities University).

（明）严从简，《殊域周咨录》，续修四库全书，史部，地理类，735 – 736册，北京图书馆藏本，齐鲁书社影印。(*Records on Foreign lands*, Qi Lu Publishing).

徐斌，《郑和下西洋对琉球贸易的影响》，载《郑和研究》，2002年第1期，中国南京郑和研究会。(*Journal of Zheng He Research*, Nanjing Zheng He Research Society).

（明）巩珍，《西洋番国志古里国》四库全书存目丛书，史部，地理类，第255册，北京图书馆藏本影印，齐鲁书社。(*Record of Countries of the West Seas — Calicut*, Qi Lu Publishing).

《西洋朝贡典录》卷下《古里国》，四库全书存目丛书，史部，地理类，第255册，暨南大学图书馆藏本影印，齐鲁书社。(*Records of Tributes from the West Seas*, Qi Lu Publishing).

Chapter 4

COMPARING THE ART OF COLLABORATION WITH THE ART OF WAR
Does the AoC Always Triumph Over the AoW?

INTRODUCTION

We already know that Zheng He was charged by Emperor Yongle with the fundamental mission of pursuing a diplomacy of peace by spreading Chinese culture and forging friendly ties between China and countries in Asia and Africa.[1] Zheng He was to lead the grand voyages to the West to spread goodwill, help others progress, and in the process, network and build bridges for trade and collaboration; this would in turn facilitate everyone coexisting peacefully and harmoniously, even as they were ruled in accordance with the ways of heaven,[2] and in this way, do justice to the grandeur and splendour of the Ming Imperial Court.[3]

Zheng He's fulfillment of this emperor-decreed mission through his grand voyages therefore carried with it the much bigger message of pursuing peace, goodwill and collaboration

108

for the benefit of all peoples. His fifteenth-century message and practices as demonstrated through his voyages represent what we consider in this book to be his fundamental contribution for the benefit of not only business leaders and managers, but for all mankind. We refer to this as Zheng He's *Art of Collaboration* (AoC) and we have introduced and presented this in chapter 2 as an alternative model to the very well-known and well studied Sun Zi's Art of War (AoW).

Interpretations and applications of Sun Zi's Art of War in the business arena have become especially popular in recent years. Managers and leaders have been awed by AoW's stratagems for winning against their competitors by managing the perception and psychology of these "enemies" on the business battlefields, something that is basically absent in the mechanistic strategic convention of western business teaching. Especially in the area of Marketing and Sales, where competition is particularly fierce, Sun Zi's AoW has become a source of inspiration for managers to formulate competitive strategies for winning markets and customers. Books such as *Sun Tzu: Strategies for Marketing — 12 Essential Principles for Winning the War for Customers*, and *Sun Tzu: Strategies for Selling — How to Use the Art of War to Build Lifelong Customer Relationships*[4] were written in an attempt to adapt Sun Zi's military strategies into guidebooks for winning in business competitions. MacDonald and Neupert even considered Sun Zi's insights in the understanding and use of geography in warfare and interpreted them in the context of competing for markets through marketing strategies.[5]

While we embrace this analogy of business competition as warfare, it is important to recognize that in today's highly connected world, business networks and relationships are much more intricate and complex than the clear lines of animosity and opposition in warfare. In other words, aggression and warfare represent only one approach, and often a less-than-ideal approach, to managing situations in business. We have chosen to highlight in this book Zheng He's *Art of Collaboration* as an alternative model, one that is clearly a less aggressive alternative to Sun Zi's Art of War. On the surface, collaboration seems to be a direct opposite of war. And so Zheng He's AoC seems to be the antithesis of Sun Zi's AoW. Intuitively, most would argue that it is helpful to embrace collaboration, and few would say that warfare is good. In this sense, is the AoC preferred over the AoW? Would the AoC always triumph over the AoW? Are they truly dichotomous strategies? Can the two models coexist?

In this chapter,[6] we attempt to provide a better understanding of the relationship between Zheng He's AoC and Sun Zi's AoW. We will examine the fundamental philosophies, assumptions and contexts of both Zheng He and Sun Zi's strategies. This chapter is therefore an attempt at a comparative analysis and understanding of Zheng He's *Art of Collaboration* and Sun Zi's Art of War.

The chapter is therefore organized as follows. We will explain in the next section that the two alternative models actually share a common philosophical root in Chinese thinking. We will then show how these two models or sets of strategies branch out from the same philosophical root into two dichotomous approaches that are essentially contrasting on the four levels of Fundamental Strategic Objective, Principles in Strategy Formulation, Execution of Strategies and Desired Outcome. The chapter will then conclude by highlighting the implications of these differences in the application of AoC and AoW in the context of today's businesses.

COMMON ROOT IN CHINESE PHILOSOPHY

Both the AoW and the AoC carry with them influences from the values and philosophical principles that are embedded in

Chinese culture. As my senior colleague Professor Wee Chow Hou, author of *Sun Zi Bingfa: Selected Insights and Applications*, has mentioned in his book, the term "Art of War" is a most commonly accepted English title of Sun Zi's book but it is not the most precise representation of Sun Zi's philosophy.

Sun Zi is not an advocate of war, and his military strategies extend beyond physical warfare. He believes the ideal scenario is not to win every war, but to "subdue the enemy without any battle".[7] This concept is an extension from the idea of "benevolence", a fundamental philosophy advocated by Confucius. According to Confucius' thinking, one who is benevolent has respect and love for all people.[8] Hence, with such a respect for people and life, Sun Zi contends that physical warfare, in which the loss of life is inevitable, should only be used as the last resort.

Ming emperors were also well versed with the *Analects* and they advocated Confucius' teachings, the essence of which is "benevolence towards all". In fact, Zheng He was sent out on his grand voyages to shower other countries and peoples with gifts and goodwill, and to ensure that all people under heaven, including those outside of China, were enjoying the prosperity of a peaceful era.[9]

Both Sun Zi and Zheng He therefore shared the same root of philosophical thinking based on Confucius' fundamental benevolence and goodwill towards all man. Upon closer examination, however, the expressions of benevolence turned out to be different in the AoW versus the AoC. In the AoW, Sun Zi emphasized on minimizing the cost of war as in the loss of lives, while in the AoC, Zheng He focused on maximizing the benefits for Ming China and her collaborative partners overseas.

Sun Zi's expression of benevolence therefore translated into his preference for not waging war. This is why Sun Zi said, "The adept in warfare is able to subdue the army of the enemy without having to resort to battles. He is able to capture the cities of others without having to launch assaults."[10] Sun Zi further ranked his preference for warfare strategies as follows:

1. Attack the plans and strategies of the enemy
2. Attack his relationships and alliances with other nations
3. Attack the army
4. Attack walled cities[11]

The first two strategies do not involve direct physical conflict with the enemy, and kept opposition at the strategic level. The third strategy attempts to limit the harm and destruction to within the army. Attacking walled cities is the least preferred strategy as it destroys infrastructure and often leads to death of innocent civilians. Hence, Sun Zi further emphasized that one should "attack walled cities [only] when there are no other alternatives".[12]

Zheng He, on the other hand, expressed benevolence by being generous in giving gifts and sharing resources, knowledge and technology with the people of foreign countries, leading to the improved lives of these natives overseas. For example, Zheng He shared the Chinese Almanacs with Champa and Ryukyu to help enhance the quality of life of locals there, and to help spread Chinese culture and customs.[13] Similarly, Zheng He distributed free medicine as he instructed his team of medical officers to treat the local patients in Siam as an expression of his care and concern for the people there.[14] Also, Zheng He's act of building win-win collaboration through his engagement in trading activities had increased the wealth of both Chinese and foreign traders, as well as the variety of products available to all in the region. According to records, foreigners since then had greater access to Chinese porcelain, silk, and medicine,[15] while China also imported more than 160 different types of goods through Zheng He's voyages.[16]

Hence, through his collaborative strategies, Zheng He brought benefits and increased the welfare of all people in the countries he visited through his grand voyages.

FUNDAMENTAL STRATEGIC OBJECTIVE

The difference in their expression of benevolence gave rise to the difference in the fundamental strategic objectives of the AoW and the AoC.

In the AoW, arising from the expression of benevolence through the minimization of loss of value, the fundamental strategic objective is therefore to subdue and dominate the enemy in such a way as to avoid the destruction of value. In this way, the victor is able to wrestle maximum value away from the enemy through a minimization of value destruction in the process.

This is so because in Sun Zi's AoW, the assumed worldview is one where a win-win situation is not possible. There is therefore a fixed or definite amount of value and the warring parties are fighting or competing to decide on who gets to own what share of the total value available, while aiming to minimize the destruction of value as a result of the warring process. In such a win-loss situation, the best scenario is to reduce loss as value creation is not possible; the objective is then one of value redistribution to the winner. Strategies are therefore designed to gain control or dominance over the enemy in order to win value. Whether to wage war or not is just a matter of the means; the fundamental objective is still to overpower the opponent and obtain more value off him.

As mentioned earlier, Chapter 3 of Sun Zi's AoW advocates that "The adept in warfare is able to subdue the army of the enemy without having to resort to battles. He is able to capture the cities of others without having to launch assaults. He is able to destroy and damage the states of others without waging protracted campaigns."[17] Here, while we can see that Sun Zi is really against any unnecessary suffering and destruction, the ultimate aim is still to conquer the enemy.

We have also seen earlier that one of the more preferred strategies is to attack the alliance of the enemy where one seeks to "overawe the other states so much that none of these allies (of his enemy) would dare to unite against him".[18] In this case, even when no physical war is waged, exerting dominance over the enemy and the allies of the enemy is still the ultimate objective in the AoW. A non-physical method is preferred and beneficial only in that it reduces the loss to the total value. If there are no other means to subdue the opponent, then war is inevitable and acceptable. Consideration for the interest of the other party is practised only to the extent that it does not deter from achieving the strategic objective.

In Zheng He's AoC, arising from the expression of benevolence through the maximization of value or benefits for all, the fundamental strategic objective is therefore to form collaborative relationships with others so as to co-create and increase the total value available for all. In this way, the parties involved in the collaboration gets to share and enjoy together a maximized total value that is co-created in the process.

This is so in Zheng He's AoC because the assumed worldview is one where win-win is not only possible but preferred and actively sought after. This is therefore a case of total value creation where the synergy of the collaborative relationships can be expected to increase value for all parties of the collaboration. In this context, parties involved in the collaboration are friends with a common objective of value creation. Strategies are therefore designed to encourage and facilitate collaborative behaviours in order to co-create and increase total value for all. The fundamental objective is always aimed at building collaborative relationships.

It is important to note that Zheng He made a very clear distinction between recognized and legitimate leaders and chieftains of the foreign states, versus the pirates and bandits. Only legitimate leaders and chieftains are targets of the AoC, while pirates and bandits were treated as obstacles to collaboration as they were not parties that will contribute towards overall total value. Zheng He therefore made special efforts to protect the interests of not just the Ming Court, but also the interests of his collaborative partners so as to ensure the sustainability of their collaboration and hence value creation. For example, Zheng He invoked his military strength to capture pirate chief Chen Zuyi in Palembang on his first voyage,[19] in order to protect all traders and envoys in the region. This is what we referred to earlier as Zheng He's act of ensuring sustainability of the collaborative environment. Quite clearly here in the AoC, consideration for the interest of the other party is much more important than that in the AoW as it directly contributes to achieving its strategic objective of building collaboration.

This is also why in Zheng He's AoC, we highlighted Zheng He's other acts of collaboration (see chapters 2 and 3) where he proactively articulated his strategic intention to build collaboration, and then followed that through with his act of generosity, and then his acts of building win-win trade and ensuring its sustainability. And undergirding all these, Zheng He also acted on cultivating trust with all the people in all the places he visited.

PRINCIPLES IN STRATEGY FORMULATION

The basic difference in the fundamental strategic objectives of the AoC and the AoW as explained above leads us to two dichotomous sets of principles upon which the AoC and the AoW strategies were formulated.

The AoC is fundamentally aimed at building collaboration with others, and for this, the principle of trust, and the associated act of cultivating and earning trust, becomes important for effective sharing of resources, knowledge and technology so as to generate synergy for the collaborators. This means that Zheng He's AoC is essentially a set of strategies formulated based on a set of principles that includes honesty, transparency, consistency, mutuality and trust.

The AoW, on the other hand, is fundamentally aimed at wrestling control over, and thereby reducing the control exercised by, the opponent. To succeed in achieving this, it is often necessary to confuse the opponent so that he loses his sight and control over the competitive environment, making it possible then for the aggressor to come in to subdue and gain dominance and victory. Therefore, the AoW is essentially a set of strategies formulated based on a set of principles that includes deception, manipulation, unpredictability, self-guardedness and suspicion.

In the 4C framework we described in chapter 2 as Zheng He's AoC, the first strategy is that of building "Capabilities" for collaboration. This is based primarily on the recognition that one must have something to contribute towards the collaborative relationship that can be of benefit to others. It is therefore hinged largely on the principle of mutuality that seeks to contribute towards common interests and benefits. The second strategy is that of "Coordination" which refers primarily to getting one's constituents to work together towards developing collaboration with others. This means the need to make it clear and transparent internally that collaboration is what is aimed for. The second strategy is therefore based largely upon the principles of internal transparency and consistency so that all may be coordinated internally to embrace and practise collaboration.

The third strategy in Zheng He's AoC is "Communication"; here, we see Zheng He putting in much efforts to communicate, in words and through actions, the intent of his visits to the many foreign countries. Indeed, the first thing Zheng He did upon arrival in a foreign state was to present and read out the emperor's edict in the presence of the local rulers, officials and people. This imperial announcement would essentially state the mission of Zheng He's trip as that of sharing in "the prosperity of peaceful times".[20] Zheng He also erected stone tablets not just to record the diplomatic events but also to communicate his goodwill to the local people. Such intention, for example, was shown in the trilingual tablet which Zheng He set up in Ceylon,[21] where the ruler and people were initially cold towards Zheng He's fleet. Zheng He actually took note of the religious complexities of Ceylon during his initial voyage there. When he returned to Ceylon on his subsequent trip, he restated his honest and friendly intention through the trilingual stone tablet inscribed in Chinese, Persian and Tamil. The Chinese portion praised Buddha, the Persian portion thanked Allah and the Tamil portion expressed a devotion to Hindu god Tenavarai-Nayanar. If the objective was only to record his visit to Ceylon, a single language inscription would have been sufficient. Zheng He's intention in erecting the trilingual tablet was to make his message clear to the Ceylonese people who were of different language and religious background, as well as to show his respect for their different religions so as to gain their trust. Of course, his words were also backed up by his actions. He made generous donations to the temples and religious institutions[22] to show his sincerity and honesty. Such gestures were consistent throughout his voyages, contributing to his success in gaining trust from his collaborative partners.

In fact, we elaborated earlier in chapters 2 and 3 that Zheng He's third strategy of "Communication" is really his 5 Acts of Collaboration on the ground: the Act of Articulating Intent for collaboration, the Act of Practising Generosity, the Act of Building Win-Win through trade, the Act of Ensuring Sustainability in the collaborative environment, and the Act of Building Trust. Therefore, quite clearly, this third strategy in Zheng He's AoC is based on the principles of honesty, transparency, consistency, mutuality and trust.

In Zheng He's AoC, the fourth strategy of "Continuity" highlights his perseverance and patience in his continual attempts at building collaboration. It is clearly based on the same set of collaboration-facilitating principles indicated above.

In contrast, the strategies in Sun Zi's AoW were designed to deceive and confuse the enemy. Within the first chapter of the AoW, Sun Zi already laid out that "military strategy is a game of deception";[23] as such, "when you are capable, feign that you are incapable. When you are able to deploy your forces, feign that you are unable to do so. When you are near the objective, feign that you are far away; and when you are far away from the objective, feign that you are near."[24] These strategies were clearly devised to deceive and confuse the opponent so that he cannot make a sound judgment for action that would lead to his own advantage.

In a specific example, Sun Zi also recommended to "use more fire and drums in battles at night, and use more flags in battles in the day, as they distract and confuse the enemy's eyes and ears".[25] In chapter 7 of Sun Zi's AoW on maneuvering, Sun Zi stated that "military tactics are based on deception, developed to gain advantage".[26] The army therefore has to be flexible: "Agility in adapting to the changing circumstances lies in uniting and dividing the armed forces, hence the army should be fast as a wind when moving rapidly, compact as a forest when moving slowly, ravaging as a fire in attack, unwavering as a mountain when halted, enigmatic as if shrouded in a shadow, and explosive as a thunderbolt when launched".[27]

In fact, the formulation of military strategies in Sun Zi's AoW is similar to that of strategy formulation in Game Theory. The AoW is designed for a "game" of imperfect information, whereby one party makes a move based on the move made by the other party, and also based on his anticipation of future moves. The constantly changing circumstance is the result of exchanges of moves and tactics in a dynamic cybernetic loop formed between the two parties in opposition. Hence, in this case, strategies are purposely dynamic and even unpredictable, rather than being transparent and consistent.

This is especially so in the deployment of troops; it is important to "use strategies and plans that are beyond the predictions of the enemy".[28] As such, "the ultimate skill in the deployment of troops is to ensure that it has no fixed or constant formation and disposition".[29] The less accurate the information the opponent gets, the greater will be the chance that he will make a mistake in his strategies, and the greater will be one's likelihood of winning.

Sun Zi's AoW strategies were therefore formulated based on the principles of deception, manipulation, unpredictability, self-guardedness and suspicion. If Zheng He were to act based on these principles, he would certainly not earn the trust he desired from his collaborative partners. And while "the expert in offence attacks where the enemy does not know how to defend, and the expert in defense guards places where the enemy does not know how to attack",[30] the expert in collaboration wants to know as much as possible the complementary strengths of his collaborators in order to work seamlessly and synergistically together.

EXECUTION OF STRATEGIES

The execution of the strategies of AoW and AoC is also different as a result of the dichotomous principles on which they were based.

In Sun Zi's AoW, since information is imperfect, and there is inherent suspicion over the opponent's moves, Sun Zi recommended a more defensive and passive mode in executing his strategies. He advocated that "a person adept at warfare places himself in a position where defeat is impossible, and then does not miss any opportunity to defeat the enemy."[31] Here, in "defeat is impossible", Sun Zi was actually referring to putting up an impeccable defence; and, in "opportunity to defeat the enemy", Sun Zi was referring to loopholes or mistakes and missteps in the enemy's strategies. Sun Zi therefore believed that defence is in one's own hands and therefore it is within one's own control; hence, with an impeccable defence, one can ensure that the enemy cannot defeat him. On the other hand, in Sun Zi's thinking, victory is dependent on the opponent. Therefore Sun Zi advocated that one should first ensure that one's own defence is impeccable, and then wait or induce the opponent into making his mistakes or exposing his weaknesses before attacking.

Taking such a passive stance can be effective in the execution of AoW strategies as it minimizes rash actions that may expose one's weaknesses to the opponent.

Zheng He's AoC, on the other hand, seems to suggest that taking the active role and making the proactive first move to establish goodwill can be helpful, and may even be necessary, in building collaborative relationships. Therefore Zheng He actually went out on his seven grand voyages, proactively announced his intention to collaborate and share Ming China's resources, knowledge and technology, and actively practised the Act of Generosity through his giving of gifts not only in accordance with royal rites and practices but also going beyond that as we have indicated earlier. Again using the example of Ceylon, Zheng He made the first move by giving gifts and erecting the stone tablet to express his intention to build a collaborative relationship. In fact, throughout his seven voyages, Zheng He was proactive in creating opportunities to collaborate or to express his goodwill. His crew imparted to the local people Chinese fishing techniques[32] and agriculture technologies[33] and also helped in treating some of the common local diseases.[34] Benefiting from Zheng He's generosity, the local people then returned his favour with gifts and shared with him their local medical knowledge. Trade became a natural outcome.

Adopting such an active stance can be effective in the practice of the AoC as spontaneity itself may be perceived as an expression of sincerity.

DESIRED OUTCOME

The last apparent contrast between the AoW and the AoC lies in the final desired outcome of these two alternative sets of strategies.

In Sun Zi's AoW, the final desired outcome is victory over the opponent, and this should be a quick, decisive victory that gives no chance for the enemy to retaliate, so as to minimize the destruction of value. In this way, the desired outcome in the AoW is a clearly defined end to war; it is a one-time transaction that should terminate itself as quickly as possible.

Within this context, it is therefore readily understandable that deception is an accepted fundamental principle in the design of warfare strategies. After all, war itself is a "purely distributive, one-time transaction".[35] Through deception, one can win the war and gain the value that gets distributed from the loser to the victor, and the relationship between the two parties comes to an end. In fact, Sun Zi clearly stated that protracted campaigns are undesirable. Chapter 2 of Sun Zi's AoW states, "While a rash battle may not be wise, a prolonged campaign has never proven to be strategic. Prolonged war never benefits the country."[36]

In Zheng He's AoC, the final desired outcome is an ongoing collaborative relationship with one's partners that continues to create value for all. In this sense, the desired outcome is one of patience and perseverance in the continuity and sustainability of collaboration and synergistic value creation.

We therefore see that one of the 4Cs strategies in Zheng He's AoC framework is that of "Continuity", as described in chapter 2. As collaboration is a value creation process, it is therefore beneficial to keep the collaborative relationship ongoing so that more value can be co-created for mutual benefit. Zheng He, therefore, apparently put in conscious efforts to maintain the collaborative relations with the foreign countries he visited. Instead of just one voyage, Zheng He made seven voyages to the south and west seas throughout his life. Also, apart from the last voyage, which was delayed due to the transition of emperors and a lack of support from Emperor Renzong, the other voyages were made essentially back to back. It was Zheng He's consistent and conscious effort to visit, communicate and trade with foreign countries regularly that kept the collaborative relationships positive and thriving.

In the case of the AoW, continuity in war would mean value destruction and this will therefore be more of a disaster than a benefit.

IMPLICATIONS

The application of Sun Zi's AoW has often been criticized as unethical business practices; this is especially so when it involves the use of deception and psychological manipulation. Such ethics-based criticisms of the AoW, however, can be problematic.

For example, in the context of war, one would readily accept that peacetime ethical standards no longer apply; otherwise, the obedient soldier who kills the enemy in battle would be labelled as immoral or unethical. Similarly, in legitimate business competition, one's gain of the market often results in the loss of another; surely it will be problematic to accuse the winner as unethical since the managers and leaders here owe no fiduciary duty to their competitors. Instead, being honest and open towards one's competitor and then losing out in the competition is not doing due diligence in the best interest of the company. This would instead constitute a breach of fiduciary duty owed to the company.

Further, we have pointed out earlier that Sun Zi's AoW is an expression of the fundamental value of benevolence. The AoW does not advocate for war; where war becomes inevitable, the AoW's desired outcome is minimization of value destruction and loss of lives. This cannot be accused of being unethical or immoral.

On the other hand, Zheng He's AoC may be criticized as naïve and unrealistic in a highly competitive market arena. When the competing party is seeking to take over your share of the business pie, being generous and showering the competitor with goodwill may just encourage him to take advantage of you.

Rather than judging these strategies by ethical standards or the yardstick of being realistic, a more useful approach would be to evaluate their applicability to different types of business contexts. The economics literature can help us in this; it has made a distinction between two types of business transactions: "market" transactions versus "administered" transactions. Market transactions are defined as transactions "governed by the competitive logic of the market" while administered transactions are defined as transactions "subject to the cooperative norms that govern collective action in a bureaucracy".[37] In our context, we can understand market transaction as one in which value is distributed in the form of competition, and administered transaction as one in which value is created through collaboration. Quite clearly then, the AoW is more applicable in the context of market transactions while the AoC is useful for administered transactions.

It is important to recognize that both types of transactions are unavoidable in the business environment. While value creation is always beneficial, a process to distribute the created value may also be necessary. Competitions are not always evil either. Healthy competitions often generate positive externalities. For example, while competition in the IT industry reduces the profit margins of the participating companies, it benefits the customers and leads to development of better technologies for the industry as a whole. Problems will arise when the cost of competition outweighs the benefits it generates. In such a situation, it will require the joint effort of the companies in the industry and the regulators to bring the competition back to a healthy level.

We should also point out that some of the management strategies in the AoC and AoW are transferable between them. For example, the two strategies of "Capability-building" and "Coordination" in Zheng He's AoC can also be important in the perspective of the AoW. Similarly, the strategy advocated in Sun Zi's AoW to "know yourself and know your enemies" can also be easily adapted to "know yourself and know your collaborators" within the context of the AoC. However, dichotomies between the AoC and the AoW lie in their contrasting strategic objectives, principles in strategy formulation, execution, and desired outcomes. As such, today's managers and leaders need not consider the AoC and the AoW as substitutes for one another. Instead, judgment can be exercised to determine if the circumstance is one of market transaction or administered transaction, and therefore apply the AoW or the AoC accordingly. Of course, if there are ways to move a competitive relationship towards that of a collaborative nature, it would appear that this will always be beneficial for both the companies and the overall industry. Also, as the AoC helps in an administered transaction through the co-creation of value, the ever growing pie of benefits may suffice in obviating the need for deliberate value distribution. In this sense, does the AoC always triumph over the AoW?

Of course, in today's reality, business relationships are complex and intricate. Companies could be both competing and collaborating with each other. Competitors today may also become collaborators in the future. Since collaboration is intuitively preferred, it often depends on the managers and leaders' wisdom to avoid unhealthy competition and to turn competitive relationships into collaborative ones. The AoC and the AoW can both be excellent references and guides for today's managers and leaders. However, they will need to be discerning and flexible in applying these strategies to ensure that win-win situations are facilitated as much as possible, while keeping the cost of inevitable competition to the minimum.

Endnotes

1. Tan Ta Sen and Chia Lin Sien, eds., *The Zheng He Epic*, 1st edition in Chinese edited by Zhou Wenlin et al. (Kunming, Yunnan, China: Yunnan People's Publishing House, Yunnan Fine Arts Publishing House, Auora Publishing House, 2006), p. 318.
2. *Zheng He Epic*, p. 316 (side bar; decree of Emperor Xuande).
3. Kuo Pao Kun (playwright of "Descendants of the Eunuch Admiral"), as quoted in Paul Rozario, *Zheng He and the Treasure Fleet, 1405–1433* (Singapore: SNP International Publishing, 2005), p. 49.

4. Both written by Gerald A. Michaelson and Steven W. Michaelson (New York: McGraw-Hill, 2004).

5. Jason B. MacDonald and Kent E. Neupert, "Applying Sun Tzu's Terrain and Ground to the Study of Marketing Strategy", *Journal of Strategic Marketing* 13 (2005): 293–304.

6. The contents in this chapter represent part of the outcome from the independent study module that my student Yuan Yi undertook with me as her supervising professor in the August-November semester of 2010.

7. 百战百胜，非善之善者也，不战而屈人之兵，善之善者也。(孙子兵法卷三谋攻篇); translation as in Chow-Hou Wee, *Sun Zi Bingfa: Selected Insights and Applications* (Singapore: Prentice Hall, 2005), p. 261.

8. 樊迟问仁。子曰："爱人"。(论语颜渊篇第十二); *The Analects of Confucius*, Chapter 12 Yan Yuan, accessible at: <http://www.guoxue.com/jinbu/13jing/lunyu/13j_lyml.htm> (accessed 30 September 2011).

9. 《郑和家谱 • 敕谕海外诸番条》，收录于《郑和下西洋资料汇编》上册，海洋出版社2005年增编本，531页。(*Compilation of Records and Materials on Zheng He's Voyages to the West Seas*, Ocean Publication); see also Emperor Xuande's imperial decree for Zheng He as in *The Zheng He Epic*, p. 316 and also in Louise E. Levathes, *When China Ruled the Seas: The Treasure Fleet of the Dragon Throne, 1405–1433* (New York: Oxford University Press, 1994), p. 169.

10. 故善用兵者，屈人之兵而非战也，拔人之城而非攻也。(孙子兵法卷三谋攻篇); translation as in Chow-Hou Wee, *Sun Zi Bingfa: Selected Insights and Applications* (Singapore: Prentice Hall, 2005), p. 264.

11. 故上兵伐谋，其次伐交，其次伐兵，其下攻城。(孙子兵法卷三谋攻篇); translation as in Chow-Hou Wee, *Sun Zi Bingfa: Selected Insights and Applications* (Singapore: Prentice Hall, 2005), p. 261.

12. 攻城之发为不得已。(孙子兵法卷三谋攻篇); translation as in Chow-Hou Wee, *Sun Zi Bingfa: Selected Insights and Applications* (Singapore: Prentice Hall, 2005), p. 262.

13. *Zheng He Epic*, p. 321.

14. （清）陈伦炯，《海国见闻录南洋记》，摘录于：《郑和与东南亚》，新加坡郑和学会出版，第19页。(*Zheng He and Southeast Asia*, published by Singapore Zheng He Society); see also *The Zheng He Epic*, p. 345.

15. 王海洲，潘望，《郑和的时代：大航海时代的反思，东西方相互的认识》，第四章：1405纵横大洋的郑和船队，古吴轩出版社，2005，第134－138页。(*The Zheng He Era: Reflections of a Era of Sea Voyages, and Mutual Understanding of the East and the West*, Gu Wu Xuan Publication).

16. 鹿世明，《郑和下西洋与中国对外贸易》，载《走向海洋的中国人》，海潮出版社，1996年，第35页。(*The Chinese on Their Path to the Oceans*, Hai Chao Publishing).

17. Translation as in Chow-Hou Wee, *Sun Zi Bingfa: Selected Insights and Applications* (Singapore: Prentice Hall, 2005), p. 264.

18. 威加于敌，则其交不得合。(孙子兵法卷十一九地篇); translation as in Chow-Hou Wee, *Sun Zi Bingfa: Selected Insights and Applications* (Singapore: Prentice Hall, 2005), p. 148.

19. （明）马欢，《瀛涯胜览》，商务印书馆影印，第26页。(*Yingya Shenglan*, Commercial Publishing).

20. 《郑和家谱•敕谕海外诸番条》，收录于《郑和下西洋资料汇编》上册，海洋出版社2005年增编本，531页; see also *The Zheng He Epic*, p. 316, and *When China Ruled the Seas*, p. 169.

21. （明）费信，《星槎胜览》，摘录于《郑和下西洋资料汇编》上册，海洋出版社2005年增编本，570页; see also *When China Ruled the Seas*, pp. 100 and 113.

22. 《布施锡兰山佛寺碑》，摘录于《郑和下西洋资料汇编》上册，海洋出版社2005年增编本，570页; see also *When China Ruled the Seas*, p. 113.

23. 兵者，诡道也。（孙子兵法卷一计篇）(*The Art of War*, Shanghai Ancient Classics Publishing).

24. 故能而示之不能，用而示之不用，近而示之远，远而示之近。(孙子兵法卷一计篇); translation as in Chow-Hou Wee, *Sun Zi Bingfa: Selected Insights and Applications* (Singapore: Prentice Hall, 2005), p. 235.

25. 故夜战多火鼓，昼战多旌旗，所以变人之耳目也。（孙子兵法卷七军争篇）。

26. 故兵以诈立，以利动。（孙子兵法卷七军争篇）。

27. 以分合为变者也，故其疾如风，其徐如林，侵掠如火，不动如山，难知如阴，动如雷霆。（孙子兵法卷七军争篇）。

28. 用兵计谋，为不可测。(孙子兵法卷九行军篇); translation as in Chow-Hou Wee, *Sun Zi Bingfa: Selected Insights and Applications* (Singapore: Prentice Hall, 2005), p. 230.

29. 故行兵之极，至于无形。(孙子兵法卷十一九地篇); translation as in Chow-Hou Wee, *Sun Zi Bingfa: Selected Insights and Applications* (Singapore: Prentice Hall, 2005), p. 243.

30. 攻而必取者，攻其所不守也；守而必固者，守其所不攻也。(孙子兵法卷六虚实篇); translation adapted from Chow-Hou Wee, *Sun Zi Bingfa: Selected Insights and Applications* (Singapore: Prentice Hall, 2005), p. 192.

31. 故善战者，立于不败之地，而不失敌之败也。(孙子兵法卷四形篇); translation as in Chow-Hou Wee, *Sun Zi Bingfa: Selected Insights and Applications* (Singapore: Prentice Hall, 2005), p. 175.

32. *Zheng He Epic*, p. 281.

33. 梁志明，《略论占城在郑和下西洋中的历史地位与作用》，收录于《郑和远航与世界文明—纪念郑和下西洋600周年纪念论文集》，北京大学出版社，2005年，第418页。

34. （清）陈伦炯，《海国见闻录南洋记》，摘录于：《郑和与东南亚》，新加坡郑和学会出版，第19页。

35. Blaine McCormick, "Make Money, Not War: A Brief Critique of Sun Tzu's *The Art of War*", *Journal of Business Ethics* 29 (2001): 285–86.

36. 兵闻拙速，未睹巧之久也。夫兵久而国利者，未之有也。(孙子兵法卷二作战篇).

37. Joseph Heath, "An Adversarial Ethic for Business: or When Sun-Tzu Met the Stakeholder", *Journal of Business Ethics* 72 (2007): 359–74.

References

Heath, Joseph. "An Adversarial Ethic for Business: or When Sun-Tzu Met the Stakeholder". *Journal of Business Ethics* 72 (2007): 359–74.

Levathes, Louise E. *When China Ruled the Seas: The Treasure Fleet of the Dragon Throne, 1405–1433*. New York: Oxford University Press, 1994.

MacDonald, Jason B. and Kent E. Neupert. "Applying Sun Tzu's Terrain and Ground to the Study of Marketing Strategy". *Journal of Strategic Marketing* 13 (2005): 293–304.

McCormick, Blaine. "Make Money, Not War: A Brief Critique of Sun Tzu's *The Art of War*". *Journal of Business Ethics* 29 (2001): 285–86.

Michaelson, Gerald A. and Steven W. Michaelson. *Sun Tzu: Strategies for Marketing — 12 Essential Principles for Winning the War for Customers*. New York: McGraw-Hill, 2004.

———. *Sun Tzu: Strategies for Selling — How to Use the Art of War to Build Lifelong Customer Relationships*. New York: McGraw-Hill, 2004.

Rozario, Paul. *Zheng He and the Treasure Fleet, 1405–1433*. Singapore: SNP International Publishing, 2005.

Tan Ta Sen and Chia Lin Sien, eds. *The Zheng He Epic*. 1st edition in Chinese edited by Zhou Wenlin et al. Kunming, Yunnan, China: Yunnan's Publishing House, Yunnan Fine Arts Publishing House, Auora Publishing House, 2006.

Wee Chow-Hou. *Sun Zi Bingfa: Selected Insights and Applications*. Singapore: Prentice Hall, 2005.

（春秋）孔子，《论语》颜渊篇第十二，载国学网。(*The Analects*, accessible at: <http://www.guoxue.com/jinbu/13jing/lunyu/13j_lyml.htm>).

《郑和下西洋资料汇编》，海洋出版社，2005年增编本。(*Compilation of Records and Materials on Zheng He's Voyages to the West Seas*, Ocean Publication).

廖建裕［编］，《郑和与东南亚》，新加坡郑和学会2005年出版。(*Zheng He and Southeast Asia*, published by Singapore Zheng He Society).

王海洲，潘望，《郑和的时代：大航海时代的反思，东西方相互的认识》，古吴轩出版社，2005年出版。(*The Zheng He Era: Reflections of a Era of Sea Voyages, and Mutual Understanding of the East and the West*, Gu Wu Xuan Publication).

鹿世明，《郑和下西洋与中国对外贸易》，载《走向海洋的中国人》，海潮出版社，1996年。(*The Chinese on Their Path to the Oceans*, Hai Chao Publishing).

（明）马欢，《瀛涯胜览》，商务印书馆影印。(*Yingya Shenglan*, Commercial Publishing).

（春秋）孙武，《孙子兵法》，上海古籍出版社，2006年出版。(*The Art of War*, Shanghai Ancient Classics Publishing).

《郑和远航与世界文明—纪念郑和下西洋600周年纪念论文集》，北京大学出版社，2005出版。(*Zheng He's Voyage and World Civilization*, Peking University Publication).

PART II

ZHENG HE AND HIS MANAGEMENT

Chapter 5

LEARNING FROM ZHENG HE
Leadership Principles and Practices

INTRODUCTION

Most, if not all, of the writings about Zheng He has been from the historical, maritime, diplomatic and cultural perspectives. Accordingly, the written literature has conferred many titles on Zheng He from these perspectives, praising him as a eunuch military commander, an admiral, navigator and explorer, a diplomatic Ming envoy, and a cultural disseminator.[1]

Which of these titles would be most apt in describing Zheng He and his vocation? His claim to fame seems to stem from the fact that he had accomplished the colossal feat of having moved and fed some 27,000 crew, spread out over 200–300 ships of unprecedented sizes, seven times across the long and wide stretches of oceans between China, Southeast and South Asia, Arabia and Africa. And much of these waters were in many places fraught with dangers and infested with pirates; and each of these voyages took place over long durations of 1.5 to 2 years, back in the early fifteenth century, without the help of modern-day communications and satellite technologies.

Was Zheng He therefore great because of his outstanding seamanship or navigation capabilities as demonstrated in these epic voyages? Given his background as a military general who was neither trained in maritime warfare nor specialized in navigation, it is difficult to come to such a conclusion.

More recently, in a 2005 video production screened over Channel NewsAsia as part of the celebrations of Zheng He's 600th anniversary of his maiden voyage, Zheng He was portrayed as a modern-day CEO.[2] Also, in his paper presented at the International Conference on Zheng He and the Afro-Asian World held in Malacca in 2010, Captain Rivers described Zheng He as follows: acting as it were as a CEO, he repeatedly directed the extensive preparations that enabled great fleets to follow previously established trade routes where only handfuls of trading vessels had plied before.[3]

Evidently, Zheng He's success in leading his emperor-decreed voyages would suggest that he had much capability in the realm of leadership and management; after all, it is obvious that these grand voyages were representative of careful and strategic planning, organization, coordination and control. In this regard, Zheng He had surely demonstrated much leadership and management capabilities, like a modern-day CEO indeed. And in this sense, it would be fair to ascribe to Zheng He the title of a successful organizational leader, in addition to his usual titles of Ming admiral, navigator, explorer and envoy.

In this chapter, we introduce Zheng He from the perspective of overall leadership and management. We will specifically highlight him in his role as a leader. We would like to be able to learn from Zheng He's leadership principles and practices that can be of benefit for today's leaders, managers and businesses.

This chapter is therefore organized as follows. In the next section, we will suggest an approach for examining Zheng He from a leadership perspective by drawing upon the primary source materials of Zheng He's inscriptions at Liujiagang and Changle.[4] We will then present a model of Zheng He's leadership that should help us understand and appreciate his leadership principles and practices. We will also attempt to draw implications and applications from this for our learning as today's leaders and managers.

ZHENG HE'S VIEW OF HIS LIFE WORK

While there exists a body of primary materials in Chinese that described Zheng He's career and work to some extent, there is really very limited primary source materials available that described Zheng He's thoughts and inner life.[5] Many of the secondary writings about Zheng He are therefore based on deduction and inferences.

There are, however, two of the earliest primary source materials in the so-called Liujiagang and Changle inscriptions that were set up by Zheng He and his associates in 1431, and which were first translated and published and presented to the world by Duyvendak[6] in 1938. These two inscriptions can be very useful for our purpose of trying to understand and learn from Zheng He in his role as a leader. In fact, Dreyer would suggest that these two original primary materials come closest to giving us insights on Zheng He's thoughts and feelings.[7]

Zheng He set up the two inscriptions on the eve of his seventh grand voyage. By that time, Zheng He was already into the sixty-first year of his life. Given that the earlier patron of his grand voyages, the Emperor Yongle, had already passed away in 1424, and that Yongle's successor, the Emperor Hongxi had put a stop to such voyages then, Zheng He knew that this seventh voyage called for by the new Emperor Xuande may likely be his last. Perhaps this was the reason why Zheng He set up the two inscriptions, spelling out quite clearly, and with sufficient details, an overall outline that served as a summary of what he and his team had done over their last six voyages. In any case, the contents they wrote on the stone steles they erected at Liujiagang and Changle carry the apparent sense of a career being summed up and the passing of an era.[8] In fact, Dreyer suggested that at this stage of Zheng He's life, one might expect to learn something of Zheng He's sense of the meaning of his life as he set forth on his seventh and last voyage.[9]

We should therefore pay attention to the contents in these two inscriptions. What do they tell us of Zheng He's own view of his lifetime work? What were the elements in his work that he considered most important and which he therefore chose to include in the inscriptions? And if we see the essence of his life work to be that of a leader in planning, organizing, commanding and controlling of the seven epic grand voyages, then Zheng He's own summary of his work here should give us insights on his leadership beliefs and practices.

The Liujiagang and Changle Inscriptions

So what did Zheng He write in the two inscriptions? We turn to Dreyer for his translation and summary:[10] both inscriptions put Zheng He as the leader of the voyages, but they also clearly made mention of his key senior team members. Both inscriptions present the composition of the fleet and the itinerary for each of the voyages, as well as some details on what had happened on each of these trips. On the three voyages where military force was exercised, these incidents were clearly detailed, while on the other three voyages, the focus appeared to be on the tributes the foreign countries offered. Both inscriptions also emphasized the purpose of the voyages: to activate the tribute system and to facilitate trade. Zheng He stated that because of these voyages, the sea lanes had become safe, and foreign peoples could use them to pursue their occupations in safety. Both inscriptions also devoted much space to the invocation of divine protection, honouring the "Heavenly Princess" or Tianfei — the goddess of sailors and seafarers. Zheng He and his associates also made mention of the installations they had helped in: the repair of the halls of Buddhas and the temples of the gods, including making the statue of the goddess shine as though it were new. They also stated their resolve to do even more for their gods.

In the Changle inscription, Zheng He and his team also explicitly stated the one concern that they carried with them in all the voyages:[11]

> While in command of the personnel of the fleet, and responsible for the great amount of money and valuables on board, one concern while facing the violence of the winds and the dangers of the nights was that we would not succeed.

This seemed to be the burden that Zheng He carried with him as the overall leader of the voyages. But he also apparently carried with him his sure conviction as he engraved in the Changle inscription the following:[12]

> If men serve their prince with utmost loyalty there is nothing they cannot do, and if they worship the gods with utmost sincerity there is no prayer that will not be answered.

Dreyer went on to provide the following as his overall summary:[13]

> The inscriptions portray Zheng He as a dedicated servant of his ruler surrounded by fellow officers who are a "band of brothers" and a crew many of whom had sailed on previous voyages with Zheng He and about whose safety and welfare

Zheng He cared. The inscriptions also suggest that the voyages by sea had become the activity that defined the meaning of his life for Zheng He, and that devotion to Tianfei, the goddess of seafarers, had become the dominant strand in his eclectic religious heritage.

ZHENG HE'S LEADERSHIP MODEL

Quite clearly, the Liujiagang and Changle inscriptions as summarized by Dreyer, and as presented above, give us a glimpse of Zheng He's own thinking about his lifetime work. And if we understand his lifetime work to be that of leading the seven epic grand voyages, then Dreyer's summary also gives us a glimpse of what Zheng He considered to be the most important components of his model of leadership.

We therefore present Zheng He's Leadership Model as comprising of five strategies described briefly as follows:

(1) *Allegiance to Authority*: his clear devotion to his ruler, the emperor;
(2) *Band of Brothers*: his co-labouring with a team of senior associates;[14]
(3) *Care for Crew*: his care and concern for his crew of workers;
(4) *Doing due Diligence*: his efforts in executing his mission on the ground; and
(5) *Embracing the Eternal*: his entrusting of his fleet and people to the divine spirits.

We will now elaborate on each of these strategies, so as to understand and appreciate Zheng He's leadership practices better, and in the process gain inspiration for our practice of leadership in today's world.

Allegiance to Authority

This *Allegiance to Authority* (A-A) strategy of Zheng He's leadership highlights his loyalty and devotion to Zhu Di, who later became the Emperor Yongle, and therefore his patron for his lifetime work of leading the seven epic grand voyages to Southeast Asia, India, Arabia and Africa. There are three aspects to Zheng He's *Allegiance to Authority* strategy.

Accountability

The first is his sense of responsibility and accountability to his higher authority, the Emperor Yongle. Though Yongle had passed away in 1424, Zheng He still explicitly stated in his two 1431 inscriptions that he and the others had been commissioned to lead the various voyages "from the beginning of Yongle until now".[15] Zheng He therefore seemed to have intuitively embraced this aspect of his accountability to his higher authority, even as he proceeded to give a report of what he had done in his various voyages as represented by the contents in the two inscriptions.

Also, because of his sense of accountability to the emperor, Zheng He consciously decided to defer the decision to the emperor on what to do with the captured culprits in the three incidents (relating to pirate chief Chen Zuyi,[16] the Ceylonese King Alagakkonara,[17] and the rebel Sekander[18]) that invoked the use of military force. Indeed, with his large military force, and being thousands of miles away from the emperor, Zheng He could have readily decided and proceeded with the execution of these individuals. However, because he was keenly aware of his emperor-decreed mission of spreading goodwill, peace and building collaboration, instead of aggression, antagonism and the use of military force, Zheng He apparently recognized the need for accountability and hence decided to defer to the emperor in these three incidents that involved his use of military force.

Continued Trust

The second aspect of Zheng He's *Allegiance to Authority* strategy of leadership is his recognition of the need to continue to earn the emperor's trust and confidence. In fact, in the incident involving the pirate chief Chen Zuyi referred to above, it should be quite obvious that he could have executed the latter without the need to defer the decision to the emperor. After all, in this incident, it was clear that he was seeking to remove the danger posed by the pirates on the free and safe passage of traders through the Straits of Malacca. Hence, by capturing the aggressor alive and leaving the final say to the emperor, Zheng He also established himself as one who respected the emperor, and thus continued to earn his trust for the leading of the voyages, one after another. Such strong emperor sponsorship is an important element that helped in Zheng He's discharge of his fundamental mission.

Similarly, Zheng He apparently made his conscious effort to honour the emperor with his allegiance and presence by being back into Beijing for the festivities that were held in celebration of the emperor's completion and designation of his massive Forbidden City as the country's capital in 1420. Zheng He was at that time in the midst of his sixth voyage; apparently, at Semudera in north Sumatra, Zheng He divided his fleet and let one of his deputies lead the main portion onto to Aden and Africa while he himself led a smaller portion of the fleet to return to China.[19] Such an action no doubt helped Zheng He to continue to win the emperor's trust, as he accorded his priorities accordingly, and with wisdom.

Motivation and Conviction

Beyond the above, there is a third aspect in Zheng He's *Allegiance to Authority* strategy that involves a much deeper level of significance. Indeed, to Zheng He, this sheer allegiance and loyalty to his higher authority represented a clear motivation and conviction that drove him forward in his work. Zheng He was convinced that *"If men serve their prince with utmost loyalty there is nothing they cannot do."*[20] At a deeper level, this first strategy of Zheng He's leadership model is therefore a fundamental principle that apparently gave him the strongest of motivation for his leadership work. He seemed to be convinced that there is nothing that he cannot accomplish as a result of his loyalty and allegiance to his higher authority, the Emperor Yongle.

To appreciate this fundamental motivation in Zheng He, we can turn to the early part of Zheng He's life to see how his background and growing up years may have contributed to this strong *Allegiance to Authority*. We already know that Zheng He was born into a noble Muslim family, with a father whom Zheng He himself described as a gentleman whom the local community looked up to.[21] In fact, Zheng He went on to describe his father Haji Ma as being one who was always ready to offer help and protection to the poor, weak and needy.[22] Zheng He's mother, whose maiden name was "Wen", was full of wifely virtues; she was described as a kind and gracious lady.[23] Zheng He had an elder brother and four sisters.[24] As he was growing up, Zheng He used to hang out at the lake near his home with his siblings and friends where they observed how fishermen built fishing boats, and returned home to build models of these boats from memory.[25] All these point to Zheng He growing up with an apparently very happy childhood within a very respectable and loving family environment.

Unfortunately, at the tender age of ten, Zheng He met with the major tragedy in his life. He lost his father to the invading Ming imperial troops while he himself was among the thousands of young boys who were captured, castrated and sent to serve the Ming Court as eunuch slaves. By then, his life was no longer his own; he lived only because his masters wanted him to live; he had no idea of where he was going and what he would eventually grow up to be.[26]

That must be the darkest moment in his life. But he would later grow up to appreciate that *Adversity can be Good*. Because, as it turned out, he was soon given basic military training and fought in a number of battles at a young age; he therefore grew up in a military environment and became a tough strong young man. And then a major turning point came when he was transferred to serve Zhu Di, the then Prince of Yan, who was based in Beijing, and who was later to become the third Ming emperor, the Emperor Yongle.[27]

Zhu Di appointed Zheng He as his bodyguard,[28] groomed and entrusted him with important responsibilities. Zheng He accompanied his master the Prince of Yan on all his military battles, learning the art of war, and fighting alongside with his master. He played a remarkably important role as a trusted bodyguard in the 1390s battle against the Mongols, where he served and protected Zhu Di at close range.[29]

Indeed, following the death of Ming's first emperor, the Emperor Hongwu (Zhu Yuanzhang) in 1398, the throne was succeeded by his eldest grandson, as his eldest son had passed away. As this succession resulted in tension and grievances among the Princes, Zhu Di staged a court revolt in 1399 referred to as the Battle of Jingnan.[30] Once again, Zheng He proved himself as a capable and intelligent eunuch supporting the Yan Prince in this battle.[31] He was described to have fought fiercely beside

Zhu Di and given him critical support in the mopping-up campaign.

Zhu Di the Prince was therefore clear and fully convinced that Zheng He was a man of high caliber,[32] a brave soldier and a capable leader.[33] Faithful, sincere and intelligent, Zheng He won the confidence of Zhu Di over the years.[34] Quite clearly, through this process, Zheng He knew that for his continued success, *Ability is Key*.

In 1402, Zhu Di entered Nanjing and declared himself the third emperor of the Ming Dynasty, taking on the title of Emperor Yongle. Given his ability in battles, Zheng He was promoted to become Grand Eunuch;[35] this was the top position a eunuch could be promoted to. In addition, regular and direct contact with the emperor accorded Zheng He an importance beyond his formal position.[36]

Emperor Yongle also appointed Zheng He as the principal envoy and commander-in-chief to lead the grand voyages to the West. Apparently this was because the emperor was convinced of Zheng He as a capable organizer of large scale construction projects, having earlier appointed and observed Zheng He as the Grand Director of the eunuch Directorate of Palace Servants, which was responsible for the construction and maintenance of all palace buildings.[37] In addition, the emperor had utmost trust in Zheng He and presented him with blank scrolls stamped with his seal, so that Zheng He could issue imperial orders at sea.[38]

So while Zheng He could have despaired when he met with his tragedy at the age of ten, this adversity did turned for the good as he was transferred to serve Zhu Di who created many opportunities for Zheng He to prove himself. Zheng He did worked hard and built his capabilities so that indeed, his proven ability led to Zhu Di's confidence and trust in him. Because of this, Zheng He must have become convinced that he owed the emperor deeply and significantly. He therefore demonstrated this through his clear loyalty and supreme devotion to his emperor. In Zheng He's leadership model, *Adversity can be Good; and Ability is the Key*. But these in turn gave rise to Zheng He's strong conviction of *Allegiance to Authority*, which then provided him with the fundamental motivation for his work of leadership.

Implications

What does this first strategy of Zheng He's leadership model suggests for us in our work of leadership?

Quite obviously, it tells us that the two elements of accountability and the need to earn the ongoing trust of one's higher authority are important. Indeed, today's emphasis on issues of good corporate governance and accountability attests to the importance of these two aspects of Zheng He's A-A leadership strategy.

In the business scene over the last few years, we have witnessed the financial excesses, greed and fraud associated with the notorious collapses of firms such as Enron, WorldCom and Lehman Brothers. At Enron, for example, "top executives cast traditional business controls by the wayside"[39] and in the process created a corporate culture of extravagance which made it simple for fraud to occur. Without a culture of integrity through accountability which helps in building and earning trust, our recent history of businesses demonstrated that leaders and managers can fall prey to unethical pursuits and practices, working to meet their own agendas rather than working in the best interests of their companies. Organizational demise and dishonour can therefore readily result from such a lack of accountability and allegiance to authority.

At the personal and more fundamental level, what drives a leader to pursue excellence in his work of leadership? For Zheng He, it was his allegiance to the emperor. However, even in Zheng He's experience, this was no simplistic or superficial allegiance. Instead, his allegiance grew out of a background of tragedy and adversity, followed by opportunities created by his benefactor which allowed him to learn and work on his abilities, and which in turned led to recognition and trust being earned and granted. All these led to a very strong loyalty and allegiance with a deep sense of gratitude that formed and steeled Zheng He's conviction that *with utmost loyalty there is nothing (that he) cannot do*.[40]

So at the personal level, today's leaders can draw inspiration from Zheng He simply because his experience tells us that *Adversity can indeed turn out to be Good*, though *Ability is the Key* to greater opportunities and higher levels of leadership work. Also, we learn from Zheng He that at the personal level, each leader must continue to find his own ways of earning trust from his higher authority. This is obviously an important element in managing our relationships with our immediate superiors.

At the deeper level, Zheng He's experience also means that for today's leaders, we must find our own *Allegiance to Authority*. This aspect of Zheng He's A-A strategy should point us to the need to identify our *Allegiance to a Higher Cause* that can give us that deeper level of conviction and motivation to want to do well. What is it that we believe in fundamentally that could provide us with such conviction and motivation? For many of us, it would be our desire to meet the expectations and KPIs set for us by our bosses. But is this sufficient motivation and deep enough conviction for us to do our work of leadership with excellence? Perhaps we need to see our work as a *higher calling* so that we may lead passionately and experience a sense of the conviction that Zheng He must have experienced through his *allegiance to his higher authority*. In the modern day maxims of leadership, perhaps this higher calling lies in leaders doing the work of investing in people and grooming the next generation of leaders, rather than merely meeting expectations and KPIs. After all, it would seem that this was what Zhu Di did with Zheng He: he created opportunities for Zheng He to come out of his adversity to learn and prove his ability. Is this indeed our higher calling as leaders: creating opportunities for grooming the next generation of leaders? What should be the *higher cause* that can serve as our *Allegiance to Authority*?

Band of Brothers

This *Band of Brothers* (B-B) strategy of Zheng He's leadership model refers to the importance Zheng He apparently accorded to his team of senior associates who travelled with and helped him in the overall leadership of his seven epic grand voyages. Zheng He explicitly made mention of them by name in his apparent "end-of-career" summary inscriptions erected at Liujiagang and Changle on the eve of his final voyage. Dreyer refers to Zheng He's senior team as his *Band of Brothers*.[41]

Apart from Zheng He himself as the leader of the overall *Xia Xiyang* (Travels to the Western Seas) enterprise, the two inscriptions mentioned his senior eunuch collaborators (his *Band of Brothers*) as including: Wang Jinghong, Zhu Liang, Zhou Man, Hong Bao, Yang Zhen, Zhang Da, Li Xing and Wu Zhong.[42]

Zheng He and Wang Jinghong were the most senior, carrying the titles of Principal Envoys and Grand Directors. The other seven were Deputy (or Assistant) Envoys while also carrying the rank of Grand Directors.

Chiu seemed to make reference to another senior eunuch Hou Xian as part of Zheng He's team of senior close associates; he made mention that Wang Jinghong and Hou Xian were particularly important to Zheng He because of their diplomatic linkages to several of the countries in the western seas then.[43]

Though Hou Xian was not named in the two inscriptions as translated by Dreyer, he was nonetheless mentioned by Dreyer as a eunuch associate of Zheng He of the same rank of Grand Director and who had accompanied Zheng He on the second and third voyages.[44] Indeed, Zheng He was personally in command of the third voyage and Wang Jinghong and Hou Xian were referred to as his principal deputies.[45]

The Changle inscription also mentioned Zhu Zhen and Wang Heng as part of Zheng He's team; they were both Regional Military Commissioners,[46] with a rank 2a that was higher than the rank 4a of Grand Directors.[47]

Why did Zheng He seemed to have paid tribute and recognition to his senior team or *band of brothers* by making mention of them by name on the inscriptions? There are apparently a number of reasons.

Sharing the Burden of Leadership

First, Zheng He knew that he had no experience when it came to maritime expeditions and leadership. He had been successful as a military ground commander, but having to lead the epic voyages across the waters represented a move out of his comfort zone. His emperor-decreed mission was made more complex by his colossal fleet that involved hundreds of ships and carried tens of thousands of crew. This meant that Zheng He must activate his senior associates to help him in command and control of his fleet and crew that were spread out in the open seas. In fact, Zheng He expressed that the one concern or burden that he carried with him while facing the violence of the winds and the dangers of the nights was that he would not succeed.[48] Zheng He therefore had to rely on his *band of brothers* to share in carrying this leadership burden and help him succeed in his overall leadership of the voyages.

Delegation of Work

Second, the emperor's decree for each voyage clearly specified the countries that need to be visited. Given the need to coordinate his fleet and crew to catch the external monsoons that will be blowing in primary directions at different times on the maritime calendar, Zheng He knew that he will have to separate his main fleet into smaller squadrons in order to complete his itinerary. This meant that Zheng He needed to delegate the leadership of his squadrons to his *band of brothers*. For example, on the seventh voyage, at Calicut, the main fleet divided into smaller fleets with Hong Bao leading the important part of the voyage to Hormuz and cities down the east coast of Africa.[49] Hong Bao also apparently authorized seven men to make a visit to Mecca.[50] Similarly, on the sixth voyage, the fleet divided at Semudera on north Sumatra, with Zhou Man leading the main fleet on to Aden and Africa while Zheng He himself led a smaller squadron to return to China to attend to other priorities.[51]

Bonding through Proximity and Time

Third, over the long and many voyages, with each voyage lasting usually for 1.5 to 2 years, Zheng He would have had much opportunity to work in close proximity with his *band of brothers* as he depended on their help on various matters. Apparently, Zheng He would have consulted with Zhu Zhen and Wang Heng, his two Regional Military Commissioners on military matters, while his fellow envoys would have been of major help to him on diplomatic issues. Similarly, over the long voyages, Zheng He would have cultivated his relationships with his various deputies as they faced the challenges and dangers associated with their travels together. For example, on the fifth voyage, Zheng He's closest deputy Wang Jinghong apparently became ill; Javanese legends described of Zheng He's efforts in personally tending to him.[52] Such episodes would certainly have helped to build the bonding amongst the *band of brothers*.

This second strategy of Zheng He's leadership model therefore highlights the importance of having a *Band of Brothers* to help in overall leadership work. Indeed, Zheng He's success in the seven grand voyages can be attributed to this team of close senior associates, the equivalent of today's management committee that supports the CEO.

Implications

It is obvious that every leader needs to cultivate his own *Band of Brothers* to help share his burden and work of leadership. No leader should need to sail on his leadership journey alone. Zheng He's experience through his B-B strategy highlights and confirms this for us. It should inspire us to actively search out and put in place our own *band of brothers*.

This is all the more so when unlike Zheng He's experience, today's leaders seldom have the chance of working and living in close physical proximity, over long durations, with his team. This should therefore suggest that today's leaders must put in conscious efforts in practising this second strategy of Zheng He's leadership model. We will need to consciously build trust-engendering and mutually-respectful relationships with our team of senior associates in leading our people and businesses. When a leader's senior team truly becomes his *band of brothers*, the leader's responsibility burden will be shared, his work can be delegated, and he will have others who can care and minister to him when the need arises.

Care for Crew

This *Care for Crew* (C-C) strategy of Zheng He's leadership model refers to Zheng He's care and concern for his crew. It highlights the basic elements of Zheng He's care for his people, as well as his depth of care which evolved through his close and direct involvement with his people in the face of life-threatening events during their many voyages.

What were the basic elements of care for his crew that Zheng He focused on?

Welfare

First, he focused his care on the welfare of his crew. This included the basic requirement of providing for the necessary supplies to meet the physical needs of his crew. This was important for Zheng He because his voyages involved travelling with a large crew of some 27,000 men. Also, because the duration of each voyage in general lasted between 1.5 to 2 years, this need for supplies and re-supplies became an extended problem. Because of this, Zheng He built and prepared for "specialty ships" to carry different types of supplies: treasure ships, battle ships, grain ships, water ships and horse ships. The grain ships carried and stored the food supplies, while the water ships were designed to carry fresh water. During the long voyages, Zheng He would activate replenishment of fresh water from rivers and lakes at ports of call and store them in water tankers.[53]

Another aspect of this basic focus on the crew's welfare included Zheng He's careful selection of a team of doctors to look after the health of his crew. Because of the large crew, Zheng He put together a specialized medical team of some 150 medical officers where on average, it was one medical officer for 150 crew members. Some of these specialists came from the palace's elite medical institution and some were famous local medical practitioners. The medical team also conducted studies of local diseases and their cures in order to help them take the necessary precautions to safeguard the health of the crew.[54]

Zheng He even considered details of his crew's welfare pertaining to their need for sewing services and haircuts. Apparently, Zheng He brought along dozens of elderly seamstress on the voyages to help in mending cloths, socks and even shoes. During Zheng He's time, shoes were made of cloth and hence they wouldn't last a month. Without the sewing services, even bringing 200,000 pairs of shoes, would not last a year. Similarly, Zheng He included barbers on board his fleet. With over twenty thousand crew members, and most of whom being in their prime years, Zheng He apparently had to bring with him more than a hundred barbers.[55]

Of course, as part of his focus on the welfare of his crew, Zheng He also ensured that his crew was well recognized and rewarded by the emperor when they returned from their voyages. There apparently existed a complex organization of formal ranks and salary for every category of crew and each was recognized with promotion in ranks and/or with monetary rewards.[56] And for crew members who were injured or who lost their lives, they or their families would be given special compensation.[57] In fact, Zheng He would always try to get any perquisites for his own subordinates when any such benefits had been given to other workers.[58]

Safety

Zheng He also specifically focused on the safety of his crew as part of his care for them.[59] This is quite natural given the nature of their mission since travelling out in the open seas can be fraught with much risk.

To protect his people against bandits and pirates, or even against aggressive and difficult local chieftains and troops, Zheng He knew that he had his massive military force which can be called upon to provide the needed help. And given his own military capability and experience, this is one dimension of crew safety that Zheng He was probably quite confident in. Nonetheless, he wanted to minimize any such dangers. And in the only three episodes where Zheng He had to exercise his military force, he had demonstrated that he had been able to care for the safety of his crew.

Zheng He also ensured that his fleet remained sea-worthy at all times, and hence he made provisions for ship repair when needed. Malacca, for example, had been set up as a depot to facilitate such repairs: "the ships which had gone to various countries returned to this place and assembled; they repaired [their vessels...and then] waited till the south wind was perfectly favourable [before setting off on the return leg]".[60] As another example, Zheng He also recruited a number of elderly experienced farmers who were apparently very sensitive and observant of pending weather changes and they would forecast fairly accurately when winds would be blowing strong and when it would be raining. Zheng He had great respect for their capability and when these farmers warned him of an incoming storm, Zheng He would give instructions for the fleet to berth in some sheltered areas nearby.[61] Similarly, Zheng He also explicitly kept a lookout for hardwoods suitable for emergency replacements of rudders since these were easily damaged on the long voyages.[62]

Deep Care

More importantly, beyond these two basic aspects of welfare and safety, Zheng He's *Care for Crew* strategy of leadership also highlights his deep sense of burden and responsibility for the many personnel of his fleet.[63]

This was due in part to the fact that many of his crew had travelled with him on previous voyages,[64] and that these voyages were each of fairly long duration. Zheng He therefore would have come to know many of his crew, as he would have lived and worked in close proximity with them. Further, they would have encountered some of the real dangers and challenges together when their ships were in the open waters. All these would have contributed to Zheng He's deeper sense of care and concern for his crew.

While Zheng He would do what he could to care for his crew, he knew that once they were on the open seas, they would need to battle against nature with her "thick fogs and high winds", and with "waves rising to heaven".[65] This was where he knew they would be quite helpless. With his deep sense of care and responsibility for his crew, Zheng He would have felt the need to turn to higher powers for help. In this context, even the emperor would not be able to help fight against the will of nature. As such, Zheng He would join his crew in invoking the protection of the divine spirits; both the Liujiagang and Changle inscriptions attested to that.

Implications

Most leaders can appreciate the need to provide the basic elements of care for their people; but to learn from Zheng He his depth of care and concern for his crew, and his practice of being with his people, will likely be a lot more difficult.

This is especially so when today's leaders hardly have the opportunity to spend any significant direct time with their people. As such, it is difficult to develop a sense of real and deep care for people. Work and businesses become largely transactional, and the use of KPIs only reinforce this. Relationships between leaders and workers are at best cursory and superficial. In this modern day context, the need for Zheng He's *Care for Crew* strategy becomes obvious.

What can today's leaders do? For a start, we can each consciously make a firm commitment to care deeply for our staff. Then the actual work of caring for the basics of people's welfare, safety and sense of long-term employment security must be put in place. Creating regular opportunities to meet, interact, help and work with our people should be called for. The recent reality-TV programme on the Undercover Boss[66] and the likes (Management by Wandering About[67]) can be very powerful in helping leaders reach out to their people and tangibly help them in their work as well as improve their work environments.

Doing due Diligence

This *Doing due Diligence* (D-D) strategy of Zheng He's leadership model refers to Zheng He's actual work of fulfilling the emperor-decreed mission on the ground: preparing for and actually travelling on the seven epic grand voyages to make manifest the wealth and power of the Middle Kingdom.[68] Zheng He's work was to spread the Chinese culture, maintain peace and forge friendly ties between China and the countries in Southeast Asia and beyond.

How did Zheng He go about doing the needed due diligence in fulfilling his mission? What can we learn from his experience in actually getting his work done?

Accepting the Job

Zheng He's background and training had been that of a fighting soldier and commander in the army. He would know a great deal about fighting on land as he was well experienced and accustomed to battles. He fought alongside Zhu Di (the subsequent Emperor Yongle) on all his military missions, playing a major role in the 1930s campaign against the Mongols in the northern steppe.[69]

However, when the Emperor Yongle appointed him to be commander-in-chief of an unprecedented fleet of hundreds of ships with tens of thousands of crew to go on the *Xia Xiyang* grand voyages down fairly uncharted maritime territories from China through Southeast Asia and India, and then towards Arabia and Africa, the new job must had appeared daunting to Zheng He. After all, in all his life till then, he had never set foot outside of China, and he had no experience whatsoever as a maritime leader, navigator and diplomat. The new assignment was clearly a challenge that went outside of his comfort zone.

Nonetheless, Zheng He accepted the job. Perhaps he had no choice since this was an emperor-decreed mission for him. Or, as we have noted earlier, Zheng He had a strong sense of allegiance and loyalty to his emperor, who was also his benefactor while he was growing up as a eunuch slave, and this had given him the motivation to accept the challenge to serve his emperor and country. Indeed, as we have indicated earlier, Zheng He held the conviction that "If men serve their prince with utmost loyalty there is nothing they cannot do."[70]

At the same time, Zheng He had a close relationship with the emperor; in fact, as we have indicated earlier, his regular and direct contact with the emperor accorded him an importance beyond his formal position.[71] This should add to Zheng He's confidence in accepting this special challenge.

Defining the Job

While the emperor would have handed Zheng He his imperial edict for Zheng He to make the epic voyages, we know that these imperial scrolls generally merely spell out the purpose for the voyage and sometimes included the associated broad itinerary. They do not spell out the details of when to set sail, who to include on the voyage, what and how much supplies and cargo to carry, etc. In fact, even with regards the specific purpose for each voyage, Zheng He had significant leeway to decide on what to do and when and how to accomplish these purposes.

The following is an example of such an edict that was issued by the Emperor Yongle to Zheng He before his third voyage in 1409:

> I, the emperor, send my words to the kings and chieftains of foreign states far in the west, that I follow the heaven's order to rule the world, to execute heaven's will to give blessing and virtue. It is my wish that on all lands showered with sunshine and moonlight, moistened by frost and dew, its people, regardless of age, will be granted a stable livelihood, and a safe shelter. Today, I send Zheng He to spread my message. All of you must obey the heaven's will and follow my words, and know your limits. Do not bully the minority. Do not attack the weak. All of you should share the prosperity of the peaceful time. If you wish to pay tribute to my court, you will be bestowed with gifts of goodwill. I send my edict to let you know my message.[72]

In this edict, we see that the emperor's intention was a fairly broad and vague instruction for Zheng He to spread his message of establishing goodwill and good relations with foreign states. There was much room for Zheng He to interpret and translate this broadly worded mission into more specific actions at his own discretion.

Given this, Zheng He was therefore not merely "doing the job" since the job for him was not defined or specified in detail. Instead, Zheng He had to first "define or make the job" as part of his overall due diligence. As an example, we know that Zheng He planned for and strategically carried out economic activities of trade with the many places that he visited while helping to "spread the emperor's message". Yet other eunuch diplomats such as Hou Xian, who had in twenty-five years also led envoys to Tibet and fifteen Southeast Asian countries,[73] did not engage in extensive economic activities like Zheng He did. This showed that Zheng He had exercised much of his own discretion and had substantial authority in planning and executing his seven voyages. In fact, for the convenience of Zheng He, the Emperor Yongle even gave him blank scrolls pre-stamped with his imperial seal so that Zheng He could issue authorized imperial orders during his many voyages.[74]

Doing the Job

Zheng He's lifetime work was indeed represented by what he eventually did through his leadership of the seven epic grand voyages. Indeed, as he "defined and made his job" within the broad scope of the emperor's edict, Zheng He's due diligence in doing his job faithfully, eventually gave rise to what we have already described as Zheng He's *Art of Collaboration* in the earlier part of this book.

However, even as Zheng He did his due diligence, he and his crew were just doing it one step at a time, embarking on one voyage at a time, riding over each wave as it came, overcoming each storm as it blew, meeting each military challenge as it arose, visiting one city after another, facilitating one trade at a time, and completing one task at a time. After all, Zheng He did not receive an edict upfront for him to make a total of seven voyages; he had no big picture of how many *xiyang* countries he will eventually be visiting; and often times, in the earlier voyages, the imperial orders for them were given in fairly quick succession. So Zheng He simply pressed on with doing his due diligence on the ground – doing his job on the ground as best as he could, and in accordance with how he had defined it.

It was only as he neared the end of his career, on the eve of his seventh and last voyage, that Zheng He looked back on what he had done and accomplished. Only then did he see his whole lifetime of work, embodied in his leadership of the seven epic grand voyages, finally being put together on the stone steles that he erected at Liujiagang and Changle,[75] for the sake of posterity.

And in this book, we attempt to represent Zheng He's body of work in his leadership of the seven epic grand voyages as his *Art of Collaboration*, for the sake of today's managers and leaders, and also for the sake of posterity.

Indeed, Zheng He's *Doing due Diligence* strategy of leadership means simply *accepting, defining and doing the job*, one step at a time. But upon completion of one's mission, this strategy would point to a lifetime body of contributions that should give the leader a sense of accomplishment and satisfaction.

Implications

Clearly for any leader, a new assignment that promises to take one out of his comfort zone will always appear to be an overwhelming and intimidating challenge. How can one prepare oneself to accept such a challenge when it comes? Learning from Zheng He, one should never frown upon adversity in one's life. Instead, as in Zheng He's case, *Adversity can turn out to be Good* as it led him to a strong and special relationship with the emperor, his benefactor. This had also gave him the chance to build his own capabilities so that again learning from his experience, indeed *Ability is the Key* to gaining trust from others and building confidence in oneself. This can help in meeting new challenges as they come along.

Today's leaders must go beyond asking for and following a detailed job description. Indeed, as one moves up the leadership hierarchy, there is often no job description available for a given position. One must learn to define or make one's job within a vaguely specified job scope, if indeed one is available. In fact, this implicit requirement for defining one's job is something that the newcomer to leadership often stumbles over. We must therefore learn from Zheng He's experience in this: the job is often as big as one can make it! In Zheng He's case, he made it all the way from China to Africa in the early fifteenth century, moving tens of thousands of crew, with an unprecedented fleet of hundreds of ships.

As today's leaders, we can also learn patience from this D-D strategy of Zheng He's leadership practices. Often times, one cannot expect to see big results from our work over a limited period of time. We must be disciplined in doing our daily due diligence over a protracted period of time. In Zheng He's case, he put his significant work on record only as he neared the end of his career.

Embracing the Eternal

This *Embracing the Eternal* (E-E) strategy of Zheng He's leadership model points to Zheng He's practice of entrusting his fleet and people to the protection that may be offered by the eternal divine spirits. It highlights Zheng He's apparent need to depend on an ultimate invisible authority bigger than himself (and his emperor). Indeed, regardless of whether one sees this aspect of Zheng He's leadership as mere superstitious belief or genuine religious faith on his part, it is nonetheless an obvious element of Zheng He's practice as he led his fleet and crew on the seven epic voyages. In fact, as Zheng He and his associates put it, both the Liujiagang and Changle inscriptions were dedicated to making manifest the virtue of the goddess or Heavenly Princess.[76]

There are two aspects to this E-E strategy of Zheng He's leadership practice.

Religious Inclusiveness

While Zheng He and several of his close associates may have been Muslims, many of his men were not.[77] A large number of his crew, including many who were recruited in Fujian, were worshippers of Mazu, the Goddess of the Sea.[78] As the leader of his fleet, Zheng He allowed altars to be set up on board, enabling his crew members to pray to Mazu and seek her protection for their journeys.[79] In fact, Zheng He went so far as to help "popularize the worship of Mazu".[80] Before embarking on his grand voyages, Zheng He would help to build Mazu temples, and join his crew in praying to Mazu, showing his understanding and acceptance of all religious beliefs and cultures,[81] as well as his desire to be one with his men.

Though this may be his practice, Zheng He nonetheless stayed true to Islam, his religion. In fact, Levathes stated that Zheng He's diligence in attending to Buddhist rituals and ceremonies for the Daoist goddess of seamen did not cause him to turn from his Muslim beliefs, and that he had not abandoned the faith of his forefathers.[82] Zheng He, for example, consciously recruited Imam Hasan to be part of his crew; he also participated in the building and renovating of mosques such as the Qingjing Mosque in Xian.[83]

Quite simply put, the historical records seemed to indicate Zheng He's practice of an eclectic spiritual faith, one that invokes and embraces the reality of divine help and protection, and also one that is all inclusive and tolerant. Dreyer made reference to the spread of Islam among the islands of Indonesia during Zheng He's time to be a tolerant variety of Islam.[84]

Personal Conviction

The other aspect of this E-E strategy of Zheng He's leadership is his personal conviction of belief in the divine.

Both the Liujiagang and Changle inscriptions clearly invoked divine protection.[85] Dreyer's translation of the Liujiagang inscription of 1431 included this:

> We have traversed over a hundred thousand li of vast ocean and have beheld great ocean waves, rising as high as the sky and swelling and swelling endlessly. Whether in dense fog and drizzling rain or in wind-driven waves rising like mountains, no matter what the sudden changes in sea conditions, we spread our cloudlike sails aloft and sailed by the stars day and night. Had we not trusted her divine merit, how could we have done this in peace and safety? When we met with danger, once we invoked the divine name, her answer to our prayer was like an echo.[86]

Similarly, in the Changle inscription, we read the following: *It is not easy to enumerate completely all the cases in which the goddess has answered our prayers.*[87]

If indeed we interpret the contents in the two inscriptions to be significant, then Zheng He's conviction of belief in the divine help that was available to him and his crew is clearly evident in the above.

In fact, even in the military success that Zheng He seemed to have secured against the pirates through the sheer strength and capability of his own soldiers, so that the sea lanes had become safe and peaceful for all foreign people to use,[88] Zheng He had nonetheless also ascribed this to the divine aid of the goddess.[89]

Perhaps it is not difficult for us to understand why. No matter how much preparations Zheng He and his crew may have done, and even with the Emperor of the Middle Kingdom of the world as their imperial patron, once the unprecedented fleet set sail with the 27,000 plus crew, they would invariably be subjected to the mercies of the winds and waves, the storms and rains, and the isolation of being out in the miles and miles of oceans without any land in sight. And when Zheng He saw himself as the overall leader of such a risky venture, and when he saw that his crew was all spread out over the 200–300 vessels around his, it became quite clear to him that indeed, he may not succeed.[90] He must have realized through such a sense of leadership loneliness and helplessness that he needed to invoke divine aid.

And indeed, in Zheng He's experience, his personal conviction of belief was inscribed clearly in the Changle tablet as follows: *"If men are able to serve the gods with utmost sincerity, then all their prayers will be answered."*[91]

Implications

Zheng He's E-E leadership strategy calls for a belief in the divine. Even if one does not or chooses not to practise such a spiritual element, Zheng He's practice here would nonetheless suggest that leaders need to be religiously inclusive and tolerant.

Such a slant towards religious inclusivity, sensitivity and harmony is clearly even more important for leaders in today's world of religious extremism and terrorism. It should therefore be helpful for leaders of today to put in conscious efforts to understand the religious beliefs and practices of their people. Pulling people to work together to achieve a mission is the fundamental task of a leader. One can choose to do this at one level through material incentives and bonuses; or, one can add to that by choosing to do this at the deeper level of supporting one's people in their respective religious beliefs and practices.

Similarly, Zheng He's apparent conviction of belief in the divine as embodied in his E-E strategy of leadership suggests that leaders can and may indeed need to find strength in something that is beyond them.

In the *Allegiance to Authority* (A-A) strategy of Zheng He's leadership model, one can find strong motivation and conviction in one's allegiance or loyalty to a higher authority or cause. Here, in the E-E strategy, Zheng He's experience and practice points to finding that deeper motivation and strength in the divine. The prescriptive management literature is traditionally quite thin in this area of leadership and faith. Perhaps, this is because management and leadership practices are largely confined to the man-made realm of businesses, processes and systems. However, the growing importance of Enterprise Risk Management today suggests that leaders must pay attention to recognition of all types of risks, including risks embedded in the realm of nature. In Zheng He's leadership work in his epic voyages, it is obvious that he had to do battle with risks associated with the natural elements of rain, wind and waves (as well as risks associated with pirates and oppressive chieftains). And this led to his practice and conviction of embracing the eternal spiritual realm. Today's leaders apparently also need to deal with earthquakes and tsunamis, landslides and floods, in addition to religious riots and terrorism. Perhaps Zheng He's E-E strategy here may deserve a closer look.

LEARNING FROM ZHENG HE ON LEADERSHIP

Zheng He apparently saw his lifelong work as that embodied in his leadership of the seven epic grand voyages he made at the emperor's decree. As he himself reflected upon this, he apparently put together a summary that is now available to us in the form of the two tablet inscriptions he made at Liujiagang and Changle. From these, it is clear that he saw the following as important elements of his leadership work: his clear devotion to his ruler, the emperor; his co-labouring with a team of senior associates; his care and concern for his crew of workers; his detailed efforts of executing his mission on the ground; and his entrusting of his fleet and people to protection by the divine spirits.

In line with these, we have therefore presented our learning on Zheng He's leadership in the form of five leadership strategies: the A-A strategy that represents Zheng He's *Allegiance to Authority* that gave him the strong motivation to do his leadership work; the B-B strategy that highlights the importance of having a *Band of Brothers* as co-labourers in leadership; the C-C strategy that calls for a leader's *Care for his Crew* of workers; the D-D strategy that requires leaders to act on *Doing due Diligence* in terms of putting in the requisite efforts in executing his mission on the ground; and the E-E strategy of *Embracing the Eternal* that suggests the need for leaders to look beyond themselves in their search for solutions.

Quite clearly then, Zheng He was more than a Ming era navigator, explorer, and diplomat. He was first and foremost the **leader** of the largest fleet and crew ever to sail the oceans, long before the likes of Christopher Columbus, Vasco da Gama and Ferdinand Magellan.

Endnotes

1. Tan Ta Sen, *Cheng Ho and Malacca* (Singapore: International Zheng He Society, 2005), p. 1.
2. Channel NewsAsia, *Zheng He the Modern CEO* (Singapore: MediaCorp News (video production), 2005).
3. Rivers, P. J., "Cheng Ho — Admiral of the Western Ocean: A Nautical Perspective, Some Practical Considerations of the Ming Voyages", International Conference on Zheng He and the Afro-Asian World, Malacca, 2010, p. 2.

4. Zheng He's Inscriptions at Liujiagang and Changle (1431), as translated in Edward L. Dreyer, *Zheng He: China and the Oceans in the Early Ming Dynasty, 1405–1433* (U.S.: Pearson Education, Inc., 2007), pp. 191–99.

5. *Zheng He: China and the Oceans in the Early Ming Dynasty*, Preface, p. xii.

6. J. J. L. Duyvendak, "The True Dates of the Chinese Maritime Expeditions in the Early Fifteenth Century", *T'oung Pao* XXXIV (1938): 341–412, as quoted in *Zheng He: China and the Oceans in the Early Ming Dynasty*, p. 217.

7. *Zheng He: China and the Oceans in the Early Ming Dynasty*, p. 145.

8. *Zheng He: China and the Oceans in the Early Ming Dynasty*, p. 32.

9. *Zheng He: China and the Oceans in the Early Ming Dynasty*, p. 145.

10. *Zheng He: China and the Oceans in the Early Ming Dynasty*, pp. 145–50.

11. *Zheng He: China and the Oceans in the Early Ming Dynasty*, p. 197.

12. *Zheng He: China and the Oceans in the Early Ming Dynasty*, p. 197.

13. *Zheng He: China and the Oceans in the Early Ming Dynasty*, p. 150.

14. We borrow this term from Dreyer's summary in *Zheng He: China and the Oceans in the Early Ming Dynasty*, p. 150.

15. *Zheng He: China and the Oceans in the Early Ming Dynasty*, p. 191.

16. Tan Ta Sen and Chia Lin Sien, eds., *The Zheng He Epic*, 1st edition in Chinese edited by Zhou Wenlin et al. (Kunming, Yunnan, China: Yunnan Publishing House, Yunnan Fine Arts Publishing House, Auora Publishing House, 2006), p. 232.

17. Louise E. Levathes, *When China Ruled the Seas: The Treasure Fleet of the Dragon Throne, 1405–1433* (U.S.: Oxford University Press, 1994), pp. 114–15.

18. *Zheng He: China and the Oceans in the Early Ming Dynasty*, pp. 79–81.

19. *When China Ruled the Seas*, p. 151.

20. *Zheng He: China and the Oceans in the Early Ming Dynasty*, p. 197.

21. From memorial tablet engraved by Zheng He in honour of his father, as quoted in *When China Ruled the Seas*, p. 62.

22. *When China Ruled the Seas*, p. 62.

23. *Zheng He Epic*, p. 48.

24. *When China Ruled the Seas*, p. 62.

25. *Zheng He Epic*, p. 57.

26. *Cheng Ho and Malacca*, p. 3.

27. *Cheng Ho and Malacca*, p. 3.

28. *Cheng Ho and Malacca*, p. 3.

29. *When China Ruled the Seas*, p. 64.

30. *Cheng Ho and Malacca*, p. 3.

31. *Zheng He Epic*, p. 69.

32. *Zheng He Epic*, p. 68.

33. *Zheng He: China and the Oceans in the Early Ming Dynasty*, p. 18.

34. *Zheng He Epic*, p. 69.

35. *Zheng He Epic*, p. 68.

36. *Zheng He: China and the Oceans in the Early Ming Dynasty*, p. 22.

37. *Zheng He: China and the Oceans in the Early Ming Dynasty*, p. 50.

38. *When China Ruled the Seas*, p. 87.

39. The New York Times Website, <http://www.nytimes.com/2002/02/26/business/enron-s-many-strands-corporate-culture-enron-lavish-excess-often-came-before.html> (accessed 3 November 2010).

40. *Zheng He: China and the Oceans in the Early Ming Dynasty*, p. 197.

41. As indicated earlier, we borrowed this term from Dreyer's summary in *Zheng He: China and the Oceans in the Early Ming Dynasty*, p. 150, to represent the second strategy in Zheng He's leadership model.

42. *Zheng He: China and the Oceans in the Early Ming Dynasty*, pp. 145–46.

43. Chiu Ling-yeong, "Zheng He: Navigator, Discoverer and Diplomat", *Wu Teh Yao Memorial Lectures 2000* (Singapore: Unipress, Center for the Arts, National University of Singapore, 2001), pp. 14–15.

44. *Zheng He: China and the Oceans in the Early Ming Dynasty*, pp. 157, 208.

45. *When China Ruled the Seas*, p. 107.

46. *Zheng He: China and the Oceans in the Early Ming Dynasty*, p. 199.

47. *Zheng He: China and the Oceans in the Early Ming Dynasty*, p. 127.
48. *Zheng He: China and the Oceans in the Early Ming Dynasty*, p. 197.
49. *When China Ruled the Seas*, p. 171.
50. *Zheng He: China and the Oceans in the Early Ming Dynasty*, p. 146.
51. *When China Ruled the Seas*, p. 151.
52. *When China Ruled the Seas*, p. 191.
53. *Zheng He Epic*, pp. 212–16.
54. *Zheng He Epic*, p. 345.
55. 陈存仁 《被误读的远行：郑和下西洋与马哥孛罗来华考》桂林市：广西师范大学出版社, 第45 and 61页. (Chen Cunren, *The misread Voyages: A Study of Zheng He's Voyages and Marco Polo's Trip to China*, published in Guilin City by Guangxi Normal University Publication, 1998, pp. 45 and 61).
56. *Zheng He: China and the Oceans in the Early Ming Dynasty*, pp. 127–34.
57. *When China Ruled the Seas*, p. 84.
58. *Zheng He: China and the Oceans in the Early Ming Dynasty*, p. 141.
59. *Zheng He: China and the Oceans in the Early Ming Dynasty*, p. 150.
60. *Zheng He Epic*, p. 248.
61. 陈存仁 《被误读的远行：郑和下西洋与马哥孛罗来华考》桂林市：广西师范大学出版社, 第62页. (Chen Cunren, *The misread Voyages: A Study of Zheng He's Voyages and Marco Polo's Trip to China*, published in Guilin City by Guangxi Normal University Publication, 1998, p. 62).
62. *When China Ruled the Seas*, p. 111.
63. *Zheng He: China and the Oceans in the Early Ming Dynasty*, p. 149.
64. *Zheng He: China and the Oceans in the Early Ming Dynasty*, p. 150.
65. *Zheng He: China and the Oceans in the Early Ming Dynasty*, p. 148.
66. "Undercover Boss: What would you want your CEO to see?", at <http://blogs.wsj.com/juggle/2010/02/07/undercover-boss-what-would-you-want-your-ceo-to-see/> (accessed 25 July 2011).
67. "MBWA after all these years", at <http://www.tompeters.com/dispatches/008106.php> (accessed 25 July 2011).
68. Zheng He's biography in *Mingshi 304.2b–4b*, as translated in *Zheng He: China and the Oceans in the Early Ming Dynasty*, p. 187.

69. *When China Ruled the Seas*, p. 64.

70. *Zheng He: China and the Oceans in the Early Ming Dynasty*, p. 197.

71. *Zheng He: China and the Oceans in the Early Ming Dynasty*, p. 22.

72. 《郑和家谱•敕谕海外诸番条》，收录于《郑和下西洋资料汇编》上册，海洋出版社2005年增编本，531页。(Compilation of Records and Materials on Zheng He's Voyages to the West Seas, Ocean Publication); (own translation into English).

73. 彭勇，《2009年郑和研究综述》，郑和研究，2010年第1期第8页，江苏省郑和研究会与太仓市郑和研究会联合出版。(Journal of Zheng He Research, Jiangsu Zheng He Society and Tai Cang Zheng He Society Publication).

74. *When China Ruled the Seas*, p. 87.

75. *Zheng He: China and the Oceans in the Early Ming Dynasty*, p. 32.

76. *Zheng He: China and the Oceans in the Early Ming Dynasty*, pp. 193 and 197.

77. Tan Ta Sen, *Cheng Ho and Islam in Southeast Asia* (Singapore: Institute of Southeast Asian Studies, 2009), p. 171.

78. *Cheng Ho and Islam in Southeast Asia*, p. 204.

79. *Cheng Ho and Islam in Southeast Asia*, p. 171.

80. *Cheng Ho and Islam in Southeast Asia*, p. 204.

81. Rosey Wang Ma, "Zheng He's contribution on the spread of Islam in the Malay World and a legacy of an open-minded peaceful multi-ethnic, multi-religious community", International Conference on Zheng He and the Afro-Asian World, Malacca, 2010, p. 7.

82. *When China Ruled the Seas*, p. 147.

83. *Zheng He Epic*, pp. 200–1.

84. *Zheng He: China and the Oceans in the Early Ming Dynasty*, p. 148.

85. *Zheng He: China and the Oceans in the Early Ming Dynasty*, p. 148.

86. *Zheng He: China and the Oceans in the Early Ming Dynasty*, p. 192.

87. *Zheng He: China and the Oceans in the Early Ming Dynasty*, p. 196.

88. *Zheng He: China and the Oceans in the Early Ming Dynasty*, p. 148.

89. *Zheng He: China and the Oceans in the Early Ming Dynasty*, p. 192.

90. *Zheng He: China and the Oceans in the Early Ming Dynasty*, p. 197.

91. *When China Ruled the Seas*, p. 90; and *Zheng He: China and the Oceans in the Early Ming Dynasty*, p. 197.

References

Chiu Ling-yeong. "Zheng He: Navigator, Discoverer and Diplomat". *Wu Teh Yao Memorial Lectures 2000*. Singapore: Unipress, Center for the Arts, National University of Singapore, 2001.

Dreyer, Edward L. *Zheng He: China and the Oceans in the Early Ming Dynasty, 1405–1433*. U.S.: Pearson Education, Inc., 2007.

Levathes, Louise E. *When China Ruled the Seas: The Treasure Fleet of the Dragon Throne, 1405–1433*. U.S.: Oxford University Press, 1994.

Ma, Rosey Wang. "Zheng He's contribution on the spread of Islam in the Malay World and a legacy of an open-minded peaceful multi-ethnic, multi-religious community". International Conference on Zheng He and Afro-Asian World, Malacca, 2010.

"MBWA after all these years", at <http://www.tompeters.com/dispatches/008106.php>.

New York Times Website, <http://www.nytimes.com/2002/02/26/business/enron-s-many-strands-corporate-culture-enron-lavish-excess-often-came-before.html> (accessed 3 November 2010).

Rivers, P. J. "Cheng Ho — Admiral of the Western Ocean: A Nautical Perspective, Some Practical Considerations of the Ming Voyages". International Conference on Zheng He and the Afro-Asian World, Malacca, 2010.

Tan Ta Sen. *Cheng Ho and Islam in Southeast Asia*. Singapore: Institute of Southeast Asian Studies, 2009.

———. *Cheng Ho and Malacca*. Singapore: International Zheng He Society, 2005.

Tan Ta Sen and Chia Lin Sien, eds. *The Zheng He Epic*. 1st edition in Chinese edited by Zhou Wenlin et al. Kunming, Yunnan, China: Yunnan's Publishing House, Yunnan Fine Arts Publishing House, Auora Publishing House, 2006.

"Undercover Boss: What would you want your CEO to see?", at <http://blogs.wsj.com/juggle/2010/02/07/undercover-boss-what-would-you-want-your-ceo-to-see/>.

陈存仁《被误读的远行：郑和下西洋与马哥孛罗来华考》桂林市：广西师范大学出版社. (Chen Cunren. *The misread Voyages: A Study of Zheng He's Voyages and Marco Polo's Trip to China.* Published in Guilin City by Guangxi Normal University Publication, 1998).

《郑和家谱•敕谕海外诸番条》，收录于《郑和下西洋资料汇编》上册，海洋出版社2005年增编本。(Compilation of Records and Materials on Zheng He's Voyages to the West Seas, Ocean Publication).

彭勇，《2009年郑和研究综述》，郑和研究，2010年第1期第8页，江苏省郑和研究会与太仓市郑和研究会联合出版。(Journal of Zheng He Research, Jiangsu Zheng He Society and Tai Cang Zheng He Society Publication).

Chapter 6

LEARNING FROM ZHENG HE
Human Resource
Management Practices

INTRODUCTION

Zheng He's grand voyages have been associated with two unprecedented, large-scale characteristics: a huge fleet of 200–300 ships, with the largest treasure ships measuring some 480ft by 194ft and the medium-sized ones measuring about 399ft by 162ft;[1] and a large crew of more than 27,000 men.[2] In putting together this large number of people, and in managing them throughout the voyages, Zheng He must have had much experience in Human Resource (HR) management practices that today's managers and leaders can learn from.

In fact, as a land-based army man rather than being a navy commander before he was appointed by the emperor to lead the grand voyages, Zheng He must have had the acute sense that without access to highly skilled maritime-oriented human capital, it would have been impossible for him to embark on his grand voyages, much less to achieve any degree of notable success. What were the major HR management tasks that Zheng

He considered to be most important and which he apparently paid special attention to in terms of planning and execution? What can we learn from Zheng He about his people skills and HR management practices that can be of relevance to us today? How did he manage his leadership team and crew to ensure that they stayed united while travelling to distant shores and peoples?

Indeed, when we ponder over these questions, and as we grapple with the sheer size of his huge crew of more than 27,000 men, we must conclude first and foremost that Zheng He saw his human resource as a very vital asset for carrying out his emperor-decreed voyages and mission. It would require much boldness on his part to decide on the need for such a large crew if he did not see it as mission-critical.

Similarly, it should also be apparent that Zheng He would have to consider how he would organize and structure his huge HR asset base so as to efficiently and effectively operationalize his mission. And given the open seas as the working environment for his crew, and with each voyage's duration of 1.5–2 years, it should also be obvious that Zheng He must figure out how to manage his HR in terms of meeting their needs and keeping them motivated.

In this chapter, we consider Zheng He's HR management practices and introduce the Zheng He's HR Role model that sees him in the following roles: Zheng He as the *Strategic HR Planner,* the *Clever HR Organizer,* and, the *Wise HR Manager.* Through these roles, we will see Zheng He's HR management practices that seemed to emphasize the following:

(1) **Human Resource** as the *Key Strategic Asset;*
(2) **Selection and Recruitment** as the *Foundation for Performance;*
(3) **Organization and Structures** as the *Required Enabler;*

(4) **Care for Crew** as the *Fuel for Performance*;

(5) **Ongoing Learning** as the *Means for Value Creation*; and

(6) **Sponsor Linkage** as the *Support for Mission Sustainability*.

This chapter is therefore organized as follows. In the next section, we will introduce Zheng He as the *Strategic HR Planner*. Here, we will highlight Zheng He's recognition of human resource as a key strategic asset for his voyages; we will also see that selection and recruitment of the needed people were apparently very important HR tasks to Zheng He. We will then introduce Zheng He as the *Clever HR Organizer* who saw "organization and structures" as the required enabler for the work of his people. Here, we will note Zheng He's efforts in organizing his people for operating in the open seas even as they travelled with him across the oceans on his unprecedented epic fleet. We then follow this by introducing Zheng He as the *Wise HR Manager*. Here, we will focus on Zheng He's apparent efforts at managing his people, caring for them as he recognized that his care for the crew can provide the fuel for continued effective performance. We will also note his efforts in facilitating ongoing learning as the means for value creation by his crew, keeping them motivated and growing in the process. We will also highlight here Zheng He's apparent efforts at building his ongoing sponsor linkage with the Emperor Yongle in order to garner support for the sustainability of his mission. In learning from Zheng He through all his work in these three HR roles, we will also attempt to draw implications for today's managers and leaders.

ZHENG HE: THE STRATEGIC HR PLANNER

Following his appointment to serve as the commander-in-chief of the emperor-decreed *Xia Xiyang* (Travel to the Western Seas) mission, Zheng He began to plan for his voyages. As we search through the existing literature on this, it is quite clear that Zheng He spent much effort on the construction of his unprecedented huge fleet that comprised some of the largest ships ever to sail the oceans. At the same time, it is also obvious that Zheng He paid much attention to planning and putting his crew together for the voyages.

Human Resource: The Key Strategic Asset

In this aspect, it is apparent that Zheng He recognized the crucial importance of people for the success of his voyages and mission. Indeed, as he moved into the details of planning for his voyages, Zheng He must have had carefully considered and interpreted his imperial mission and translated that into requirements for human resource. And in his planning, it is now a fact that he had decided to sail with a crew of more than 27,000 men. This is a huge requirement of human resource by any standard, even in today's business landscape and in terms of today's businesses' requirements of human resource.

Zheng He must have been convinced that his large crew was indeed needed and necessary, and indeed even strategic, in terms of ensuring the success of his emperor-decreed mission. Otherwise, it would be foolish boldness on his part to sail with more than 27,000 men, since such a huge crew would mean Zheng He needed to put in extra efforts and resources in planning for and managing the actual movement and feeding of his people throughout the long voyages.

We already know that a fundamental element of Zheng He's mission was to demonstrate and share Ming China's splendour and glory, a kind of projection of Ming China's power.[3] Both the unprecedented scale of Zheng He's fleet, and the equally huge crew of tens of thousands of men, would therefore add to the vision of a powerful and glorious Ming China.

At the same time, we also know that Zheng He was tasked with delivering imperial gifts to the local rulers and chiefs in the countries he visited. Many of such gifts would be quite valuable as a demonstration of the wealth of the Ming Court. Zheng He must have felt the need to guard and protect such gifts, and the large quantities of the many other goods and items that he also carried for the purpose of trade. Indeed, in the Changle inscription, Zheng He indicated that he felt a sense of responsibility for the great amount of money and valuables on board.[4] In this context, together with his knowledge of the issue of piracy and bandits that could endanger the lives of his crew, Zheng He must have had wanted to provide for safety and security. His crew was therefore purposely assembled to include a fairly large component of military officers and soldiers.

In addition, we have already pointed out in chapter 3 that Zheng He had planned to carry out large scale trade, and he had also apparently planned for and executed this very systematically, including the setting up of logistics bases in different countries,[5] the building of *guanchangs* or warehouses as in Malacca,[6] and the conscious separation of his fleet into different squadrons and sending them out to execute independent trading activities.[7]

In Zheng He's HR planning, all these needs described above necessitated a large crew. And making the decision to sail with a large crew of more than 27,000 men, in spite of the obvious logistics burden of having to house, move and feed this large number, would suggest that it was apparent to Zheng He that *Human Resource* is a *Key Strategic Asset* for the success of his mission. Indeed, to Zheng He as a Strategic HR Planner, it was apparent that Human Resource is a mission-critical resource.

Selection and Recruitment: The Foundation for Performance

In our literature search, it is also apparent that Zheng He as a Strategic HR Planner paid much attention to the matter of Selection and Recruitment of his people. Zheng He had to put his people together at two levels: the leadership team that supported his leadership work directly, as well as the specialist experts and the rest of the crew.

The literature recorded a team of senior associates and envoys who accompanied Zheng He to the western seas: Wang Jinghong, Hou Xian, Li Xing, Zhu Liang, Zhou Meng, Hong Bao, Yang Chen, Zhang Da and Wu Zhong. These men were either experienced sailors or "old hands" in dealing with affairs of foreign countries. Of these men, Wang Jinghong and Hou Xian were particularly important to Zheng He because of their diplomatic linkages to several of the countries in the western seas then.[8] Zheng He also explicitly made mention in the Changle inscription of Zhu Zhen and Wang Heng as part of his leadership team; they were both Regional Military Commissioners,[9] with a Ming Court rank that was higher than the rank of Grand Directors (as carried by the envoys mentioned here).[10] No doubt these men were included in Zheng He's leadership team because of what Zheng He saw in their particular capabilities and background experiences.

Zheng He also paid attention to the selection and recruitment of specialist experts and the rest of the crew so as to provide expertise and support in various mission-specific areas.

For example, in one of the grand voyages, the *Zheng He Jiapu* (Genealogy of Zheng He) recorded these specialists and crew as including: 7 grand eunuchs serving as chief envoys; 10 lesser eunuchs serving as deputy envoys; 63 eunuchs; 2 brigadiers; 93 captains; 207 military officers; 2 secretaries; 1 financial officer; 1 protocol officer; 5 astrological-cum-meteorological officers;

180 medical officers; and 26,803 others (including navigators, compass-men, technicians, soldiers, clerks, buyers, manual workers, etc);[11] another reference specifically included strong men, cooks and interpreters within this group of 26,803 others.[12]

On interpreters and knowledge of foreign languages in particular, Emperor Yongle saw the need for capability in proper communication with the foreigners. He therefore had a *Siyi Guan* set up in Nanjing to train people to be proficient in foreign languages. Zheng He appointed well-known interpreters including Ma Huan and Feixin to be part of his fleet.[13] In fact, as preparation for his fourth voyage where Zheng He was to visit the Arab countries in the far west for the first time, Zheng He personally went into Shaanxi to look for interpreters and he recruited Hasan, the imam of the Qingjing Mosque.[14]

From the Taicang area, Zheng He apparently readily recruited marine engineers and technicians, experienced traders with specialist knowledge of foreign ports and the associated geography, and navy personnel to provide security for his fleet.[15]

From the Changle and neighbouring area, Zheng He recruited helmsmen, technicians, interpreters and medical officers.[16]

In Quanzhou, Zheng He recruited marine technicians with knowledge of the sea routes and skilled navigators and shipbuilders; he also recruited interpreters knowledgeable in foreign languages and foreign affairs.[17]

And on the medical specialists, to look after the health of his approximately 27,000 crew members, Zheng He carefully put together a specialized medical team where on average, he had one medical officer looking after the health needs of some 150 crew members. Some of these specialists came from the palace's elite medical institution and some were actually well-known local medical practitioners.[18] For example, there were principal professionals like Senior Medical Officer Chen Yicheng, and

Medical Officers Chen Chang, Peng Zheng, and Kuang Yu on board Zheng He's fleet on his voyages to the Western Ocean.[19]

Zheng He also leveraged on his earlier network in selecting people to support him on his mission. As an example, Zheng He had Yao Guangxiao join him on his voyage to the West in 1411.[20] Yao Guangxiao was apparently the most significant strategist who had worked closely with Zhu Di in the successful Battle of Jingnan;[21] Zheng He had during that time established a close relationship with Yao Guangxiao, and he had therefore called on him when he embarked on his voyages.

Quite clearly, Zheng He's apparent careful and personal efforts in all these would suggest that he saw the *Selection and Recruitment* of the right people as critically important in laying the *Foundation for Performance* once his voyages were on the way.

Implications

If we go with Zheng He's strategic considerations as a HR planner, then the obvious implication for today's managers and leaders is to see *Human Resource* as a *Key Strategic Asset* for our organizations. This means paying attention to HR as a strategic mission-critical resource which forms the intellectual asset base of our companies. In this context, we are no longer mere bean counters in viewing HR through the question of "how many workers or staff do we need to hire for efficiency?", even as we keep a keen eye on total payroll cost; instead, we will consider this same question and go out of the way to hire the required number of workers and staff needed to ensure our strategic mission success.

In the same way, we will need to ask the question: how are we currently selecting and recruiting people for our companies? Zheng He's apparent efforts at seeking out the relevant right people would suggest that we should not merely be hiring to fill up our job vacancies. Apparently, if we intend to do more than lip service to Zheng He's practice here, we will need to set up a rigorous process for our selection and recruitment of leaders, specialists, and also to some extent, our rank and file staff. We may think that for Zheng He, when he had a wrong person on the job while out at sea, it could spell disaster; and so in Zheng He's context, getting the right crew and team in place would be critical. While most of us may not be operating in a similar setting as that of Zheng He's, would our need to see *Selection and Recruitment* as the *Foundation for Performance* be anything less?

ZHENG HE: THE CLEVER HR ORGANIZER

Having strategically selected and recruited his people and hence laid the foundation for future performance, Zheng He paid attention to cleverly organizing them to effectively fulfill his mission. This task of organizing his HR was important because Zheng He recognized that his crew will essentially be operating out in the open seas and in foreign lands. Also, given the significantly large total crew size, and the unprecedented scale of his fleet, Zheng He knew that he must cleverly assign his different people to the different types of ships, organize and manage his fleet to facilitate this, as well as institute some structured means for communication with his people while out at sea. Zheng He also knew that he needed to divide his crew and fleet into sub-fleets or squadrons in order to visit more places on a given voyage. All these called for Zheng He to be clever in his role as the HR organizer of his grand enterprise of travelling to the western seas.

Organization and Structures:
The Required Enabler

Quite clearly in this role, Zheng He recognized the importance of putting in place organizational structures that would enable the effective accomplishment of his mission through his voyages.

Departments

Zheng He therefore cleverly organized his entire crew into four functional departments or groups:[22]

(1) Command Centre, which included the envoys, deputy envoys, senior eunuch associates of Zheng He and the lesser eunuchs: this group served as the decision and command centre of the entire fleet and was responsible for all policy matters and decision-making;

(2) Navigational Affairs Department, which included the navigators, compass-men, vessel captains, astrological officers and technicians: this group clearly helped with the actual navigation and travel of the fleet during the different voyages;

(3) Foreign Affairs and Supplies Department, which included the foreign affairs and trade officers, protocol officers, language interpreters, financial officers, supplies officers and medical officers: this group helped with diplomacy and foreign trade, tributary matters, food and water supply and resupply, and the health of the crew; and

(4) Military and Defence Department, which included the brigadiers, captains, soldiers and other military officers: this group provided for the security and safety of the fleet throughout the voyages.

Ships

Zheng He also cleverly organized his fleet of ships according to their functions,[23] and assigned his people from the different departments to these accordingly:

Treasure Ships: these were the largest and grandest ships in Zheng He's fleet; they were the flagships and therefore essentially carried Zheng He and his senior associates and staff from the Command Centre group;

Horse Ships, Grain Ships and Water Ships: these functioned as supplies ships, carrying different types of supplies including food and water, horses and other animals; these ships also served as accommodation cabins for mid-level officials, interpreters and medical officers from the Foreign Affairs and Supplies Department; and

Command Ships and War Ships: these were also referred to as battle ships and they carried the military personnel (soldiers and commanders) from the Military and Defence Department.

Quite logically, the crew from the Navigational Affairs Department would be distributed across the various types of ships to help in the actual navigation during the voyages.

Communications

To facilitate communication with his people while out at sea, Zheng He set up an elaborate but simple sight and sound system involving the use of flags and banners, bells and drums, colours and lanterns.[24]

And in conjunction with this system of sight and sound communication, Zheng He also cleverly organized his fleet to sail with a formation that looked like a bird with its two wings spreaded out;[25] with his own Commander-in-Chief Ship being set right in the centre of the formation, facilitating his oversight of, and communication with, all his people. Zheng He also separately named each ship (such as 'Qing He', meaning Pure Harmony), and attached a number following each name (such as 'Qing He 1', 'Qing He 2', etc). Such a naming convention helped with overall communications.

Sub-fleets

On his various voyages, as Zheng He himself could not visit all the countries, he had to cleverly organize his deputies and crew to act on his behalf. For this purpose, he explicitly created a structure comprising the main fleet (called the *dazong*) to be led by himself and the sub-fleets or branch-fleets (called the *fenzong*) to be led by his deputies. The latter would leave the former in places like Champa and Calicut and sail to their assigned countries. Then all the *fenzong* and the *dazong* would assemble in a base like Malacca after accomplishing their respective missions. The base in Malacca was carefully set up and fortified; and while they waited for the arrival of the summer monsoon for their homeward journey, various treasures and materials, including important documents, were kept safely there in the base depot.[26]

All these examples demonstrated Zheng He in his role as the Clever HR Organizer; here, he had clearly recognized the importance of setting up *Organization and Structures* to serve as the *Required Enabler* for the accomplishment of his mission.

Implications

The more complex business becomes, the more important it is to establish "organization and structures" to facilitate the smooth running of the business. Zheng He's experience with his huge fleet and large crew out in the tough environment of a long journey in the open seas clearly necessitated him to be clever in terms of organizing his human resources and capital assets. To Zheng He, he apparently knew intuitively that such "organization and structures" will enable his accomplishment of his emperor-decreed mission.

In today's environment, businesses operate in a global competitive marketplace, with long supply chains that cut across national boundaries and oceans. And in many large organizations, the total human resource headcount is also huge. And analogous to the fleet and ships of Zheng He's voyages is today's network of organizational units and multi-site operations belonging to a single business group. While today's businesses can appear to be complex and challenging, Zheng He's fifteenth-century HR organization work can point us to the simple necessities of "organization and structures". When done well, these efforts here can help an organization accomplish its mission effectively. Zheng He's experience points us to the power of "real organizational structures" as represented in today's "org charts"; they also highlighted the necessity of setting up simple and straightforward communication systems for all staff and leaders; and, Zheng He's *fenzongs* demonstrated the inevitable need to organize our people into smaller focused units which, when supported well as through Zheng He's establishment of regional bases, can in turn lead to greater productivity and results.

ZHENG HE: THE WISE HR MANAGER

With his crew selected and recruited, and having set up the various organizational structures to facilitate the work of his people, Zheng He then proceeded to play his role as the Wise HR Manager where he apparently focused his efforts at managing his people, caring for them and recognizing and rewarding them, catering to their needs and facilitating ongoing learning to keep them motivated while adding value to his fundamental mission. In this role as the Wise HR Manager, Zheng He also apparently paid attention to managing his "boss" as he put in effort at building his ongoing linkage with the Emperor Yongle in order to garner support for the continuation of his mission.

Care for Crew: The Fuel for Performance

As he managed his crew on the voyages, Zheng He quite obviously worked on providing for their various needs. As indicated in some detailed manner in chapter 5, Zheng He provided for the welfare of his crew in terms of meeting their physical need for food and water, ensuring the adequate supply and resupply of these throughout the long duration of each of the voyages. At the same time, Zheng He also looked after the health needs of his people, putting his specially assembled team of some 150 medical doctors to work on his crew as the need arose. We also noted earlier that Zheng He even paid attention to minute, detailed level needs including that for barbers and needlework services as in the repair of clothes, socks and shoes. Of course, Zheng He also provided for the safety and security needs of his crew through the military and defence department he had assembled and organized, and the command and war ships he had consciously included in his fleet. All these demonstrated Zheng He's care for the basic hygiene needs of his crew.

Zheng He also paid attention to the crew's higher level needs; for example, he carefully ensured that his crew was well recognized and rewarded by the emperor when they returned from their voyages. In fact, as also indicated earlier in chapter 5, Zheng He would always try to get any perquisites for his people when any such benefits had been given to other workers. Zheng He also supported and facilitated private trade between his crew and the locals,[27] granting them material benefits through such, thereby helping to motivate them as they worked for him throughout the voyages. We should further highlight that Zheng He also paid attention to the spiritual needs of his people. As many of his crew comprised of non-Muslims who were worshippers of Mazu (the Goddess of the Sea), Zheng He set up Mazu altars on board the treasure ships for prayers to be offered by his crew for a safe voyage out at sea.[28] In fact, Zheng He would often join his crew in invoking the protection of the divine spirits, as both the Liujiagang and Changle inscriptions attested to.[29] We have earlier indicated in chapter 5 that this involvement of Zheng He with his people in seeking divine protection through prayers demonstrated his deep care for his crew, as he felt a sense of deep burden and responsibility towards them in terms of their safety.[30]

Zheng He also cared for his team of senior associates who travelled with and helped him in the overall leadership of his voyages. In fact, Zheng He explicitly gave them recognition by making mention of their names in his summary inscriptions erected at Liujiagang and Changle on the eve of his final voyage. As we indicated earlier, Dreyer referred to Zheng He's senior team as his *Band of Brothers*,[31] suggesting the closeness in their relationships as they voyaged and led together.

All these efforts by Zheng He demonstrated his role as the Wise HR Manager in terms of his people management skills. He apparently recognized that his constant and deep *Care for his Crew* would continue to provide the *Fuel for effective Performance* by them which would then in turn help him in fulfilling his mission and responsibility toward the emperor.

Ongoing Learning: The Means for Value Creation

Zheng He also apparently kept his crew motivated by facilitating ongoing learning so that they could also continue to add value to the basic mission entrusted to them by the emperor.

As an example, we have earlier highlighted in chapter 2 that Zheng He apparently coordinated his seven grand voyages in two phases. The first phase comprised the first three voyages; in his first voyage, the main destinations were Champa, Java, Sumatra, Ceylon, Calicut and Palembang. Gradually, he increased the main destinations over subsequent voyages to include visits to Malacca, Siam, Brunei, Quilon, Cochin, Kayal, etc. Only in the second phase from the fourth expedition onwards did he lead his fleet to venture out towards places like Hormuz, Mogadishu,

Aden, and Malindi on the African coast.[32] This suggested that Zheng He facilitated the ongoing learning of his crew by moving gradually from the closer known places out towards the farther away places. In fact, we provide more details on this in the next chapter on Zheng He's gradual growth of his supply chain from China out towards Africa.

We have also highlighted in chapter 2 that the medical team on Zheng He's voyages conducted studies of local diseases and their cures, and collected local medicinal herbs and learned of local medical treatment methods. They also helped promote the exchange of medicines between China and the Afro-Asian countries by opening the door to import foreign herbs to China.[33]

Similarly, Zheng He's crew conducted "market surveys" in the various places they visited. They collected first-hand ground data on the demand for China's products and these showed that China's products had much potential in the many overseas markets. Zheng He therefore apparently built ground knowledge pertaining to each country he visited through his people, thereby preparing Ming China for the long-term development of peaceful foreign trade.[34]

All these represented the *Ongoing Learning* of Zheng He's people as they continued *to Create Value* to add to Zheng He's basic mission. They also demonstrated Zheng He's wisdom as the HR Manager in managing his people's ongoing motivation through learning and value creation.

Sponsor Linkage: The Support for Mission Sustainability

This is yet another aspect of Zheng He as the Wise HR Manager, namely his careful and wise management of his relationship with the sponsor and patron of his grand voyages, the Emperor

Yongle. This is what we commonly refer to as "managing the boss" in today's language.

Zheng He knew quite clearly that he must have the continuing support of the emperor in order to ensure the sustainability of his mission and voyages. In this context, he therefore practised accountability, built and earned continuing trust, and stayed in close and regular communications, with the emperor.

Accountability

This is evidenced by Zheng He's actions on the ground that proved him to be a man of integrity. In all his voyages to the West, Zheng He did not engage in conquests, killings, looting or destruction.[35] Instead, Zheng He faithfully carried out Emperor Yongle's policy of harmony and friendliness by respecting the local rulers and their people, and establishing friendly ties with them. Evidence can be found in the Padmanabhapura Palace in India where paintings on the bloody battle between the king's troops and the Portuguese were displayed, but no Chinese weapons were displayed; instead, only porcelain pieces, urns and wooden chairs were seen there, suggesting that Chinese voyagers like Zheng He had maintained a diplomacy of harmony and friendliness in contrast with their western counterparts.[36] Zheng He's diplomacy of peace and goodwill was at odds with western imperialism over maritime Asia that began with the voyages of Vasco da Gama (1497–99) and Pedro Cabral (1500–01).[37]

As we saw in the last chapter, another example of Zheng He's practice of accountability to the emperor was in his decision to let Emperor Yongle decide on the fate of pirate chief Chen Zuyi,[38] the Ceylonese king Alagakkonara,[39] and the rebel Sekander[40] (captured in the three incidents where Zheng He invoked the use of military force). While Zheng He could have readily decided and proceeded with the execution of these individuals, he was keenly aware of his emperor-decreed mission of spreading goodwill, peace and building collaboration, instead of aggression, antagonism and the use of military force. Zheng He therefore apparently recognized the need for accountability and hence decided to defer to the emperor in these three incidents.

Trust

In fact, we indicated earlier that in the incident involving the pirate chief Chen Zuyi, it was clear that Zheng He was helping to remove piracy that infested the Straits of Malacca. Hence, by capturing the aggressor alive and leaving the final say to the emperor, Zheng He established himself as one who respects the emperor, and thus continued to earn the emperor's trust in his leading of the voyages, one after another.

Similarly, we pointed out in the previous chapter that when Zheng He was in the midst of his sixth voyage, while at Semudera in north Sumatra, he divided his fleet and let one of his deputies lead the main fleet onto Aden and Africa while he himself led the smaller sub-fleet to return to China.[41] Zheng He apparently wanted to honour the emperor with his presence by being back into Beijing for the celebration of the emperor's massive Forbidden City as the country's new capital in 1420. Such an action no doubt helped Zheng He to continue to win the emperor's trust and confidence.

Of course, Zheng He's ability in leading and managing the grand voyages in fulfillment of the emperor-decreed mission would also help to earn the emperor's continuing trust. Apparently, after having observed the first three successful voyages led by Zheng He, the Emperor Yongle was confident enough with the financial position of the Ming Court that he ordered the construction of the Dabao En Temple, including an extravagant porcelain pagoda to show his gratitude to his mother, the Empress Ma. The overall Bao'en project eventually cost over 2.5 million ounces of silver and this bill was apparently met by the surplus revenues brought back by Zheng He's treasure fleet.[42]

Close Links

Throughout his voyages, Zheng He had sought to maintain close and frequent linkages with the emperor. In fact, by deferring important decisions to the emperor as in the examples of the three incidents involving the use of military force, Zheng He had gained the attention of the emperor on a fairly regular basis.

Indeed, the Emperor Yongle did pay careful attention to Zheng He's grand voyages to the West and had given him his fullest imperial support. When Zheng He successfully returned from his second voyage, for example, the emperor issued a special edict which called for the building of the Jinghai Temple in Xiaguan, Nanjing to commemorate this.[43] This, of course, was also part of Zheng He's overall efforts to keep himself in touch with his emperor.

Even in his selection of Taicang as the ideal port and logistics assembly point for his fleet before it set off on the grand voyages, Zheng He also consciously recognized that Taicang gave him the opportunity to keep close contact with the Ming Court as it took just about a day's voyage to reach Nanjing from Taicang.[44]

Through all these efforts, Zheng He played the role of a Wise HR Manager in maintaining his ongoing *Sponsor Linkage* and therefore ensuring his sponsor's ongoing *Support for the Sustainability of his Mission*.

Implications

Learning from Zheng He, the wise HR manager of today will need to pay attention to caring for his people, helping them to learn and grow continually, as well as building an ongoing linkage with his superior in order to gain his continuing support and sponsorship. The wise HR manager should recognize that care for staff serves as fuel for continuing effective performance, and that facilitating staff learning actually creates value for the organization.

All these essentially mean that as wise HR managers, we will be building human capital where we pay attention to each individual staff, providing for his individual skills training and specific capabilities development. It will also mean we need to build information capital where the wise HR manager pays attention to building a knowledge management system to facilitate sharing of knowledge and learning among our people. Finally, this will also mean today's wise HR manager will need to build organization capital by nurturing a care-based organizational culture supported by tangible welfare policies and provisions.

LEARNING FROM ZHENG HE ON HUMAN RESOURCE MANAGEMENT

In this chapter, we focused specifically on learning from Zheng He about his human resource management practices. We presented our understanding of Zheng He from this human resource management perspective by introducing what we refer to as the Zheng He HR Role model.

In this model, we highlighted Zheng He in his role as the Strategic HR Planner who saw his crew as the key strategic asset of his overall enterprise, and the careful selection and recruitment of people as laying the foundation for superior performance. We also presented Zheng He in his role as the Clever HR Organizer who paid attention to putting organization and structures in place to enable effective work to be done by his crew to fulfill the emperor-decreed mission. Finally, we also saw Zheng He in his role as the Wise HR Manager where his care for the crew served as fuel for their ongoing positive performance, where he facilitated their ongoing learning to create further value for the overall mission, and where he maintained his sponsor linkage with Emperor Yongle in order to gain his continuing support for that mission.

Endnotes

1. Tan Ta Sen and Chia Lin Sien, eds., *The Zheng He Epic*. 1st edition in Chinese edited by Zhou Wenlin et al. (Kunming, Yunnan, China: Yunnan's Publishing House, Yunnan Fine Arts Publishing House, Auora Publishing House, 2006), p. 352.

2. Louise E. Levathes, *When China Ruled the Seas: The Treasure Fleet of the Dragon Throne, 1405–1433* (U.S.: Oxford University Press, 1994), p. 87.

3. Edward L. Dreyer, *Zheng He: China and the Oceans in the Early Ming Dynasty, 1405–1433* (U.S.: Pearson Education Inc., 2007); see Author's Preface.

4. *Zheng He: China and the Oceans in the Early Ming Dynasty*, p. 197.

5. 郑一钧，《郑和下西洋对15世纪初期世界文明的发展》，收录于《郑和远航与世界文明—纪念郑和下西洋600周年纪念论文集》，北京大学出版社，2005年，第32页。(Zheng He's Voyages and World Civilization, Peking University Publication).

6. 陈达生，《马六甲'官厂'遗址考》，收录于《郑和与东南亚》，新加坡郑和学会2005年出版，第97－105页; also in Tan Ta Sen, *Cheng Ho and Malacca* (Singapore: International Zheng He Society, 2005), p. 44.

7. 郑一钧，《郑和下西洋对15世纪初期世界文明的发展》，收录于《郑和远航与世界文明—纪念郑和下西洋600周年纪念论文集》，北京大学出版社，2005年，第32页。

8. Chiu Ling-yeong, "Zheng He: Navigator, Discoverer and Diplomat", *Wu Teh Yao Memorial Lectures 2000* (Singapore: Unipress, Center for the Arts, National University of Singapore, 2001), pp. 14–15.

9. *Zheng He: China and the Oceans in the Early Ming Dynasty*, p. 199.

10. *Zheng He: China and the Oceans in the Early Ming Dynasty*, p. 127.

11. *Cheng Ho and Malacca*, pp. 14–15.

12. *Zheng He: Navigator, Discoverer and Diplomat*, p. 10.

13. *Zheng He Epic*, p. 96.

14. *Zheng He Epic*, p. 200.

15. *Zheng He Epic*, p. 128.

16. *Zheng He Epic*, p. 159.

17. *Zheng He Epic*, p. 185.

18. *Zheng He Epic*, p. 345.

19. *Zheng He Epic*, p. 218.

20. *Zheng He Epic*, p. 161.

21. *Zheng He Epic*, p. 69.

22. *Cheng Ho and Malacca*, p. 15.

23. *Cheng Ho and Malacca*, pp. 11–12.

24. *When China Ruled the Seas*, p. 83; *Cheng Ho and Malacca*, p. 13.

25. *Cheng Ho and Malacca*, p. 13.

26. *Zheng He: Navigator, Discoverer and Diplomat*, pp. 13–14.

27. *Zheng He Epic*, p. 8.

28. Tan Ta Sen, *Cheng Ho and Islam in Southeast Asia* (Singapore: Institute of Southeast Asian Studies, 2009), p. 204.

29. *Zheng He: China and the Oceans in the Early Ming Dynasty*, pp. 191–99.

30. *Zheng He: China and the Oceans in the Early Ming Dynasty*, pp. 149–50.

31. *Zheng He: China and the Oceans in the Early Ming Dynasty*, p. 150.

32. *Zheng He Epic*, pp. 226–29.

33. *Zheng He Epic*, p. 345.

34. *Zheng He Epic*, p. 320.

35. *Zheng He Epic*, p. 315.

36. *Zheng He Epic*, p. 284.

37. *Zheng He: China and the Oceans in the Early Ming Dynasty*, pp. 7–8.

38. *Zheng He Epic*, p. 232.

39. （清）张廷玉，《明史》，卷三百二十四，列传第二百十二，外国五，爪哇传，载于：<http://www.guoxue.com/shibu/24shi/mingshi/ms_324.htm>.

40. *Zheng He: China and the Oceans in the Early Ming Dynasty*, pp. 79–81.

41. *When China Ruled the Seas*, p. 151.
42. *When China Ruled the Seas*, p. 121.
43. *Zheng He Epic*, p. 71.
44. *Zheng He Epic*, p. 130.

References

Chiu Ling-yeong. "Zheng He: Navigator, Discoverer and Diplomat". *Wu Teh Yao Memorial Lectures 2000*. Singapore: Unipress, Center for the Arts, National University of Singapore, 2001.

Dreyer, Edward L. *Zheng He: China and the Oceans in the Early Ming Dynasty, 1405–1433*. U.S.: Pearson Education Inc., 2007.

Levathes, Louise E. *When China Ruled the Seas: The Treasure Fleet of the Dragon Throne, 1405–1433*. U.S.: Oxford University Press, 1994.

Tan Ta Sen. *Cheng Ho and Islam in Southeast Asia*. Singapore: Institute of Southeast Asian Studies, 2009.

———. *Cheng Ho and Malacca*. Singapore: International Zheng He Society, 2005.

Tan Ta Sen and Chia Lin Sien, eds. *The Zheng He Epic*. 1st edition in Chinese edited by Zhou Wenlin et al. Kunming, Yunnan, China: Yunnan's Publishing House, Yunnan Fine Arts Publishing House, Auora Publishing House, 2006.

郑一钧,《郑和下西洋对15世纪初期世界文明的发展》, 收录于《郑和远航与世界文明—念郑和下西洋600周年纪念论文集》, 北京大学出版社, 2005年。(Zheng He's Voyage and World Civilization, Peking University Publication).

陈达生,《马六甲'官厂'遗址考》, 收录于《郑和与东南亚》, 新加坡郑和学会2005年出版。

Chapter 7

LEARNING FROM ZHENG HE
Logistics and Supply Chain Management Practices

INTRODUCTION

From 1405–33, Zheng He led the world's largest ocean-going fleet in seven epic grand voyages to the West. The voyages were epic in terms of their unprecedented fleet and crew sizes, and the long distances travelled; they were grand because of the sheer size of the so-called "treasure" ships.

For every voyage, Zheng He mobilized over 100 (sometimes even more than 300) ships, including approximately 60 large ships to form the main body of the fleet, and over 20,000 crew members.[1] In his maiden voyage, for example, Zheng He had a crew of more than 27,000 men and a fleet of 317 ships.[2] His largest ships measured about 480ft by 194ft while the medium-sized ones measured about 399ft by 162ft.[3] Such vessels were clearly considered colossal, and especially so in the context of the world in the fifteenth century.

Over the seven voyages, Zheng He made calls at more than thirty countries and territories, including present-day Vietnam,

Thailand, Pahang, Kelantan, Java, Sumatra, Sri Lanka, India, Dhufar (Arabian Peninsular), Hormuz (Persian Gulf), Yemen, Mecca and Mogadishu in East Africa.[4] These voyages covered a total mileage of over 300,000 kilometres.[5]

In essence, each of Zheng He's grand voyages was a floating fifteenth-century supply chain designed to pick up, store and deliver Chinese products (including the imperial gifts) to the many states and countries that Zheng He would visit and trade with. At the same time, each voyage was also a supply chain of the needed daily provisions of food and water to support the movement and sustenance of Zheng He's massive fleet and crew. Of course, each voyage also served as the supply chain that brought back to China the foreign products picked up through trade, including the tributary gifts for the Ming emperor from the vassal states.

From today's twenty-first century perspective, operating in a world supported by widespread wireless communications and satellite technologies, and with global supply chains that literally networked the entire globe, a fundamental, puzzling question on Zheng He's seven voyages to the West remains: how were these voyages undertaken? How did Zheng He manage to move and feed his 27,000 plus men, spread out over 200–300 ships of unprecedented sizes, seven times across the long and wide stretches of oceans that were in many places fraught with dangers and infested with pirates, and over long durations of 1.5 to 2 years,[6] back in the early fifteenth century?

Logistics and Supply Chain Management

It should be obvious that there is much we can learn from Zheng He in terms of the logistics and movement of people and materials. Preparing for and moving his massive fleet and crew over long distances and durations across the unknown oceans must have been a massive challenge, even for today's leaders and managers.

So what preparations did Zheng He made in putting his supply chain together before he could embark on his voyages? For one thing, he must begin to build and put his fleet of ships together quickly. What did Zheng He's fleet look like? What fleet design would be necessary to help him fulfill his emperor-decreed mission of spreading Ming China's goodwill and splendour through collaborative trade and generous exchanges? How and where did he build them? We already know that by the time they were ready for deployment, Zheng He's ships were considered colossal, and they reflected the advanced shipbuilding capabilities in China in the fifteenth century.[7] So designing and building these ships (in the hundreds) must have been a massive endeavour in itself.

Then there is the large scale logistics of what, how and where did Zheng He make arrangements for provisioning of food, water and other supplies for sustenance of his large crew during the long voyages anticipated. For example, we know that for his maiden voyage, Zheng He must ensure that his 27,000 plus crew were well-fed and kept healthy over the entire two-year duration of that voyage. How did Zheng He source, store, protect and manage his supplies over each of such long voyages, including precious royal gifts and the large quantities of items to be used for trade?

Then there is the crew itself: what types of crew members would Zheng He need for the voyages? Where and how did he recruit or select them?

And then when he was ready to set sail, what navigational tools and technologies did Zheng He use? What routes did he choose and how did he plan out his voyages? How did Zheng He communicate and exercise command and control over his people during the actual movements across the open waters?

As an example, we know that amongst the various ships on Zheng He's fleet, communications was made possible by an elaborate system of sound and sight signals.[8] And where and how did Zheng He set up his supply and re-distribution centres along his long itinerary route?

What relevance do all these suggest for today's managers? Surely there must be rich lessons we can distill from the logistics and supply chain management practices of Zheng He for the benefit of today's logistics and supply chain managers and leaders.

In the rest of this chapter, we will present what we refer to as Zheng He's 7S Model of Importance in logistics and supply chain management. The Model will highlight what we consider to be the seven important aspects of Zheng He's logistics and supply chain management practices. We will also provide some key implications and modern-day examples in each of these elements of the model. In so doing, we also seek to provide some answers to the many questions raised above on how Zheng He actually designed, implemented, managed and extended his fifteenth-century "global" supply chain.

ZHENG HE'S 7S MODEL OF IMPORTANCE

From the literature that apparently described Zheng He's logistics and supply chain management practices, we highlight seven aspects that seemed to be of particular importance to Zheng He. We present these as Zheng He's 7S Model of Importance in logistics and supply chain management as follows:

(1) **Strategic Intent and Clarity**: the *Importance* of Supply Chain Mission and Vision;
(2) **Supply Ecosystem**: the *Importance* of Supply Chain Capabilities;

(3) **Specialists Recruitment**: the *Importance* of Supply Chain People and Knowledge;

(4) **Sights and Sound of Navigation**: the *Importance* of Simplicity in Operations;

(5) **Selection of Regional Bases**: the *Importance* of Supply Chain Collaboration;

(6) **Supply Growth and Development**: the *Importance* of Continual Learning; and

(7) **Storage and Guanchang**: the *Importance* of Physical Supply Chain Assets.

Strategic Intent and Clarity: The Importance of Supply Chain Mission and Vision

What should Zheng He envision his voyages to be like? How large should his fleet be? How big should each ship be? How many crew members should he travel with? To answer such questions, Zheng He must first be clear of the purposes of his voyages; this means he must first be clear of his emperor-decreed mission for the voyages. Only then can he envision what his voyages should be like and therefore proceed to design and plan for these voyages. Then in executing or implementing these carefully designed voyages, Zheng He can then indeed fulfill the emperor's mission for him.

This is the essence of this first element of Zheng He's 7S Model of Importance: Zheng He apparently had clarity of the strategic intent of his voyages (the mission for his supply chain), and this gave him the boldness to design his voyages on an unprecedented scale (his vision of the type of supply chain to design and build), which then led to his success in fulfilling his emperor-decreed mission.

Vision: Building the Largest and State-of-the-Art Fleet

Zheng He was appointed by the Emperor Yongle as the principal envoy and commander-in-chief to lead the grand voyages to the West. Apparently this was because the emperor was convinced of Zheng He as a capable organizer of large-scale construction projects, having earlier appointed and observed Zheng He as the Grand Director of the eunuch Directorate of Palace Servants, which was responsible for the construction and maintenance of all palace buildings.[9]

Once appointed, Zheng He proceeded with detailed planning for the maiden voyage. We had already described in chapter 2 that Zheng He interpreted his emperor-decreed mission as spreading Ming China's goodwill and splendour through generous exchanges and collaborative trade. Zheng He therefore had clarity of his mission and clarity of the strategic intent for his voyages.

Zheng He therefore envisioned that he needed to plan for the voyage on an unprecedented scale (in terms of fleet and ship sizes, and crew to be carried) so as to both impress and awe the peoples in the countries that he will visit (what Dreyer referred to as "projection of power" of the Ming Court[10]), as well as to carry the large volumes of imperial gifts and Chinese product items needed for trade. With the large crew envisaged, Zheng He will also need to provide for capacity to carry the associated need for provisions of food and water,[11] and other supplies.

In essence then, Zheng He had to plan for a supply chain to deliver imperial gifts and Chinese products to the many states and countries that he will visit and trade with. At the same time, he also had to plan for the needed logistics and supplies to support the movement and sustenance of his massive fleet and crew, as well as the storage and transport of imperial gifts and tributes from vassal states.

Zheng He's first task was therefore to build the fundamental element of his supply chain: the design and construction of his massive, state-of-the-art fleet of more than 300 ships to house, transport and provide for a crew of more than 27,000 men. And many of these ships were huge in size, the largest ever to sail the seas then.

It is therefore apparent that Zheng He's clarity of his mission and vision gave him the boldness to design, plan, embark and complete a maiden voyage (and supply chain) that would involve the largest fleet ever assembled to sail the waters from China to South Asia, through Southeast Asia and back. Together with his subsequent voyages, it was also clear that Zheng He succeeded in meeting his emperor-decreed mission given the large-scale trade that took place through his voyages, and the many vassal states that sent tributes and envoys to the Ming Court.

Implications

Zheng He's clarity of strategic intent, which led to the vision and building of the necessary (and unprecedented) supply chain, has much implications for today's supply chain managers and leaders.

One does not simply build and operate a supply chain similar to what other companies possess. One also does not simply outsource the company's supply chain work to third party logistics service providers without a consideration of strategic fit. To help the company succeed, the supply chain that is designed and built, either in-house or by a third party, must be strategically purpose-driven. It must be aligned with the company's strategic intent for the supply chain.

A more current example of this is clearly represented in the experience of modern day Wal-Mart. How did Wal-Mart become the largest successful retailer in the world that it is today?

This question is especially relevant when we note that back in 1979, Kmart was the industry giant with some 1,891 stores compared with Wal-Mart's 229 stores.

From the operations perspective, the key to Wal-Mart's success "was to make the way the company replenished inventory the centrepiece of its competitive strategy". This clear strategic intent led to a series of supply chain innovations by Wal-Mart, including the early use of electronic point-of-sales technology and data; investment in, and use of, private satellite communication technologies that include online linkages to its 4,000 suppliers; the development and installation of cross-docking points and systems that command and control the use of up-to-date information of actual sales in Wal-Mart stores so as to bring about quick and accurate replenishment of inventories; and the management of a dedicated fleet of some 2,000 company owned trucks serving some nineteen distribution centres spread out across the United States.

All these innovations took Wal-Mart almost ten years to experiment and put in place, but it did so deliberately because of the clarity of its strategic intent: to use quick inventory replenishment as its competitive weapon. As one measure of the success of its inventory supply system, Wal-Mart was able to replenish its stores twice a week on average, compared with the industry norm of once every two weeks. This in turn meant an overall reduction of inventory carried at the stores, and hence helped in overall cost reduction, facilitating Wal-Mart's well known Everyday Low Prices at the stores.[12]

Quite clearly, we can learn from Zheng He's (and Wal-Mart's) experience in this first aspect of his 7S Model: the importance of supply chain vision through clarity of its strategic intent or purpose as contained in its mission. Paying attention to this first strategic and important element of Zheng He's supply chain practices can yield significant competitive advantages for a company, not just productivity enhancements.

Supply Ecosystem: The Importance of Supply Chain Capabilities

This second element of Zheng He's 7S Model for supply chain management highlights the importance and necessity of an overall ecosystem of supply chain capabilities. In Zheng He's case, when he was called upon to travel to the West, this ecosystem of supply chain capabilities was already in existence for Zheng He to use.

Relevant Historical Capabilities

In fact, long before the Ming Dynasty, the rulers of the Song and Yuan dynasties had already adopted an open-door policy to encourage foreign trade in China. For example, the Song Government set up offices of the Commissioners of Foreign Trade in various parts of China like Guangzhou, Mingzhou, Quanzhou and Mizhou Banqiao to facilitate foreign trade; they also sent envoys to foreign countries; and, for their people, they offered incentives to attract foreign ships to do business in China.[13]

During Emperor Gao Zong's tenure in the Song Dynasty, the emperor himself rallied the merchants to help build a new fleet of ships which would challenge that of Persian and Arab traders in the Indian Ocean. He also allocated funds to improve harbours, widen canals to facilitate ocean-going vessels, and build warehouses.[14] The emperor also established China's first navy, and by the early thirteenth century, the Song navy had controlled the East China Sea from Fujian to Japan and Korea, and provided patrol of all China's main rivers. By the same time, the Chinese had the best ships and had captured much of the sea trade from the Arabs, with the ocean-going merchant ships measuring some 100ft long and 25ft wide, and carrying 120 tons of cargo and a crew size of 60.[15]

By the time the Mongols conquered the Song and established the Yuan Dynasty, their merchants had sailed vessels that far surpassed Song vessels in size and grandeur. Towards the end of the thirteenth century, Marco Polo had reported sightings of four-masted Yuan vessels each with at least 60 individual cabins and carrying a crew of between 150 and 300.[16]

All these would mean that by the time of Emperor Yongle and Zheng He, Ming China already had comprehensive capabilities in shipbuilding and maritime trade. Indeed, by the time Zheng He was issued the imperial decree to embark on his grand voyages, he could readily proceed to design and build the largest fleet of state-of-the-art ships.

Ship Construction Capabilities

Some of Zheng He's ships were built in Fujian; many of them were built in the well-known Ming Dynasty Treasure Ship Shipyard in Nanjing[17] (also apparently referred to as the Longjiang shipyard[18]). The neighbouring Suzhou, Jiangsu, Jiangxi, Zhejiang, Hunan and Guangzhou provinces were also involved in the imperial shipbuilding.[19]

For lumber supplies, the coastal provinces were supplemented by lumbering operations in the outer reaches of the Yangtze and Min rivers, with timber floating downstream to the shipyards.[20]

The Treasure Ship Shipyard itself was constructed in the early Ming period; it was conveniently located with the Yangtze river to its west and the Qinhuai river to its east. This was one large shipyard built on a total area of 500,000 sqm. It was subsequently divided into two smaller ones referred to as the front shipyard and the back shipyard. The two separate shipyards had their own floodgates and waterways that link them to the Longjiang river, so that when the ships were built, the floodgates were then opened to allow water to flow in and enable the ships to float out to the river.[21]

In the shipyard, there were various departments with managers and workforce supervisors. There were also workshops for carpentry, painting, iron and steel, sails and ropes, and others. There were also ten rows of sixty houses in a sail-making factory northeast of the shipyard.[22] The shipyard drew its skilled shipbuilding workers from the provinces of Zhejiang, Jiangxi, Hunan, Hubei, Fujian and Jiangsu.[23] At its peak, some twenty to thirty thousand people worked and lived in the yards.[24]

Zheng He's vessels built here were considered colossal, and they reflected China's very advanced shipbuilding technology.[25]

Port and Supply Logistics Capabilities

Another crucial part of Zheng He's detailed preparation for his grand voyages was the availability of an ideal port to serve as a supply logistics assembly point. This was important because of the magnitude and duration of the voyages, the considerable manpower to be mobilized and the large amount of provisions to be acquired. The Emperor Yongle and Zheng He made the wise choice of Taicang because of its political, economic and cultural strengths, and also because of its excellent port facilities.[26]

Liujiagang in Taicang had a natural deep water harbour with wide and spacious berths to cater to Zheng He's fleet both before they set sail and also when they returned. Because of the massive amount of provisions (food and daily necessities) required to feed the 27,000 plus crew and the cargo (silver and gold coins, ceramics, spices, tools etc.) to be used as gifts and for trade with other countries, Zheng He must select a viable supply collection and distribution centre of these provisions and cargo.

Quite readily, Taicang fitted the bill; indeed, Taicang had the entire Yangtze basin as its economic hinterland. It also had an advanced land and sea transportation network that linked it to its economic interior.[27]

In addition, Taicang could offer skilled manpower and expertise in navigation; it had a ready pool of marine engineers and technicians, and being part of the entire Jiangnan region, it also had many seasoned and experienced seamen and navigators. Taicang also had a navy base since the Song and Yuan dynasties and this provided Zheng He the ready opportunities to recruit the necessary navy crew to help provide security for his fleet. Further, many traders dealing in foreign trade congregated in Taicang; these people had for generations sailed between the Pacific and the Indian oceans and they were therefore very familiar with foreign ports and geography. They were therefore readily available to join as part of Zheng He's crew.[28]

Finally, Taicang also allowed Zheng He to keep close contact between the Ming Court and his fleet as it took just a day's voyage to reach Nanjing from Taicang (which was 696 *li* by road and 712 *li* by sea from Nanjing).[29]

In building his supply chain and preparing for his voyages, Zheng He therefore had an entire ecosystem of supply chain capabilities at his disposal. If this had not been the case, Zheng He would not had built his unprecedented fleet, recruited his huge crew of workmen and navigation experts, sourced for the needed provisions of food, water and trade supplies, gathered and moved his fleet and people out from the port and into the open seas.

Implications

The importance of an overall ecosystem of supply chain capabilities is clear from Zheng He's experience and practices.

It should be equally important, if not more important, for today's logistics and supply chain managers and leaders, given today's global nature of supply chains and the keen level of business competition.

This second element of Zheng He's 7S Model would suggest that companies need to build a comprehensive set of supply chain capabilities for themselves, or choose to base and build their supply chains within an environment that offer ready access to such capabilities.

In this sense, this aspect of Zheng He's model affirms Singapore's attempt to build its own version of a modern-day ecosystem of supply chain capabilities to attract companies to set up their operations headquarters here. Similarly, for companies seeking to access the emerging Asian markets, Zheng He's model would suggest that these companies choose from amongst the regional locations one that has a more comprehensive ecosystem of supply chain capabilities.

In this context, Singapore seeks to continually upgrade its capabilities to serve as a Leading Global Integrated Logistics Hub, with Robust Maritime, Aviation, and Land Transport Capabilities Supporting the Global Economy; it aims to serve as the Nerve or Brain Centre controlling and managing activities and assets of global supply chains across an expanded hinterland.[30] It therefore regularly upgrades its airport, seaport and land transport infrastructure, connectivity and services to support and help companies manage their regional business operations from Singapore. It therefore also constantly strengthen its ecosystem of supply chain players by hosting over 8,000 logistics establishments, including 17 of the world's top 25 Third Party Logistics (3PL) companies.[31]

But quite clearly, this second aspect of Zheng He's model also emphasizes the importance of building supply chain capabilities in a given company. If a company is clear of its strategic intent, and knows the kind of supply chain it should design and develop to meet its strategic purpose, but recognizes that it does not yet have the capabilities to build such a supply chain, then it must proceed to begin to invest in and develop such capabilities over time. The availability of an ecosystem of supply chain capabilities in its operating environment can help in this. But this does not mean that the company needs to completely outsource its supply chain requirements to other service providers available in the ecosystem, as this may lead to strategic vulnerability for the company. The company can instead seek to maintain its control on the design and subsequent management of its supply chain, but with help from the entire ecosystem.

Otherwise, the company will need to compromise on its supply chain performance and end up with a less efficient and effective supply chain when compared to what it should be in terms of meeting its strategic intent.

We can note one other implication from this aspect of Zheng He's experience. In the specifics of shipbuilding practices at the Treasure Ship Shipyard described earlier, we saw the big shipyard actually being divided and operated as two smaller ones. This seemed to represent the modern-day practice of operating a "Focused Factory" in the form of organizing and managing a "Plant within a Plant", resulting in overall increase in productivity and gaining competitive advantages.[32] We also note the organization of different workshops within the shipyard, together with the setup of ten rows of sixty houses in a sail-making factory northeast of the shipyard.[33] This part of the shipbuilding practice may be seen as a forerunner of what we know today as building a "Toyota City" of suppliers near to the Toyota Factory itself. Again, such a practice can lead to much improvement in productivity and competitive advantages as demonstrated in

Toyota's experience. Learning from the Chinese experience in the fifteenth century, it may be helpful to today's managers and leaders to consider these two specific operations practices.

Specialists Recruitment: The *Importance* of Supply Chain People and Knowledge

This third aspect of Zheng He's 7S Model for supply chain management highlights the importance of supply chain people and the knowledge embodied in these people. In Zheng He's case, this refers to the crew and specialists that Zheng He apparently specially recruited for his voyages. These crew and specialists became part of Zheng He's overall supply chain, and they clearly played an important role in working to deliver the imperial gifts and trade product items to the far away countries and peoples.

Putting Supply Chain Leadership in Place
The Emperor Yongle had already appointed Zheng He as the commander-in-chief for the voyages. Zheng He then needed to put in place the rest of the supply chain leadership team, the equivalent of today's senior leadership team that supports Zheng He the CEO. We already pointed out that the literature recorded a team of senior associates who accompanied Zheng He to the western seas: Wang Jinghong, Hou Xian, Li Xing, Zhu Liang, Zhou Meng, Hong Bao, Yang Chen, Zhang Da and Wu Zhong. These men were either experienced seamen or diplomats.[34]

Also, as Zheng He could not visit all the countries himself, he had on different voyages divided up the fleet where he himself would lead the main fleet, and his senior associates would lead the branch fleets. There were at least five branch fleets, leaving the main fleet at Champa, Sumatra, Ceylon, Calicut and Quilon, to sail directly to their assigned countries.[35]

Each branch fleet represented a branch supply chain to its assigned countries, and Zheng He's deputies therefore provided the necessary leadership for them.

Recruiting People with Specialist Skills

Beyond the leader and his team of close senior associates, Zheng He also recruited a specialist team that provided expertise in various specific areas to support the mission. These included diplomatic envoys, military officers, medical doctors, navigators, technicians, soldiers, buyers, cooks, manual workers and strong men.[36]

Zheng He also specifically recruited specialists who were proficient in foreign languages. Ma Huan and Feixin, for example, were recruited as interpreters.[37] Zheng He even personally went into Shaanxi to look for interpreters and here he recruited Hasan, the imam of the Qingjing Mosque[38] to help him in his fourth voyage when he began visiting the Arab countries.

From the different areas around Taicang, Changle and Quanzhou, Zheng He apparently readily recruited marine engineers and technicians, experienced traders and navy personnel,[39] helmsmen, technicians, interpreters and medical officers,[40] and also marine technicians with knowledge of the sea routes and skilled navigators and shipbuilders.[41]

And on the medical specialists, Zheng He put together a well-organized medical team with the requisite knowledge and medical facilities on board which was unprecedented in maritime history then. During the voyages, the team also collected local medicinal herbs and learned of local medical treatment methods; they also helped promote the exchange of medicines between China and the Afro-Asian countries.[42]

Organizing the Crew and Specialists

Zheng He essentially organized his entire crew into four functional groups:[43] the Command Centre group; the Navigational Affairs

Department; the Foreign Affairs and Supplies Department; and the Military and Defence Department.

All these functional groups of carefully recruited crew and specialists meant that Zheng He's floating supply chain to the West was well staffed with the necessary supply chain knowledge to ensure its success: the Command Centre group provided the needed supply chain leadership for planning and making decisions; the Navigational Affairs group provided the specialist knowledge to ensure smooth transportation and movement of the entire fleet; the Foreign Affairs sub-group provided the needed knowledge to help build collaboration with the foreign supply chain partners, namely the local traders and rulers; the Supplies sub-group provided the necessary knowledge on food and water re-supplies for the crew on board Zheng He's supply chain; and the Military and Defence group provided the knowledge for supply chain security and risk management.

All these different people and knowledge sets were clearly very important for Zheng He's supply chain work. Gong Zhen, who travelled with Zheng He on the seventh voyage, subsequently returned and wrote the *Xiyang Fanguo Zhi*; in his writing, he made reference to the importance of provisions of food and water: (1) the treasure ships were huge in size; a few hundred men were needed to work the sails, manage the anchors and control the rudders; if these lack the necessary food and drink, then the labour and hard work on the ships cannot be done; and (2) all ships went to the streams, marshes and creeks to gather new supplies of fresh water; the water tankers were then used to transport the water and the grain ships carried the grains for the crew.[44]

Similarly, the interpreters provided the language knowledge to communicate and understand the ground at the different supply chain markets visited; and the doctors provided the medical knowledge to look after the health of the crew who were all part of the overall supply chain of Zheng He's voyages.

In fact, we can interpret the doctors as offering medical services to the locals as well, and in that sense, Zheng He's supply chain carried and delivered imperial gifts and Chinese products for trade, as well as offer special services, including medical, cultural and even religious services. For example, Zheng He's supply chains presented the Chinese almanacs to the people of Champa and Ryukyu that helped them to enhance their quality of life as well as to understand Chinese custom; they also helped delivered a coronation service to Malacca's ruler Parameswara with the imperial gifts of a royal hat, robe and girdle that symbolically upgraded his status from being a local chief to that of head of state under the protection of Ming China; and they also provided building services when they helped build a temple using Chinese architectural style in Siam, as well as built mosques in Palembang, Java and the Malay Peninsula.[45]

Implications

While Zheng He had access to a significant supply chain ecosystem which could supply him with the crew he needed readily, he apparently paid attention to the specifics of the types of crew and specialists he needed for his envisioned supply chain. He even carefully organized them into clear functional areas or departments.

This would suggest that for a given supply chain with its stated mission and strategic intent, one must carefully put together the needed personnel and the associated knowledge sets to ensure that the supply chain will succeed in fulfilling its purpose.

This would include putting a key leadership team in place for the specific supply chain, much like the key account officers in today's organizations, in order to pay specific attention to a particular customer or market's needs and demands. Beyond this leadership level, this element of Zheng He's model would also suggest that we must then pay attention to the specifics of the types of logistics and supply chain crew we put in place.

Today's logistics and supply chain managers and leaders should already know Fisher's model of what constitutes a right supply chain: the functional type of products that their supply chains deliver will need an efficient supply chain that can be readily cost effective; on the other hand, when the products their companies provide to the market tend to be innovative in nature, with much changes to product design and functionalities, then the supply chain that will provide a strategic fit will be a responsive type of supply chain.[46]

Zheng He's attention to recruitment of supply chain people suggests that we need to go one step further: for an efficient supply chain, we must pay attention to recruiting cost efficient personnel (less skilled, more specific-task oriented); while for responsive supply chains, we will need to recruit personnel who are more flexible and general-purpose oriented.

It is clear then that we need to carefully consider the required specifics of people and knowledge in this area of logistics and supply chain work. Often in organizations, logistics and supply chain operations are seen as backroom work and the specifics and importance of personnel are often relegated to a less than strategic level.

Sights and Sound of Navigation: The *Importance* of Simplicity in Operations

We have earlier asked the puzzling question: with an unprecedented fleet of hundreds of ships; with many of the ships much larger than any that sailed before; and, with a crew of tens of thousands of men; how did Zheng He actually move his fleet and people? Without the benefit of today's technologies, how did Zheng He communicate with his fleet and crew throughout his voyages?

Navigational Operations on the Ground

Zheng He made use of an elaborate system of sight and sound signals to communicate among the various ships of his unprecedented epic fleet when they were out in the open seas:[47]

All his ships carried with them one large flag, some signal bells, five banners, one large drum, gongs and ten lanterns.

Sound signals were activated when commands needed to be issued on board a ship, while gongs and drums were used to create audible signals between ships so as, for example, to issue a warning for the fleet to take shelter in a safe harbour when a storm was imminent, or to communicate during war or even bad weather.

In the darkness of night, and in bad weather, lanterns were used to convey signals that were visible over some distances. Carrier pigeons were used for longer-range communication.

Each of Zheng He's ships was also identified by its special colour and a black flag with a large white character that indicated which squadron it belonged to. During the day, flag signals were used for communication.

Apparently to support this system of sight and sound communication, Zheng He also carefully sailed with a fleet formation that looked like a bird with its two wings spreaded out:[48] in the middle will be the large treasure ships that carried the imperial gifts and Zheng He and his senior associates; then surrounding these will be command ships which functioned as the navigational operations centre; then the supplies ships (carrying grains and water supplies) will be positioned to the front, back, left and right; and all these were guarded by the war ships.

With Zheng He's Commander-in-Chief Ship right in the centre of the formation, he could more easily oversee and communicate and hence command the entire fleet.

This is the fourth aspect of Zheng He's 7S Model: Zheng He's system of sight and sound signals which he used in his command and control of his fleet and people when he set sail with them on his voyages. As it turned out, this was an elaborate but simple communication system because once they were out in the open seas, Zheng He and his people must be able to communicate with each other readily. The sight and sound signals may have been elaborate, but they were easy to understand by all crew and leaders so that in the thick of danger out in the seas, no time was lost through unnecessary questions, misunderstanding and miscommunication.

Zheng He's sights and sound of navigation therefore point to the importance of simplicity in supply chain operations on the ground. It is the fourth aspect in Zheng He's 7S model of what Zheng He apparently considered to be of importance in his supply chain practices.

Navigational Expertise in the Ops Room

Of course, for navigation of his fleet, Zheng He also needed specialized knowledge, tools and techniques of navigation. In fact, since the Tang and Song dynasties, the Chinese had developed an advanced navigational system and charted detailed sailing manuals which were available for Zheng He's navigators and engineers.[49]

Some of the navigational technologies developed and used by Zheng He included: the Water Floating Compass, the Landmark Piloting Method in conjunction with the Zheng He Navigational Map, Astronomical Navigation (the "Star Observation Across Oceans" technique), and the use of "Geng" and a "Sand Hour-Glass" to measure the depth of water, speed and time.[50]

The Chinese compass used, for example, had twenty-four directional points and it utilized the magnetic needle for accurate direction. The "star observation across oceans" technique was used to calculate the ship's longitude and it was a fairly complex method using ivory-made blocks as well as wooden blocks.[51] And Zheng He's Navigational Map in particular reflected China's high level of technological development in the sphere of maritime navigation.[52]

Quite clearly, these navigational tools and techniques were advanced and complicated and would certainly require the expert specialists in order to understand and make full use of them. They were not meant for the general crew on board but were instead limited primarily for use by the expert specialists in the navigation room.

But for the other operations systems, tools and processes meant for the general operating crew, such as the system of sight and sound signals that Zheng He instituted and used for communicating with all his people, these may be tedious and even elaborate, but they were simple and easy to understand and follow through.

Implications

Of course, Zheng He was limited by fifteenth-century technology which forced him to be creative in setting up the elaborate system of sight and sound signals for communication. With today's satellite based wireless technologies, we will not need Zheng He's type of manual system.

Nonetheless, the implication is straightforward. Short of running fully automated supply chain operations, as in a modern AS/RS type of warehouse with full robotic pick and place cranes and Automated Guided Vehicles (AGVs), many of the supply chain operations will still need to be carried out by the general operations staff. Zheng He's experience with his crew suggests that for much of such operations on the ground (in the factory, warehouse or anywhere else within the supply chain), they should be designed for simplicity of implementation.

This simplicity of operations on the ground turned out to be a fundamental practice of the hugely popular and successful Japanese JIT (Just-in-Time) system and TQM (Total Quality Management). The focus in JIT and TQM is on continual improvements in operation practices; and this depends very much on the production operators on the ground. As such, many of the operation practices on the ground were designed by the engineers to be simple and visual so that the average operator can manage them without the need for supervision. Further, whenever a problem arises on the shop floor, these operators will come together in their quality control circles to investigate the cause or source of the problem. They would then help solve the problem once and for all by targeting the cause. To achieve this, the operators are trained and equipped with the tools of TQM: scatter diagram, run chart, upper and lower control limits, etc. As it turns out, all these tools are simple and visual-based. The reason: they are meant to be used by the mass of operators on the production floor; and for most of these operators, their education level can be quite limited. The bottom-line of the JIT and TQM systems is this: they can be run on a day-to-day basis by the operators themselves, including the element of problem identification and solution for ongoing improvement.

What we now learn from these Japanese practices was what Zheng He apparently also embraced in his navigation sights and sound system back in the fifteenth century: the importance of ensuring simplicity in supply chain operations.

Indeed, taking this one step further, what this also suggests is for operations processes to be standardized as standard operating procedures (SOPs) so that all operators can readily follow and execute them without the need for supervision. Once the operations personnel are introduced to (and trained where needed) on the SOPs, these operations processes can be decentralized and implemented by all. This means that SOPs represents another manifestation of this practice of "simplicity in operations" that Zheng He apparently embraced as important in his voyages. In today's supply chains, as we go global in our production and delivery with multi sites in different cities and countries, such SOPs and the practice of simplicity in supply chain operations become even more important.

Selection of Regional Bases: The *Importance* of Supply Chain Collaboration

In his voyages over long distances and duration, Zheng He visited more than thirty countries and territories, including present-day Vietnam, Thailand, Pahang, Kelantan, Java, Sumatra, Sri Lanka, India, Dhufar, Hormuz, Yemen, Mecca and Mogadishu in East Africa.[53] It is clear that Zheng He would need to set up bases or depots in some of these places in order to break journey, regroup his crew, collect, store and upload new provisions and supplies, and even to repair his ships or wait for favourable monsoon winds to set sail again.

In his selection of such regional bases or depots, it is obvious that Zheng He would consider certain cities to be more logistically favourable than others, in terms of their strategic geographical locations, accessibility to ports, harbours and berths, availability of sources of supplies and provisions, amount of trading activities that were already taking place there, etc.

Yet where Zheng He actually set up his regional bases or depots, he apparently considered one other factor to be just as important, or perhaps even more important, than location and logistical favourability or superiority. And that was whether the local rulers and peoples were welcoming and collaborative towards Zheng He and his crew, as well as towards Ming China.

Our search of the literature seemed to indicate that Zheng He had set up his regional bases in five of the foreign cities along his route to the western seas. Each of these places clearly had a strategic geographical location; each also seemed to possess favourable logistical and/or economic characteristics; but each also had a personal relationship with Zheng He or a special relationship with the Ming Court.

This highlights the fifth aspect that Zheng He apparently considered to be important in his supply chain management practices: namely, in selecting locations to set up regional bases, supply chain collaborators must be available there.

Base in Changle: Location, Logistical and Economic Advantages

In Zhu Yunming's *Qianwenji*, which recorded details about Zheng He's seventh voyage to the West, after the fleet left Nanjing, it sailed from Taicang to Changle; and by the time it arrived in Taiping port in Changle, it was already near the end of the northeast monsoon season. As such, Zheng He and his fleet waited for some nine months in Changle until the beginning of the next season of the northeast monsoon before it finally set sail off China towards the West.[54]

But as it turned out, Changle's Taiping port was an ideal natural port for ships to take refuge and to wait for seasonal monsoon changes. Along China's southeastern coast, Taiping port also had the least chance of being hit by typhoons because of its location in the north of Taiwan Straits and between two hills, the Beiqiu Hill and Fufeng Hill. Because of this, Taiping port was actually ideal for Zheng He's fleet to take shelter there.[55]

Also, while Zheng He's fleet was berthed at Taiping, Zheng He would carry out maintenance work on the ships so that they would be ready to move out when the northeast monsoon blew again. Similarly, upon the fleet's return from its overseas visits, it would be berthed in Taiping port again for repairs and also for the crew members to rest.[56]

Beyond this, Changle was Fujian's gateway and it was only sixty miles away from Fuzhou which served as a collection and distribution centre for much of the silk, porcelain, tea, textiles, umbrellas and camphor that were produced in Fujian. So Zheng He could pick up some of such supplies while his fleet was berthed at Taiping port.[57] Also, Taiping port received fish and salt from Zhanggang, jasmine from Wufeng Hill, seafood from Nanxiang and fish, rice, melon and fruits from Beixiang and hence Zheng He's fleet can pick up these items as well as fresh water and other provisions while berthed at Taiping port.[58]

Quite clearly, Taiping port in Changle had much location, logistical and economic advantages as described above. Zheng He was therefore clearly aware of the importance of such factors and was therefore wise to base his fleet at Taiping port in Changle before he finally set sail for the foreign places.

Bases Outside China: Importance of Collaboration

However, once Zheng He was off China, he apparently paid attention not only to such location, logistical and economic factors, but also to whether he could find collaborators who could support him in the setting up of regional bases. Zheng He apparently set up five such regional bases, where each had a special relationship with either Zheng He himself, or with the Ming Court.

Base in Champa

Zheng He's first port of call in all his seven voyages was in Xinzhou in Champa, today's modern city of Qui Nhon in Vietnam.[59] Apparently, Zheng He set up a regional base there to store provisions and to use it to send out his main fleet and sub-fleets to visit Brunei, the Malay Peninsula, Java, Bengal and Malacca.[60] Indeed, Champa had been identified as one of the two most important bases in Southeast Asia for Zheng He's fleet (the other base was Malacca).[61]

Champa had built a friendly relationship with China even before Zheng He and his voyages. In fact, during Ming Taizu's reign, the Ming emperor had issued instructions to his descendents that Champa and other friendly neighbouring countries must not be invaded.[62] Champa had also sent envoys who had an audience with Emperor Yongle in 1407, at Zheng He's return after his first voyage.[63] And by the time of Zheng He's second voyage, the ruler of Champa had made it a matter of policy to cooperate with Ming China.[64] And on his fourth voyage, Zheng He brought imperial gifts of crowns and girdles for the king of Champa. It was apparently following this that Zheng He set up his base in Champa.[65]

We should also note that the ancient kingdom of Champa had been at war with ancient Vietnam; and during Zheng He's first voyage, Ming China started its attempt to annex Vietnam; and while Ming China continued to be at war with Vietnam, Champa as an enemy of Vietnam was China's friend, and China continued to support Champa throughout this period.[66]

Given all these, it is clear that Champa had a special friendly collaborative relationship with Ming China during Zheng He's voyages. It is also apparent that Zheng He selected Champa to set up one of his foreign bases because the King of Champa was cooperative with Ming China and therefore supportive of Zheng He's work.

Base in Malacca

Zheng He also set up a regional base in Malacca; this was apparently a large base,[67] and was probably the most important one to Zheng He.[68] It was also apparently the one with the strongest collaborative support provided by the local king and people.

In fact, even before Zheng He's voyages, Emperor Yongle had already sent eunuch Yin Ching to visit Malacca in 1404.[69] At that time, Malacca was a vassal state under Siam and so the local Malacca chief Parameswara was not a king as yet. Parameswara was therefore quite happy to have the Ming Court envoy visit him as he was hopeful of getting support and recognition from mighty Ming China. Parameswara sent his envoys to accompany Yin Ching back to China to pay tribute to the Ming emperor. In 1405, Emperor Yongle put forth an edict to appoint Parameswara as King, and Malacca became a kingdom under the patronage of Ming China. Parameswara was given a seal, together with an official hat, a royal girdle and robe. The Malaccan envoys, having received VIP treatment at the Ming Court, were returned home on board Zheng He's epic fleet during its first voyage in 1406. Parameswara in turn welcomed Zheng He on this first voyage through Malacca with much hospitality.[70] And by the time of Zheng He's second voyage, the King of Malacca had made it a matter of policy to cooperate with Ming China.[71]

In fact, from 1403, the first year of Emperor Yongle's reign, to 1435, the tenth year of Emperor Xuanzong's reign, Malacca and Ming China would continue to grow this relationship with frequent exchanges of official visits. Over these thirty-two years, the *Ming Shi Lu* recorded that since 1409, Zheng He and his fleet had called at Malacca five times and had established a regional base by building a highly secured stockade or depot by the Malacca River to store treasures and trade items. The Malaccan sultans had also made several personal visits to China as well as sent envoys to pay tribute to the Ming Court on some twenty different occasions.[72]

Malacca and Ming China therefore had a strong harmonious relationship; the Malacca sultanate benefited from the political insurance offered by Ming China, especially in the context of Malacca's strained relationship with Siam, while the local people enjoyed the economic benefits of the entrepot trade brought along by the Chinese. In return, Zheng He could establish a base in Malacca for his epic fleet and conduct his regional diplomatic and economic trade activities throughout Southeast Asia.[73]

Of course, it was clear to Zheng He that Malacca occupied a strategic location on the Straits of Malacca, and that since ancient times, the Malaccan Straits had been the lifeline of the East-West sea route.[74] Malacca as a regional base for Zheng He's fleet in its voyages between the eastern Chinese seaboard and the West would therefore be logistically viable and locationally strategic.

However, it is also apparent that Zheng He chose Malacca to set up as a regional base because he was confident of the long-term support and collaboration that will be offered by Malacca. Zheng He knew that he could make full use of his personal relationship with King Parameswara, having given the King his fullest support and help to develop Malacca into an international entrepot, and to prevent Majapahit and Siam from invading Malacca. Because of this, Zheng He was confident enough to build a major *guanchang* (warehouse) in Malacca to serve as a base for his fleet and voyages.[75]

Base in Samudra

In addition to Malacca, Zheng He also apparently established a *guanchang* in Samudra to serve as a regional base in the north of the Malacca Straits.[76] On the sixth voyage, for example, Samudra was the base at which Zheng He's fleet was divided into sub-fleets or squadrons which sailed to Ceylon and then to one or more of the southern Indian countries of Jiayile, Cochin, Ganbali and Calicut.[77]

Samudra (or Semudera) is present-day Aceh; it clearly occupied a strategic location in the northern end of Sumatra,[78] and it was a key port controlling the northern part of the Straits of Malacca during Zheng He's time.[79] Samudra was therefore a logistically viable location to serve as a regional base for Zheng He; it was referred to more as a "way station" en-route to southern India;[80] it was important for its location more than for its wealth or economic products, and it was described by Ma Huan as the most important place of assembly for ships going to the western (Indian) ocean.[81] It served like a last port of call before the ships set off on the long (and often times difficult) voyage across the Indian ocean to Ceylon and southern India.[82]

Nonetheless, Zheng He's decision to set up a base there seemed to be also influenced by Samudra's friendly relationship with Ming China and his own personal relationship with the local Samudra king.

Samudra had sent envoys to visit the Ming Court during the return leg of Zheng He's first voyage; they had presented tribute in local products to the Ming emperor, in accordance with the usual practice of Chinese tributary relationships; and in return, the Samudra envoys were given paper money and copper coins.[83] This would suggest that from the first voyage of Zheng He, Samudra had decided to forge a friendly relationship with Ming China.

At a more personal level, Zheng He himself had helped the King of Samudra by getting rid of the rebel named Sekander. Apparently the latter had led a rebellion against the Samudra King who had asked for help from the Ming emperor. When Zheng He visited Samudra during the fourth voyage, he brought with him imperial gifts and presented these to the King of Samudra; this apparently enraged Sekander who led a large force against Zheng He. Sekander was captured by Zheng He and was sent back to the Ming Court where he was subsequently executed.[84] It is therefore understandable that Zheng He would have had a very strong, supportive relationship with the King of Samudra.

Given this positive personal relationship, and Samudra's tributary relationship with Ming China, and Ma Huan's description of the people of Samudra as very honest and genuine,[85] Zheng He apparently proceeded to set up a regional base in Samudra, including the building of a *guanchang* there.

Base in Calicut

Zheng He also apparently set up a regional base in Calicut, on the southwestern coast of India. For the first three voyages, Calicut was the westward limit for Zheng He's journey; Fei Xin referred to it as the "matou" or "great harbour" of the Western Ocean;[86] and as the end point for the initial voyages, this was where Calicut served as the location for the turnaround of the fleet.

In fact, by the time of Zheng He's second voyage, the new King of Calicut and his officials, together with the rulers of Malacca and Champa, had given Zheng He's fleet this series of bases in their three countries from which to traverse the fairly well established sea routes of the South China Sea and the Indian Ocean.[87]

On Zheng He's sixth voyage, for example, while the main fleet stopped at Calicut before going on to Hormuz, the rest of the fleet sailed on in sub-fleets or squadrons to locations further west; one squadron, for example, under Zhou Man went on to Aden, and would likely had visited Djofar and Lasa on the way. Subsequently, the different squadrons regrouped either at Samudra (also known as Semudera), or earlier at Calicut, before the combined fleet made its way back to China.[88]

Similarly, on the seventh voyage, it was apparent that Calicut served as a regional location for the detachment, as well as for the rejoining or assembly, of squadrons.[89]

All the above indicated that Zheng He had established some form of a base in Calicut. This was not only because of its location as the westward limit on Zheng He's first three voyages, but also that Calicut was the most dominant among the nearby Indian trading port cities, including Cochin and Quilon. In fact, Ma Huan in his *Yingyai Shenglan* had referred to Calicut as the Great Country of the Western Ocean; its port was like a free trade emporium and an economic exchange centre for the trans-Indian Ocean maritime trade. And because of the geography of the Indian Ocean and the seasonal character of the monsoon winds, trade in the vicinity was segmented into two halves: the western half comprising trade from and to the Red Sea and the Persian Gulf; and the eastern half comprising trade from and to Sumatra and Malaya; and Calicut had outperformed all its rivals on the western Indian coast to become the port where these two halves of trade met. Beyond these geographic and economic advantages, Ma Huan also praised the Calicut authorities for their careful attention to weights and measures and the regulation of fair trade.[90] So Calicut was clearly a wise choice in terms of location and economic standing for the establishment of a regional base for Zheng He's voyages.

Beyond these reasons, however, Zheng He apparently selected Calicut also because of its strong and friendly ties with Ming China, and its support for Zheng He's voyages. In fact, even before Zheng He's first voyage, Calicut had already sent a first mission of its own envoys, on the return leg of Ming envoy Yin Ching, to pay tribute to the Ming Court. The Ming Emperor Yongle granted audience to the Calicut envoys, and sent out an edit to appoint the local ruler of Calicut as King. The Calicut King was given the imperial gifts of a royal seal, an official hat, and also a royal girdle and robe. Calicut was therefore recognized as a kingdom under Ming patronage, like Malacca and Samudra, in 1405.[91]

And apparently when Emperor Yongle ordered the second of Zheng He's voyages in 1407, it was also for the purpose of conferring Ming recognition on the new king of Calicut.[92] And as indicated earlier, by the time of Zheng He's second voyage, the new king of Calicut and his officials had granted Zheng He their support which apparently helped Zheng He to decide to set up a regional base in Calicut.[93]

And to Zheng He, this base in Calicut was also important because of the potential animosity of Ceylon whose rulers had become openly hostile towards Zheng He during the third voyage.[94]

Base in Hormuz

Zheng He had also set up a fifth regional base in Hormuz from which he sent out separate missions to the neighbouring countries in the Persian Gulf and Arabian Peninsula to conduct diplomatic matters and foreign trade. Hormuz was strategically located at the mouth of the Persian Gulf and was a key international trading centre during the time of Zheng He's voyages. Zheng He apparently used Hormuz as a base to meet traders from Asia, Europe and Africa.[95]

The Chinese apparently knew of the wealth of Hormuz;[96] Ma Huan in fact described Hormuz as the place where foreign ships from everywhere met with foreign merchants travelling by land, to come together to buy and sell, and therefore the people of Hormuz were all rich.[97]

It may be that the Ming emperor wanted to tap on the wealth of Hormuz to help with his various projects back in China, including the move of his capital city from Nanjing to Beijing (apparently also known as Beiping).[98]

It was through his diplomatic and trading activities here that Zheng He collected gems, spices, minerals, drugs and plants, as well as animals presented by the vassal states as tributes to the Ming Court. Some of these animals included the lions, leopards, giraffes, zebras, camels and ostriches, several of which were rarely seen in China.[99]

So quite clearly, Zheng He had set up a base in Hormuz because of its strategic location, its strong economics, and its international trading hub status. But again, as in the earlier bases, Zheng He also apparently had confidence in doing so because of the friendly ties between Hormuz and Ming China.

The *Taizong Shilu*'s entry of 3 March 1421 had stated that "the envoys of sixteen countries including Hormuz" were given gifts of paper money and coin and also ceremonial robes and linings on their return to their countries. And Zheng He was to go on his sixth voyage to bring imperial letters and gifts to the rulers of these countries.[100] This would indicate that Hormuz had paid homage to the Ming Court and so had established a friendly relationship with Ming China. This would no doubt have added to Zheng He's decision to set up a base in Hormuz.

Implications

It is clear that the literature had indicated that Zheng He set up regional bases in five of the thirty plus foreign cities or countries he visited along his route to the western seas. Each of these five foreign regional bases clearly had a strategic geographical location, and each also possessed favourable logistical and/or economic characteristics; but just as clearly, each also had a personal relationship with Zheng He or a relationship with the Ming Court that was reverent and cordial.

This highlights the fifth aspect that Zheng He apparently considered to be important in his supply chain management practices: namely that in selecting locations to set up regional bases, the availability of supply chain collaborators or partners is just as important, if not more important, than location, economic and logistical factors.

This may be all the more important for today's logistics and supply chain managers and leaders. Given the global nature of today's supply chains, and the strong competitive arena, one cannot simply add a node, such as a new warehouse in a new location, to one's supply chain just so as to be nearer to the market. This is so even if the new location had all the usual, favourable, economics and logistics factors. Should one instead site the new warehouse in another farther location where one finds a more suitable or committed partner as collaborator, even if this means a tradeoff in terms of additional transportation cost? The call for the presence of a known collaborator in that location may be just as important if not critically important.

Indeed, we already know today that many supply chains compete against each other, rather than just a company competing against another. Therefore on a given supply chain, innovations such as Vendor Managed Inventories (VMI), Collaborative Planning, Forecasting and Replenishment (CPFR) and Continuous Replenishment Program (CRP) will work only when we can find truly committed and faithful collaborators. For Efficient Consumer Response (ECR) to work within the Fast Moving Consumer Goods (FMCG) business, suppliers must come together and work closely with retailers as collaborators. Zheng He seemed to have recognized this in his fifteenth-century experience.

Of course, collaborators do not surface overnight. All these therefore suggest that today's managers and leaders could benefit from embracing and practising Zheng He's overall *Art of Collaboration*, working hard at building collaboration with others instead of seeing them as competitors or enemies.

From a third party logistics (3PL) service provider perspective, the common strategy that 3PLs offer of "going where our customer goes" would seem to make sense in the context of Zheng He's experience here. If a 3PL can indeed add to its capability on a given supply chain to support the move of its customer to a new market, for example, then that customer will continue to have the collaboration of the same 3PL in that new market location. Unfortunately, what the 3PL may need is to build its own warehouse, for example, in that new location where its customer has moved to. But where this is not feasible or economical, then the 3PL must seek out a collaborator who already owns a warehouse in any location that is near to where the customer has moved to. The search for this collaborator is presumably more important that to look for an existing warehouse that is nearest to the new market location.

And if indeed we need to identify where to locate a regional base or hub for a supply chain, then Zheng He's experience would imply that we must pay attention to looking first for a partner rather than looking first for the logistically ideal location. And that would in turn suggest that we must begin to cultivate and develop our relationships with others so that we may find that suitable partner as collaborator before the need arises.

Supply Growth and Development: The *Importance* of Continual Learning

Zheng He did not travel from China to the shores of Africa on his first voyage. He apparently adopted a phased approach in extending his voyages. When we see a given Zheng He's voyage as a floating supply chain that carried imperial gifts and trade products to the West, it would seem that Zheng He extended the reach of his supply chain gradually.

This is the sixth element in Zheng He's 7S Model of Importance in terms of his supply chain practices: that Supply Chain Growth and Development depends upon Continual Learning of the ground and market conditions.

Phased Extension of Voyages

The seven grand voyages of Zheng He could apparently be divided into three phases: the first phase comprised the first three voyages where the fleet was essentially confined to the journey from China's Changle to the western-most point of Calicut on the west coast of India. At Calicut, Zheng He learned of Hormuz as the important and prosperous international trading centre, and so he apparently extended his fourth voyage from Calicut to the destination of Hormuz on the mouth of the Persian Gulf; this would constitute Zheng He's second phase of travel. In the third phase, Zheng He continued to extend his voyages (and hence his supply chains) to include visits to places like Aden and Dhofar on the Arabian Peninsula and Mogadishu, Brava and Malindi on the east coast of Africa.[101]

This phased approach would have allowed Zheng He and his crew to learn continually and progressively about making the epic voyages with the large fleet and huge crew across the seas from China to Africa.

In fact, we know that in Zheng He's first three voyages, each of these voyages took the same basic route from Changle to Champa, then up the Straits of Malacca towards northern Sumatra, and then straight across the Indian Ocean to Ceylon and Calicut and other countries on the southwestern Indian coast; and the outward journey was made in the presence of the winter northeast monsoon, and the return leg with the summer southwest monsoon of the following year.[102] Also, on these first three voyages, Zheng He's fleet sailed to the same group of countries, of which Calicut was the furthermost.[103] This consistency of the basic route, timing and countries visited, essentially facilitated continual learning by

Zheng He and his men so that they were able to build up their ground knowledge of the seas and surrounding geography, and their own confidence, gradually with each voyage.

And then on the fourth voyage, Zheng He provided learning for himself and his crew, as he extended his supply chain to the final destination of Hormuz. And on his fifth voyage, Zheng He's fleet followed the path they sailed in the first three voyages as far as Calicut, and from Calicut to Hormuz, they followed the path they took during the fourth voyage. And going south and west of Hormuz, on the Arabian and African coasts, Zheng He and his fleet and crew finally went to places they had never gone before this fifth voyage.[104]

As a further insight, we should note that though the main route as highlighted above remained the same, nautical charts published in the *Wubeizhi* by Mao Yuanyi showed that there were actually twenty-seven detailed routes taken by Zheng He's fleet in sailing from Taicang to Changle, and twenty-nine detailed routes from Changle's Wuhumen to sail to the foreign countries. And for the return legs of the voyages, there were actually thirty-one detailed routes from overseas back to Wuhumen and twenty-two such detailed routes from Wuhumen to Taicang.[105] So there were many opportunities (and necessities) for continual learning through all these detailed routes. But keeping to the same main basic route would have made all the detailed learning much easier; this seemed to be what Zheng He apparently knew and adopted so as to facilitate continual learning by all.

Continual Learning of Local Markets

In Zheng He's interpretation of his emperor-decreed mission, Zheng He initiated and pursued commercial trade activities with the local traders in the different countries he visited so as to open up new markets and extend Ming China's influences. Zheng He was therefore focused on preparing Ming China for long-term development of large-scale private trade, even as he continually extended his supply chain to new markets through his phased voyages as described earlier.

In the various ports of call in the countries Zheng He visited, his men were conducting market surveys in order to collect information pertaining to the local methods of trading, local produce, local currency and the demand for the different Chinese products. Through their study tours and market surveys, Zheng He and his men were able to acquire much real and ground information on the competitiveness of China's products in the Southeast Asian, Indian, Persian and East African markets.[106]

Medical Learning

To look after the health of his 27,000 crew members, Zheng He recruited for his voyages a specialized medical team comprising some 150 medical officers. Many of these were famous local medical doctors in their own right, while others were recruited from the elite medical institution of the palace.

Apart from treating his own crew members, Zheng He also gave instructions for these medical officers to treat local patients at the various ports of call. No doubt this would allow Zheng He's doctors hands-on opportunities to learn much about local illnesses and diseases. At the same time, Zheng He's medical team also conducted surveys of local diseases and their cures; their learning here would then help to formulate precautionary practices so as to help safeguard the health of all the crew members.[107]

If we see these doctors as providing a medical service to the locals, then Zheng He's supply chain also carried with it the provision of Chinese medicine and healthcare services. But these were augmented through the continual learning by the doctors of the local illnesses and diseases as indicated above.

In fact, during the voyages, Zheng He's medical team regularly collected local medicinal herbs and learned local methods of medical treatment. As an example, Kuang Yu was a medical officer who travelled with Zheng He on three of the voyages; he had collected local medicinal herbs such as rhinoceros and antelope horns, cloves, fragrant incense and myrrh, and had incorporated them into the body of traditional Chinese medicine.[108]

Implications

First, Zheng He apparently grew and extended his supply chain in a phased manner in order to support learning by his crew and people on the ground. He apparently gradually and carefully visited more and further away places over his many voyages. This would suggest that one needs to be careful about extending one's business too quickly to new markets in overseas locations. Putting a supply chain together to deliver one's products to overseas markets may be helped with a phased approach in terms of extending the supply chain gradually from one market to another. There is much learning that must be supported consciously as the supply chain reach is extended.

Second, and quite clearly, as Zheng He sought to grow and extend the reach of his trading supply chains, he had to continually learn about the markets that he visited: what the locals wanted, and the competitiveness of the Chinese trade products. This is of course what today's managers and leaders must also do.

Market research and surveys, data collection and analysis, new product design and introduction to meet new market demands, or to meet existing market needs more closely; all these require conscious efforts and resources. It may be surprising to note that Zheng He actually paid attention and apparently attached importance to such continual learning of the marketplaces.

And learning from Zheng He's medical specialists, this need to continually learn about market needs would apply to the offering of new services as well.

Third, the importance of continual learning in itself: Zheng He's practice here is apparently a forerunner of the Japanese JIT and TQM system that we know today. The fundamental tenet in such JIT/TQM systems is that of waste reduction through continual improvements; the surfacing of problems in production and supply chains are considered to be good as they serve as opportunities for continual learning so that new solutions to clearly identified problems may be implemented to remove the causes of these problems. What we therefore learn from the Japanese JIT/TQM system through the 1990s in terms of the importance of continual learning and improvement in production and supply delivery was what Zheng He seemed to have practised and believed in as well. In managing today's supply chain growth and extension, managers and leaders should therefore pay attention once again to the important practice of providing for continual learning within the supply chain.

Storage and *Guanchang*: The *Importance* of Physical Supply Chain Assets

For each of Zheng He's voyage, Zheng He's fleet was essentially providing storage space for the imperial gifts and trade products, as well as transportation service in moving these to the various countries he visited. In essence then, Zheng He's fleet was a floating supply chain that delivered the gifts and trade items from Ming China to the countries in the western seas.

While Zheng He was out on his voyages, we indicated earlier in this chapter that he had also established regional bases in some of the countries he visited. In at least two of these bases, it was explicitly recorded that Zheng He actually built *guanchangs* there (in Samudra and Malacca[109]). A *guanchang* refers to an official (government) factory, warehouse or godown; as described by Ma Huan in his *Yingya Shenglan*, Zheng He's *guanchang* was actually a warehouse.[110]

Quite clearly to Zheng He, his *fleet* and *guanchangs* were important physical supply chain assets which he paid attention to, in terms of their construction and management. These elements represent the last aspect of Zheng He's 7S Model of Importance in supply chain management practices.

Zheng He's Fleet: A Floating Supply Chain

Once Zheng He was appointed as Commander-in-chief for the grand voyages, Zheng He proceeded to oversee the construction of the fleet that he had envisioned: a state-of-the-art fleet on an unprecedented scale in terms of both the number, as well as the size, of his ships.

Zheng He designed and categorized his fleet of ships into six different types according to their specification and use:[111]

Treasure Ships: these were the largest in terms of size; they represented the flagship of Zheng He's fleet. The treasure ship usually had 9 masts with 9 sails, and each measured about 480ft long, 194ft wide, 12 metres deep and had a draught of 8 metres. Each had a full load capacity of 7,000 tons. They carried Zheng He and his senior associates, and other envoys and diplomats. They also stored the many imperial gifts, the vassal states' tributes for the emperor and other valuable treasures. Treasure ships were generally designed with 4 decks. The upper decks were offices and bedrooms while the lower decks were designed as storage spaces. Zheng He's Commander-in-Chief Ship was the largest of such treasure ships and it had 12 sails. On the top deck of the Commander-in-Chief Ship was Zheng He's office where he received his guests as well.

Horse Ships: these functioned as supplies ships. They were the second largest ships in the fleet. Each horse ship had 8 masts, 10 sails, and measured some 400ft by 162ft. As supplies ships, they carried household supplies, military supplies, tools and equipment, horses and other animals. These ships also served as accommodation cabins for mid-level officials, interpreters and medical officers.

Grain Ships: these were also supplies ships used for storing food supplies. They generally had 7 masts each and measured 302ft by 130ft.

Water Ships: this was another type of supplies ship with the same size specifications as grain ships. They were designed as water tankers and used for the specific purpose of storing fresh water.

Command Ships: these were also referred to as battle ships and they each had 6 masts and measured 259ft by 102ft. They served as the operations centre during crisis that involved the use of military force. These command ships therefore carry the military personnel (soldiers and commanders) and they were like the land-based army camps.

War Ships: these constitute another form of battle ships with 5 masts each and measured 194ft by 73ft. They were lighter and smaller and more handy, and were equipped with advanced arms and weapons (including gun powder, cannon balls, flaming arrows, and exploding shells) to protect the fleet where needed.

Guanchangs: the official warehouses

Ma Huan, who was Zheng He's interpreter, provided a vivid description in his book (the *Yingya Shenglan*) of the *guanchang* that was built in Malacca:

> Whenever the treasure ships of the Middle Kingdom arrived there, they at once erected a line of stockading, like a city-

wall, and set up towers for the watch-drums at four gates; at night they had patrols of guards carrying bells; inside, again, they erected a second stockade, like a small city-wall, [within which] they constructed warehouses and granaries; [and] all the money and provisions were stored in them. The ships which had gone to various countries returned to this place and assembled; they repaired [their vessels] and marshaled the local goods and loaded them in the ships; [then] waited till the south wind was perfectly favourable.[112]

How big was this *guanchang*? According to estimate:

...the fleet would carry not less than one million tons of cargo in each trip to Melaka. If half of his crew stayed offshore to handle the cargo, then 14,000 crew members would put up in the guanchang...there could not be just a few godowns within the guanchang. If we take the measurement of an ordinary single building structure, say, 10m x 45m, there were at least 100 godowns. If roads and empty spaces were added, the guanchang would have an area of 50,000 square meters or 5 hectares.[113]

Implications

Building and managing such a large *guanchang* or warehouse, and building and organizing the unprecedented epic fleet which served as a floating supply chain, must have demanded much of Zheng He's attention. Clearly, these huge physical supply chain assets were very important to Zheng He.

And their equivalents today must be equally important to today's supply chain managers and leaders. Not only because such warehouses and transportation fleets are generally large and expensive to build and manage, but also because in today's supply chain networks, these can become very complex and difficult to manage and use optimally. This will be especially obvious in the context of the FMCG business where the number of SKUs to be managed is huge and the speed of delivery and replenishment must be quick and yet efficient. When designed and used well, with the support of strong systems and computing analytics, these assets can generate very real strategic and competitive advantages for today's businesses and leaders.

We have earlier described what Wal-Mart did in its quest to become the largest and most successful retailer in the world today. From the operations perspective, the key to Wal-Mart's success "was to make the way the company replenished inventory the centerpiece of its competitive strategy". As explained earlier, this required Wal-Mart to attach much importance to its major physical assets of cross-docking points (special warehouses), a private satellite, nineteen distribution centres, and a dedicated fleet of some 2,000 company owned trucks. On the latter for example, while Wal-Mart was building up its ground fleet, Kmart was getting out of trucking because it felt that a subcontracted fleet would suffice. As Wal-Mart paid attention to its physical assets and proceeded to link them up with the support systems of data and analytics, it became possible for Wal-Mart to bring about quick inventory replenishment as its competitive weapon.[114]

Clearly then, today's managers and leaders must recognize the importance of learning to strategically manage and use their physical supply chain assets well.

There is another implication from Zheng He's supply chain practice of Storage and *Guanchangs*. It is clear that Zheng He's fifteenth-century technologies and environment necessitated that his supply chain be mobile: a moving, floating supply chain comprising of ships used as storage spaces as well as transportation means. Today's technologies and environment tend to see warehouses as storage spaces that are fixed in location on land, while movement is provided for by actual transportation fleet of planes, or ships or railway carriages. Yet integrating these physical assets to provide a mobile seamless supply chain could be an important application area for today's businesses.

We provide an example from the iron ore mining industry as an illustration. In this industry, the supply chain is really that of delivering the iron ore from the mines to the steel mills. It is common that transportation means will serve to link mining spots to actual port facilities on land; there the iron ore will be uploaded onto ocean crossing vessels to transport them to the steel mills (ore from Australia, for example, being carried across the oceans to steel mills in China). Current applied research have led to a proposed "port-in-ocean" seamless supply chain involving the use of tipper and conveyor barges as substitutes for the port-on-land; as such, when a mining spot is no longer economically viable, the entire proposed "port-in-ocean" can be redeployed, something which is impossible for the fixed port-on-land.[115]

On Zheng He's *guanchang*, it would seem that this is a forerunner of today's integrated distripark (distribution park), except that Zheng He's *guanchang* also included repair and maintenance facilities, and possibly living quarters for the crew. In that sense, Zheng He's *guanchang* practice is even bigger than today's distribution park. Do we have need for such an idea in today's supply chain environment? Perhaps the *guanchang* idea has evolved into today's cross-docking points. What would be the next state-of-the-art practice? The creation of Wal-Mart's supercentres at the retail end may have its equivalent in the upstream portion of the supply chain.

Finally, we should also highlight that Zheng He's supply chain already had the physical expertise of storing and moving exotic animals from the West back into China. This is the realm of today's exhibition or special logistics services, an area of business that will require importance and attention to be placed on physical supply chain assets. With growing affluence, this is a business area that may be worthy of consideration.

LEARNING FROM ZHENG HE ON SUPPLY CHAIN MANAGEMENT

Razeen Sally wrote recently that in the last sixty years, the world has witnessed an economic renaissance in East and South Asia; here, "commercial clusters in and around coastal cities, connected with each other across seas and oceans, are its economic lifeblood. Its networks are complex manufacturing and services supply chains linking them to global markets".[116]

In fact, in the same article, Sally also referred to this as "a recreation of the Golden Age of Indian Ocean commerce". Sally was of course pointing us back to the fifteenth-century Indian Ocean trade of Zheng He's era.

Using fifteenth-century technology, Zheng He's supply chain was really his huge fleet and crew bringing a large supply of Chinese trade items to the world of Southeast and South Asia, and Persia and East Africa, and returning to Ming China every 1.5–2 years to pick up new stock, and stopping along the way for re-supply of provisions and water, and for trade. This long-distance trade, as Sally would put it, certainly contributed to the economic buzz in the Indian Ocean, as well as in the South China Sea, the Malacca Straits, and the Persian Gulf.

What can we learn from Zheng He's fifteenth-century supply chain practices? We considered Zheng He's supply chain work and highlighted what Zheng He apparently paid attention to as important in his logistics and supply chain practices. We have therefore sketched out in this chapter what we referred to as Zheng He's 7S Model of Importance in his logistics and supply chain practices:

(1) **Strategic Intent and Clarity**: the *Importance* of Supply Chain Mission and Vision;

(2) **Supply Ecosystem**: the *Importance* of Supply Chain Capabilities;

(3) **Specialists Recruitment**: the *Importance* of Supply Chain People and Knowledge;

(4) **Sights and Sound of Navigation**: the *Importance* of Simplicity in Operations;

(5) **Selection of Regional Bases**: the *Importance* of Supply Chain Collaboration;

(6) **Supply Growth and Development**: the *Importance* of Continual Learning; and

(7) **Storage and *Guanchang***: the *Importance* of Physical Supply Chain Assets.

We have also highlighted some implications and suggestions from these "supply chain factors of importance" for today's logistics and supply chain managers and leaders.

Endnotes

1. Tan Ta Sen and Chia Lin Sien, eds., *The Zheng He Epic*, 1st edition in Chinese edited by Zhou Wenlin et al. (Kunming, Yunnan, China: Yunnan's Publishing House, Yunnan Fine Arts Publishing House, Auora Publishing House, 2006), p. 352.

2. Louise E. Levathes, *When China Ruled the Seas: The Treasure Fleet of the Dragon Throne, 1405–1433* (U.S.: Oxford University Press, 1994), p. 87.

3. *Zheng He Epic*, p. 352.

4. Tan Ta Sen, *Cheng Ho and Malacca* (Singapore: International Zheng He Society, 2005), pp. 16–17.

5. *Zheng He Epic*, Preface.

6. Chiu Ling-yeong, "Zheng He: Navigator, Discoverer and Diplomat", *Wu Teh Yao Memorial Lectures 2000* (Singapore: Unipress, Center for the Arts, National University of Singapore, 2001), p. 8.

7. *Zheng He Epic*, p. 86.

8. *When China Ruled the Seas*, p. 83.

9. Edward L. Dreyer, *Zheng He: China and the Oceans in the Early Ming Dynasty, 1405–1433* (U.S.: Pearson Education Inc., 2007), p. 50.

10. *Zheng He: China and the Oceans in the Early Ming Dynasty*, pp. 1 and 3.

11. *Zheng He Epic*, p. 212.

12. G. Stalk, P. Evans, and L. Shulman, "Competing on capabilities: the new rules of corporate strategy", *Harvard Business Review*, March–April 1992.

13. *Zheng He Epic*, p. 8.

14. *When China Ruled the Seas*, p. 41.

15. *When China Ruled the Seas*, pp. 42–43.

16. *When China Ruled the Seas*, p. 49.

17. *Zheng He Epic*, p. 85.

18. *When China Ruled the Seas*, pp. 75–76.

19. *When China Ruled the Seas*, p. 75.

20. *When China Ruled the Seas*, p. 76.

21. *Zheng He Epic*, p. 84.

22. *Zheng He Epic*, p. 84.

23. *Zheng He Epic*, p. 85.

24. *When China Ruled the Seas*, p. 76.

25. *Zheng He Epic*, p. 86.

26. *Zheng He Epic*, p. 121.

27. *Zheng He Epic*, p. 126.

28. *Zheng He Epic*, p. 128.

29. *Zheng He Epic*, p. 130.

30. "Developing Singapore into a Global Integrated Logistics Hub", <http://app.mti.gov.sg/data/pages/507/doc/ERC_SVS_LOG_MainReport.pdf> (accessed 20 August 2011).

31. "Logistics and Supply Chain Management: Facts and Figures", <http://www.edb.gov.sg/edb/sg/en_uk/index/industry_sectors/logistics_supply/facts_and_figures.html> (accessed 20 August 2011).

32. Wickham Skinner, "The Focused Factory", *Harvard Business Review*, May–June 1974.

33. *Zheng He Epic*, p. 84.

34. *Zheng He: Navigator, Discoverer and Diplomat*, pp. 14–15.

35. *Zheng He: Navigator, Discoverer and Diplomat*, pp. 13–14.

36. *Cheng Ho and Malacca*, pp. 14–15; and *Zheng He: Navigator, Discoverer and Diplomat*, p. 10.

37. *Zheng He Epic*, p. 96.

38. *Zheng He Epic*, p. 200.

39. *Zheng He Epic*, p. 128.

40. *Zheng He Epic*, p. 158.

41. *Zheng He Epic*, p. 185.

42. *Zheng He Epic*, p. 345.

43. *Cheng Ho and Malacca*, p. 15.

44. M. Torck, "The matter of provisioning in Zheng He's Fleets: a reconstructive attempt", in *Chinese Diaspora since Admiral Zheng He with Special Reference to Maritime Asia*, edited by Leo Suryadinata (Singapore: Chinese Heritage Center, 2007), p. 52.

45. *Zheng He Epic*, pp. 321–22.

46. M. Fisher, "What is the right supply chain for your product?" *Harvard Business Review*, March–April 1997.

47. *When China Ruled the Seas*, p. 83; *Cheng Ho and Malacca*, p. 13.

48. *Cheng Ho and Malacca*, p. 13.

49. *Cheng Ho and Malacca*, p. 13.

50. *Zheng He Epic*, pp. 221–22.

51. *Cheng Ho and Malacca*, p. 14.

52. *Zheng He Epic*, p. 225.

53. *Cheng Ho and Malacca*, pp. 16–17.

54. *Zheng He Epic*, p. 220.

55. *Zheng He Epic*, p. 150.

56. *Zheng He Epic*, p. 157.

57. *Zheng He Epic*, p. 163.

58. *Zheng He Epic*, p. 167.

59. *Zheng He: China and the Oceans in the Early Ming Dynasty*, p. 52.

60. *Zheng He Epic*, p. 231.
61. Tan Ta Sen, *Cheng Ho and Islam in Southeast Asia* (Singapore: Institute of Southeast Asian Studies, 2009), p. 173.
62. *Zheng He Epic*, p. 230.
63. *Zheng He: China and the Oceans in the Early Ming Dynasty*, p. 59.
64. *Zheng He: China and the Oceans in the Early Ming Dynasty*, p. 65.
65. *Zheng He Epic*, p. 231.
66. *Zheng He: China and the Oceans in the Early Ming Dynasty*, p. 52.
67. *Cheng Ho and Malacca*, p. 50.
68. *Cheng Ho and Malacca*, p. 47.
69. *Cheng Ho and Malacca*, p. 37.
70. *Cheng Ho and Malacca*, pp. 37–41.
71. *Zheng He: China and the Oceans in the Early Ming Dynasty*, p. 65.
72. *Cheng Ho and Malacca*, p. 41.
73. *Cheng Ho and Malacca*, pp. 40–41.
74. *Cheng Ho and Malacca*, p. 46.
75. *Cheng Ho and Malacca*, p. 47.
76. *Cheng Ho and Malacca*, p. 44.
77. *Zheng He: China and the Oceans in the Early Ming Dynasty*, p. 93.
78. *Zheng He: China and the Oceans in the Early Ming Dynasty*, p. 153.
79. *Cheng Ho and Malacca*, p. 46.
80. *Zheng He: China and the Oceans in the Early Ming Dynasty*, p. 61.
81. *Zheng He: China and the Oceans in the Early Ming Dynasty*, p. 153.
82. *Zheng He: China and the Oceans in the Early Ming Dynasty*, p. 77.
83. *Zheng He: China and the Oceans in the Early Ming Dynasty*, p. 59.
84. *Zheng He: China and the Oceans in the Early Ming Dynasty*, pp. 79–81; *When China Ruled the Seas*, p. 139.
85. *Zheng He: China and the Oceans in the Early Ming Dynasty*, p. 53.
86. *Zheng He: China and the Oceans in the Early Ming Dynasty*, p. 155.
87. *Zheng He: China and the Oceans in the Early Ming Dynasty*, p. 65.
88. *Zheng He: China and the Oceans in the Early Ming Dynasty*, p. 94.
89. *Zheng He: China and the Oceans in the Early Ming Dynasty*, pp. 155–60.
90. *Zheng He: China and the Oceans in the Early Ming Dynasty*, p. 54.

91. *Cheng Ho and Malacca*, p. 39.

92. *Zheng He: China and the Oceans in the Early Ming Dynasty*, p. 59.

93. *Zheng He: China and the Oceans in the Early Ming Dynasty*, p. 65.

94. *Zheng He: China and the Oceans in the Early Ming Dynasty*, p. 61.

95. *Cheng Ho and Malacca*, p. 18.

96. *When China Ruled the Seas*, p. 138.

97. *Zheng He: China and the Oceans in the Early Ming Dynasty*, p. 78.

98. *When China Ruled the Seas*, p. 138.

99. *Cheng Ho and Malacca*, p. 19.

100. *Zheng He: China and the Oceans in the Early Ming Dynasty*, p. 91.

101. *Cheng Ho and Malacca*, p. 19; and *Zheng He Epic*, pp. 226–29.

102. *Zheng He: China and the Oceans in the Early Ming Dynasty*, p. 49.

103. *Zheng He: China and the Oceans in the Early Ming Dynasty*, p. 73.

104. *Zheng He: China and the Oceans in the Early Ming Dynasty*, p. 84.

105. *Zheng He Epic*, p. 145.

106. *Zheng He Epic*, p. 320.

107. *Zheng He Epic*, p. 345.

108. *Zheng He Epic*, p. 345.

109. *Cheng Ho and Malacca*, p. 44.

110. *Cheng Ho and Malacca*, p. 46.

111. *Cheng Ho and Malacca*, pp. 11–12.

112. *Zheng He Epic*, p. 248.

113. *Cheng Ho and Malacca*, p. 50.

114. G. Stalk, P. Evans, and L. Shulman, "Competing on capabilities: the new rules of corporate strategy", *Harvard Business Review*, March–April 1992.

115. C. T. Foo, S. F. Loke, and S. Graham, "Towards a future of mobile, competitive 'port-in-ocean' system for evolving seamless supply chains", *Port Technology International*, Edition 43, <http://www.porttechnology.org/journal_archive/edition_43> (accessed 4 September 2011).

116. R. Sally, "European twilight, Asian sunrise", *Straits Times*, 15 August 2011, p. A22.

References

Chiu Ling-yeong. "Zheng He: Navigator, Discoverer and Diplomat". *Wu Teh Yao Memorial Lectures 2000*. Singapore: Unipress, Center for the Arts, National University of Singapore, 2001.

"Developing Singapore into a Global Integrated Logistics Hub". <http://app.mti.gov.sg/data/pages/507/doc/ERC_SVS_LOG_MainReport.pdf> (accessed 20 August 2011).

Dreyer, Edward L. *Zheng He: China and the Oceans in the Early Ming Dynasty, 1405–1433*. U.S.: Pearson Education, Inc., 2007.

Fisher, M. "What is the right supply chain for your product?". *Harvard Business Review*, March–April 1997.

Foo, C. T., S. F. Loke, and S. Graham. "Towards a future of mobile, competitive 'port-in-ocean' system for evolving seamless supply chains". *Port Technology International*, Edition 43. <http://www.porttechnology.org/journal_archive/edition_43> (accessed 4 September 2011).

Levathes, Louise E. *When China Ruled the Seas: The Treasure Fleet of the Dragon Throne, 1405–1433*. U.S.: Oxford University Press, 1994.

"Logistics and Supply Chain Management: Facts and Figures". <http://www.edb.gov.sg/edb/sg/en_uk/index/industry_sectors/logistics_supply/facts_and_figures.html> (accessed 20 August 2011).

Sally, R. "European twilight, Asian sunrise". *Straits Times*, 15 August 2011.

Skinner, Wickham. "The Focused Factory". *Harvard Business Review*, May–June 1974.

Stalk, G., P. Evans, and L. Shulman. "Competing on capabilities: the new rules of corporate strategy". *Harvard Business Review*, March–April 1992.

Tan Ta Sen. *Cheng Ho and Islam in Southeast Asia*. Singapore: Institute of Southeast Asian Studies, 2009.

———. *Cheng Ho and Malacca*. Singapore: International Zheng He Society, 2005.

Tan Ta Sen and Chia Lin Sien, eds. *The Zheng He Epic*. 1st edition in

Chinese edited by Zhou Wenlin et al. Kunming, Yunnan, China: Yunnan's Publishing House, Yunnan Fine Arts Publishing House, Auora Publishing House, 2006.

Torck, M. "The matter of provisioning in Zheng He's Fleets: a reconstructive attempt". In *Chinese Diaspora since Admiral Zheng He with Special Reference to Maritime Asia*, edited by Leo Suryadinata. Singapore: Chinese Heritage Center, 2007.

Chapter 8

ZHENG HE AND HIS FAITH
Implications for Management Practices

INTRODUCTION

When we explore the existing literature on Zheng He and his grand voyages, it is difficult to miss the observation that Zheng He and his men were significantly involved in praying for divine help and protection. For example, in two of the few primary sources of writing on Zheng He, namely the Liujiagang and Changle inscriptions of 1431, much space were devoted to their invocation for divine protection and honouring of the "Heavenly Princess" or Tianfei — the goddess of sailors and seafarers. In fact, Zheng He and his associates also made mention of the religious buildings they had helped in: the repair of the halls of Buddhas and the temples of the gods, including making the statue of the goddess shine as though it were new. They also stated their resolve to do even more for their gods.[1]

To Zheng He then, his faith practices were therefore both prominent and real throughout his grand voyages. Perhaps it is not difficult for us to understand why. Once Zheng He and

248

his men were out in the open seas, his own vulnerability to the natural elements, and that of his tens of thousands of men, became helplessly obvious. Zheng He must have realized very quickly through such a sense of leadership loneliness that he needed to invoke divine help. At the same time, throughout his grand voyages, Zheng He would have encountered rulers and peoples of various nationalities, cultures and religions. Even his own crew comprised men of different religious faith and beliefs. These would no doubt have added to Zheng He's sense of spiritual awareness, and the importance he attached to religious beliefs and practices.

In today's context, the relationship between religion and business appear to be a complex one.[2] Any mention of the two elements together would tend to bring about a generally negative response from many. Indeed, most would think that the two should be kept separate and should never be mixed. To some extent, this is true as religion can pose real problems with regard to management of the company and its employees.[3] And with today's globalization, talents and skills are mobile across borders, and this would add to the personnel diversity and hence complexity in managing a multi-religious workforce.

Yet in Zheng He's context and experience, he seemed to have managed his faith practices and the emperor-decreed mission quite well. Zheng He seemed to be able to effectively deal with the potential problems associated with the different religious beliefs and practices of his crew who travelled with him. At the same time, his personal faith and those of his crew seemed to be an underlying contributory factor to his mission success in spreading goodwill and peace, and building collaborative ties with other countries and peoples.

What can we learn from Zheng He and his faith practices? From our reading of the Zheng He faith-related literature, it is apparent to us that learning from Zheng He and his faith can take place at two levels: there is the individual level of personal faith and beliefs, and there is the corporate level of managing diverse faith and its associated practices. We therefore introduce in this chapter what we refer to as Zheng He's *PC* model for managing religious beliefs and faith practices; to Zheng He, it was apparent that *Personal Faith can be a Significant Plus* for his sea-faring enterprise, while *Corporate Inclusiveness is an Important Must* for mission success.

This chapter is therefore organized as follows. In the next section, we will provide a brief description of Zheng He's personal faith through his family background and religious upbringing. Here, our focus is on Zheng He as a Muslim with a rich family Islamic faith heritage. We will then follow in the subsequent section where we will consider learning from Zheng He's experiences on how *Personal Faith can be a Significant Plus* for any enterprise. Here, we will highlight Zheng He's personal faith practices and conviction and how that shaped his leadership practices and added value to his overall mission. We will also similarly consider how the personal faith and beliefs of his crew contributed towards the success of Zheng He's emperor-decreed mission. We will then introduce Zheng He's faith practice of *Corporate Inclusiveness* and explain how this is an *Important Must* which contributed to religious harmony among his crew and therefore helped ensure success of his mission of reaching out to the countries in the western seas. We will then conclude the chapter by suggesting implications from this Zheng He's PC model of managing faith practices for today's managers and leaders.

ZHENG HE'S ISLAMIC FAITH HERITAGE

Zheng He was born in 1371 to a virtuous Muslim family, in Hedai Village located in the larger province of Yunnan. His family name was "Ma",[4] the Chinese version of "Mohammed",[5] and he was originally called "Ma He" from birth.[6] Ma He was brought up in his devout Muslim family, with strong Islamic faith and an awareness of Islam's heritage; both his father Milijin, and his grandfather Chaermidena, had travelled to Mecca to perform the pilgrimage[7] and they were revered as "Haji".[8] Ma He's father, Haji Ma, was highly respected by the local community for his selflessness as evidenced by his acts of kindness and generosity.[9] Ma He's mother, whose maiden name was "Wen", was described as a gracious lady;[10] he had an elder brother, Ma Wen Ming, and four sisters.[11]

As a child, Ma He often asked his father and grandfather about their adventures to Mecca;[12] no doubt he would have learned from them about the long and adventurous journeys across the Indian Ocean, as well as the religious significance of the pilgrimage.

However when Ma He was ten years old, Yunnan was attacked by the Ming army led by General Fu Youde. His father Haji Ma was killed and Ma He himself was taken prisoner and castrated by the Ming soldiers and sent to the Ming Court as a eunuch. He was eventually given to Zhu Di, the Prince of Yan, who grew to favour him greatly.[13]

Even though Haji Ma was killed before Ma He reached adolescence, he apparently had a great impact on the young Ma He. This was seen years later, when Zheng He, having rose to prominence in the emperor's service, had a memorial tablet engraved in his father's honour. The inscription on the tablet is shown below:[14]

> The title of this gentleman was Haji. His surname was Ma...The gentleman was by birth tall, husky, and unusually good looking, of imposing and redoubtable demeanour and bearing, unwilling to compromise himself...By nature being especially fond of doing good, [on] encountering those who were impoverished

or distressed — including widows, orphans, and others with no one to rely on, he routinely [offered them] protection and aid...[It was] for this reason that there was no one in the local community who did not look up to [this] gentleman...Verily, by observing his offspring one surely can see what the father accomplished during his life and taught by his righteous ways. By imperial decree — composed on the day of the Dragon Boat Festival in the third year of Yongle [June 1, 1405] by...the president of the Ministry of Rites...Li Zhigang.

The inscription on the tablet suggested that Haji Ma had played an important role in shaping Ma He's character as well as his early religious beliefs. It is probably valid to say that Zheng He was quite aware of his Islamic faith as he was growing up, given the good example set by his father in words and in deeds.

PERSONAL FAITH: A SIGNIFICANT PLUS

Zheng He's Personal Faith

As an adult, Zheng He continued to practise his Islamic faith. However, he also made contributions to Buddhism and had certainly also joined his men in their faith practices relating to the Mazu folk religion.[15] Indeed, the eclectic nature of Zheng He's faith is quite apparent.[16]

Islamic Practices

Zheng He certainly continued to uphold the Islamic beliefs of his forefathers. As a Muslim, for example, he continued to visit and pray in mosques, even while he was on his grand voyages. In Quanzhou at the beginning of his fifth voyage, Zheng He worshipped at the city's main mosque located on Tumen Street; he also visited and burnt incense and prayed at the tomb of two Muslim prophets located outside the city. In fact, to commemorate this episode, a tablet erected at the site carried the following message:[17]

The imperial envoy and commander-in-chief, the grand Eunuch Zheng He, proceeding on official business to Hormuz and other countries in the Western Ocean, has on the 16th day of the 5th month of the 15th year of Yongle [May 31, 1417] here burnt incense, wishing [to procure] the Divine Sacred protection, in memory of which Judge Pu Heri has set up [this tablet].

Zheng He therefore apparently continued to seek for Divine protection through his Muslim faith even as he readied his crew for the start of this particular fifth voyage. Similarly, when his fleet stopped in Semarang, Zheng He, together with some of his Chinese Muslim companions, would go to the mosque for prayer.[18] All these would indicate that Zheng He placed a personal emphasis on his Islamic faith, as he would still take time for prayer while on his voyages.

He had therefore not abandoned the faith of his fathers; in fact, he may even have played a part in fighting against the persecution of Muslims in the early years of Emperor Yongle's reign.[19] Apparently in early Ming China, there was considerable persecution of Muslims. A 1407 inscription near the Ashab Mosque in Quanzhou, where Zheng He also visited and prayed, recorded the Emperor Yongle's description of Muslims as "sincere", "good" and loyal subjects "most deserving of commendation"; it also carried the emperor's decree that "official, military and civilian [households] and other categories of people shall not maltreat, insult, cheat or bully [Muslims]". Zheng He may have used his influence with the emperor to bring about such an imperial decree on the protection of the Muslim community in Quanzhou, which Zheng He also visited in 1407 during his second voyage.

As a Muslim, Zheng He was also personally involved in building and renovating mosques. Some of the mosques that he renovated included the Jingjue Mosque in Nanjing and the Qingjing Mosque in Xian.[20] In 1413, prior to his fourth voyage where Zheng He was to begin visiting Hormuz and other primarily Muslim countries in the Middle East, Zheng He made a personal visit to Xian in Shaanxi Province to recruit Hasan, the Imam of the Qingjing Mosque, to serve as an Arabic language interpreter on the voyage.[21] Of course, given Hasan's high religious standing as an imam, Zheng He had apparently involved him as his religious advisor on board as well. And so when the fleet was caught in storms on the homeward journey, Zheng He would have rallied Hasan's help to pray for the divine protection of all his crew. The Inscription at the renovated Qingjing Mosque recorded that "Hasan prayed to Allah and the sea became calm. Hence Zheng He vowed to renovate the mosque…".[22] As his gesture of thanksgiving to his God, Zheng He therefore did indeed renovate the Qingjing Mosque.

Zheng He also helped to build mosques outside of China. The *Malay Annals* recorded that Zheng He had built mosques in Semarang, Ancol, Tuban, Gresik, Cerebon, etc. These were primarily catered to the growing Hanafite Chinese Muslim communities in Java.[23]

Indeed, Zheng He's grand voyages ushered in a new era of islamization of Southeast Asia.[24] For example, according to the *Malay Annals*, Zheng He played a key role in the spread of Islam among the Chinese communities in the Malay Archipelago. He helped to set up the administrative structure for managing the Chinese Muslim and Overseas Chinese communities in Java and Sumatra. And throughout the 1420s, Zheng He personally guided the significant growth of all these Chinese Muslim communities.[25]

Zheng He's significant involvement in all these demonstrated that he had strong ties with his Islamic faith even as an adult. In fact, many Muslims in Southeast Asia considered Zheng He as a Muslim hero.[26]

Buddhist Faith

Although Zheng He was basically a Muslim as described above, he apparently had good knowledge of the Buddhist faith and made contributions towards Buddhism, as well as joined his men in Buddhist faith practices.

For example, the Emperor Yongle directed Zheng He to publish a large number of Buddhist classics for mass circulation.[27] Zheng He printed the *Dazang Jing* Buddhist Classics nine times (in 1407, 1410, 1411, 1415, 1420, 1424, 1429 and 1430), and he donated them to Linggu Temple, Wuhua Temple, Tianjie Temple, Jinshan Temple, Jinghai Temple etc. in Beijing, Jiangsu, Yunnan and Fujian.[28]

An Inscription on Zheng He's printing and donation of the *Dazang Jing* Buddhist Classics actually recorded the following:

> ...Grand Eunuch Zheng He...printed the Dazang Jing Buddhist Classics, a total of 635 scripts, and donated to the Wuhua Temple for keeping and wished the empire strong and prosperous, the emblem of Buddha shining, people healthy and with abundance of food. Sanbao was grateful to the God for his safe voyages. Inscribed in the 18th year of Yongle's reign.[29]

"Sanbao" was the Buddhist nickname of Zheng He, and the inscription apparently noted that Zheng He made the printing and donation of the Buddhist Classics in gratitude to the Buddhist God for protection over his voyages.

Zheng He was also tasked by the emperor in the reconstruction of the Opaque Pagoda of the Buddhist Dabao'en Temple in Nanjing.[30] Zheng He personally supervised this project from 1428 on,[31] after it was first started in 1412. This was quite contrary to the notion that Buddhist temples should be built by the monks themselves.[32] The emperor was unhappy that after sixteen years, the project was still uncompleted; he therefore commanded that

Zheng He and his team complete this work quickly, and then to organize a Buddhist celebration and vegetarian feast that would last for seven days and nights.[33]

Apart from this Baoen project, Zheng He had apparently also put in efforts to repair "the halls of the Buddhas and the temples of the gods" when his ships were moored at Changle.[34] He had also joined his men in making offerings to Buddha in the cluster of three temples near the harbour.[35]

Because of all these, Zheng He had been described as "a pious Buddhist in his adult life".[36] In his biography in the *Ming Shi*, he was referred to as the "Grand Director of the Three Treasures".[37] Indeed, Zheng He's nickname "Sanbao" refers to the Buddhist Three Treasures or *Triratna*,[38] which comprised of the Buddha, the Buddhist law (*dharma*), and the community (*sangha*) of Buddhist monks.[39]

Mazu Practices

Zheng He had also been described as a good example of a faithful Mazu believer.[40] Apparently throughout his grand voyages, a majority of his faith practices were associated with the worship of Mazu or Tianfei, the Goddess of the Sea. He visited the Mazu Temple at Meizhou; helped build and renovate the Nanshan Mazu Temple, San Qing Baodian Temple, San Feng Pagoda Temple and the Yunmen Temple; built a large well at the Tianfei Temple; and erected the Liujiagang and Changle inscriptions where much space were devoted to praising the efficacy of Tianfei's protection of his fleet and crew.

More obviously, this area of Mazu faith practices was the most relevant to Zheng He on a day-to-day basis as many of his crew members were believers of the Goddess of the Sea. This was therefore where we would see many of Zheng He's men faithfully praying at Mazu altars on board their ships to ask for the Goddess' protection for their journeys[41] since their basic belief was in the Goddess coming to their rescue when they met with storms and dangers at sea.[42] And indeed for Zheng He and his men, they would have encountered too many storms and dangers in all their grand voyages that they must have had desperately invoked the divine protection of this Goddess of the Sea.

This was therefore where Zheng He's personal faith practices became the most relevant to him. Once he was out at sea with his tens of thousands of men, Zheng He would have recognized his own obvious vulnerability as well as that of his men. It would be quite clear to him very quickly that he may not succeed.[43] He must have realized through such a sense of leadership helplessness that he needed to invoke divine help. And so he would join his men in praying to Tianfei for help and guidance.[44] And no doubt he would also have rallied his other crew members to pray to their gods for protection, including the Imam Hasan's call to Allah[45] for help for the entire venture.

And his experience of the efficacy of divine help had been good. Both the Liujiagang and Changle inscriptions attested to this.[46] The Liujiagang inscription, for example, described it this way: "When we met with danger, once we invoked the divine name, her answer to our prayer was like an echo."[47] Similarly, in the Changle inscription, we read the following: "It is not easy to enumerate completely all the cases in which the goddess has answered our prayers."[48]

And Zheng He saw the divine efficacy also on his men: after their prayers for protection in the midst of encountering "great wind-driven waves", the Goddess came to their rescue as "this miraculous light appeared", and he saw it in his men as their "apprehension turned to calm, and even in danger of foundering we all trusted we had nothing to fear".[49] In fact, Zheng He went on to inscribe on this tablet erected at Changle that: "With the gods at rest and men rejoicing, this truly is a remarkable place."[50]

All these led to Zheng He's personal conviction of belief which he also inscribed clearly in the Changle tablet as follows: "If men are able to serve the gods with utmost sincerity, then all their prayers will be answered."[51] He must have experienced a deep sense of confidence based on this clear personal conviction that the gods will be there to provide him with help and answers. He seemed also convinced that even for his men, as their personal faiths were being practised, they would all serve their gods diligently and sincerely.

Learning from Zheng He's Personal Faith

From all that we observed in Zheng He's personal faith practices, including that of his crew, it should be clear that the reality of *Personal Faith can indeed be a Significant Plus* for mission success. In Zheng He's case, it was most apparent that his joint invocation with his men for help from Sea Goddess Tianfei, and all the other gods, had added to the successful completion of his voyages and mission.

Emperor Yongle's Perspective

We can also see the reality of this *"Significant Plus of Personal Faith"* from Emperor Yongle's perspective. The emperor knew that Zheng He had much knowledge about the Buddhist faith; this led him to task Zheng He with the printing of the Buddhist Classics for mass distribution, thereby apparently helping the emperor to promote Buddhism.[52] Further, because of Zheng He's knowledge of Buddhism, he was selected by the emperor to lead the grand voyages as many of the states he would visit in the West were Buddhist countries.[53] Apparently the emperor was of the view that one's personal faith can help to connect with others of the same faith at a deeper and more effective level.

In a similar manner, Zheng He's Islamic faith and upbringing was a significant plus from Emperor Yongle's perspective for facilitating the success of his imperial decree to spread Ming China's splendour and glory to the West. Again, to the emperor, Zheng He being a Muslim would enable him to engage more easily with the Muslim rulers in Asia and Africa.[54] Indeed, Zheng He's efforts had contributed significantly to the widening and strengthening of Ming China's relationships with the Islamic world; many of the Islamic states then had sent envoys to the Ming Court on a regular basis, including Champa, Malacca, Aru, Samudra, Aceh, Java, Cochin, Calicut, Bengal, Brunei, Maldive, Hormuz, Dhofar, Aden, Mecca and Mogadishu. And their trade relations with Ming China had also flourished.[55]

We should also note that several of Zheng He's senior associates (Wang Jinghong, Hou Xian, Hong Bao, Yang Zhen, and even Ma Huan, Fei Xin and Gong Zhen[56]) were also Muslims in terms of their personal faith, and their presence on Zheng He's voyages would lend similar added advantages towards mission success. In this context, as we have pointed out earlier, prior to his fourth voyage out to Hormuz, Zheng He made his special trip to Xian in Shaanxi to recruit Imam Hasan.[57] This was because Zheng He apparently believed that an Imam of high religious standing would be better able than he himself could in connecting with the Muslims out in the Middle East.

Still from Emperor Yongle's perspective, the emperor would know Zheng He quite well. He would therefore be quite confident that Zheng He could rally his many crew members who were worshippers of Mazu during their voyages across the seas. Indeed, as it turned out, "to worship Mazu was to follow the wishes of the masses", and Zheng He apparently joined his men in embracing the divine help available in the Sea Goddess; and, he even helped in promoting the development of the Mazu culture.[58] This close link between Mazu and Zheng He's voyages suggested that Zheng He "relied on the faithful worship of Mazu and the spirit of the Mazu culture to lead a large crew of several thousands to complete his missions". With their Mazu belief, both Zheng He and his men were able to forge friendly ties more readily with the countries they visited as the Sea Goddess "has numerous believers among different races spread all over the world...in the west and in India".[59] Clearly then, Zheng He and his men's personal faith practices relating to Mazu had helped contribute towards mission success. The Emperor Yongle was once again wise in selecting Zheng He to be the commander-in-chief of the grand voyages; for once again, the emperor had recognized that *Personal Faith can indeed be a Significant Plus* for the overall success of his imperial mission.

Zheng He's Perspective

We can also see how *Personal Faith can be a Significant Plus* for mission success from Zheng He's perspective as the overall leader of the grand voyages. First, his personal conviction of belief (that "if men are able to serve the gods with utmost sincerity, then all their prayers will be answered"[60]) had given him a personal sense of confidence that he can rely on his faith practices for help and guidance in his leadership of the grand voyages. This was surely a plus and a boost for the completion of his emperor-decreed mission. Second, Zheng He's faith practices had given him a deep empathy and understanding of the spiritual needs of his men. This would have helped make him a better and more religiously tolerant leader, adding value to his overall mission success. Third, Zheng He being seen as one with his men through their joint faith practices would also add value to his leadership and therefore to his mission success.

Crew's Perspective

Similarly, from the perspective of Zheng He's crew, it was apparent that their personal faith practices on board the voyages had helped to contribute to their sense of personal safety and security. Further, with support from Zheng He, the crew members had been able to practise their personal faith freely and had therefore felt their spiritual needs being met. Indeed, as described earlier, with the efficacy of the divine help they had prayed for, Zheng He and his men were apparently at peace and with joy ("with the gods at rest and men rejoicing, this truly is a remarkable place"[61]). Such a crew functioning at peace and with joy would surely be a potent workforce that would add value to the overall enterprise. Men then, when encouraged and supported in their personal faith practices, can indeed be a significant contributor to overall mission success.

CORPORATE INCLUSIVENESS: AN IMPORTANT MUST

Quite clearly, we see from the example of Zheng He and his men that personal faith practices can indeed be a significant plus for an enterprise's overall mission success. But to facilitate this, there must be a sense of corporate inclusiveness or acceptance of all types of religious faith practices. This means that there must be a corporate practice of sensitivity, tolerance and acceptance of the different personal faith practices of the people. *Corporate Inclusiveness* is therefore an *Important Must* for capitalizing on the benefits that can accrue from personal faith practices.

Zheng He's Inclusiveness

Zheng He apparently exercised corporate religious inclusiveness at two levels: within and among his crew, and also in relation to forging ties with the countries he visited.

With His Crew

Although Zheng He practised his personal faith as a Muslim, he was not hostile to other faiths.[62] We have already pointed out that a large number of his crew, including many who were recruited in Fujian, were worshippers of Mazu, the Goddess of the Sea.[63] As the leader of his fleet, Zheng He allowed Mazu altars to be set up on board, enabling his crew members to pray to Mazu and seek her protection for their journeys.[64] In fact, Zheng He went so far as to help "popularize the worship of Mazu".[65]

Although inclusive and tolerant of other faiths, Zheng He nonetheless stayed true to his own religion Islam; he had not abandoned the faith of his fathers.[66] Zheng He, as indicated earlier, recruited Imam Hasan to be part of his crew, and Hasan's call to Allah for help when the fleet met with storms on route home[67] was all part of Zheng He's corporate inclusiveness on board his fleet. In fact, Mazu worship may be seen to be more of a maritime culture rather than a religion, and the Mazu belief is said to have stemmed from Chinese traditional culture, traditional values and morality.[68] Taking this view, Zheng He's Mazu practices would then be an indication that Zheng He possessed high cultural wisdom,[69] which would then explain the ready tolerance and inclusiveness of his faith practices.

We highlight one other example of Zheng He's corporate religious inclusiveness. Apparently on board Zheng He's ships, there were included among the crew three other groups of religious personnel: Taoist priests, Buddhist monks, and a few Prophets or Fortune Tellers. To help maintain the psychological and emotional health of his crew, Zheng He would instruct the monks to chant and perform rituals with the affected crew if they were Buddhists. For the other crew members, Zheng He would instruct them to seek help from the Taoist priests or the Prophets/Fortune Tellers. Since most of his crew members were devoted to Mazu, the captains of each ship would pray to Mazu for help and safety.[70]

Zheng He therefore clearly demonstrated his desire for understanding and acceptance of all religious beliefs and cultures,[71] providing an environment of corporate inclusiveness that would help to capitalize on the personal faith practices of all his crew members to support his overall emperor-decreed mission.

With Other Countries

Zheng He also exercised his religious inclusiveness in his attempt to forge ties with other countries. As we have indicated earlier, he would visit countries that were primarily Buddhist in religious orientation, or that were Muslim states, or whose people would worship Mazu as a folk religion. In fact, we have explained earlier that it was because of Zheng He's faith knowledge and inclusive faith practices at this level that had enabled him to become the emperor's top choice of commander-in-chief for the imperial mission of visiting the countries in the West.

And where the local people worshipped and practised multiple religions, Zheng He would make special attempts to connect with them inclusively. One example was his linkage with Ceylon. Zheng He had visited Ceylon on his first voyage but he was not well received and this was likely because he had failed to give equal consideration to the three religious communities residing in Ceylon then: the Buddhists, Hindus and Muslims. Not realizing the strong religious undercurrents in Ceylon, Zheng He did not bring offerings for the Buddha and Allah on his first visit.[72]

Learning from his mistake, Zheng He actually erected a trilingual stone tablet in Ceylon during his third voyage to express his respect for all religions and his appreciation of the friendship with all the local people.[73] The Chinese portion of the tablet praised Buddha and offered thanks for his protection, and spelled out the gifts brought by Zheng He for the Buddhist god. The Tamil portion of the tablet carried similar praises to the Hindu god Tenavarai-Nayanar, and the Persian portion hailed the glory of Allah in a similar manner. Zheng He was also careful that he gave to each god an equal tribute so that none would be slighted in any way: 1,000 pieces of gold, 5,000 pieces of silver, 100 bolts of silk and more than 3,000 pounds of perfumed oil and other worship ornaments.[74] Zheng He had intended for this trilingual tablet to help him connect better with multi-religious Ceylon.

Zheng He's practice of corporate religious inclusiveness had therefore helped him to rally his multi-religious crew to work together for achieving what he had set out to do through his seven grand voyages. To be more accurate, Zheng He's faith inclusiveness had allowed him to support all his people in their personal faith practices, and this in turn had helped to connect with the foreign countries and peoples at a deeper and more effective level, leading to Zheng He's overall mission successes. *Personal Faith can indeed be a Significant Plus*, but *Corporate Inclusiveness is an Important Must* to draw out the efficacy of all religious practices of an organization's people.

IMPLICATIONS

Religion has always been a difficult issue because each person has his own personal faith practices and beliefs which can be different from that of others. When we seek to consider religion in the context of businesses, the general thinking is to keep the two separate.

Yet from what we see in Zheng He's faith practices and experience, there can be value in personal faith as this can become a contributory factor towards mission success. A person's religious knowledge and faith conviction can help the organization connect and transact business with others at a deeper level and in a more effective manner. At the same time, a person's faith can lend him inner strength and conviction that can become a potent source of value creation for the organization, whether at the individual level as a worker or as a leader in the organization, or at the collective level where the entire team or workforce becomes a powerful contributor to mission success.

But as we also saw in Zheng He's example, his corporate religious inclusiveness was an important ingredient that supported the practise of faith at the personal level. Without corporate tolerance and inclusiveness, it would have been difficult for individuals to practise their faith freely. The consequence of that would then be a loss of the value that could have accrued from personal faith practices.

What does all this mean for today's managers and leaders?

First, we may have to recognize that indeed, there can be value that accrues from personal faith practices of individuals within our organizations. Our people can become healthier spiritually and emotionally, and our leaders can become more convinced and confident of their capabilities and sources of help. All this can add to our corporate success. Also, our people can connect better and more effectively with others and this can help us in our organization's business with others.

Second, we must act on creating the all-inclusive environment that would not only encourage tolerance but also support acceptance of different personal faith practices of our people. Such corporate religious inclusiveness can become a uniting factor for our multi-religious organizations as our people would then work together harmoniously through mutual respect and acceptance of each other. This is all the more important in today's business environment as religious respect and acceptance can be quietly more potent than noisy religious extremism and jihadist inclinations.

Third, it would help significantly as we learn from Zheng He to become knowledgeable about different religions and faith practices. Zheng He's eclectic faith practices had their value. We need not advocate for eclecticism. We need only to be open to learning about others' faith practices and beliefs.

Fourth, we should consider Singapore's example on this matter; it will add to our understanding and appreciation of Zheng He's PC model where *Personal Faith* is encouraged as it can indeed be a *Significant Plus* but *Corporate Inclusiveness* is an *Important Must* in order for personal faith to lend its value.

At the individual level, Singapore's model supports and encourages personal faith practices and beliefs. Here, the Singapore model acknowledges that spiritual beliefs and practices can strengthen the individual and hence adds value to the overall fabric of society. In this context, the Singapore model recognizes and accepts a multi-religious Singapore.

At the national corporate level, the Singapore model calls for religious tolerance and inclusiveness. It believes that religious harmony can be safeguarded through mutual respect, understanding and acceptance. As such, the call has often been to encourage Singaporeans to join in each other's religious events and festivities so as to build a better understanding and appreciation for each other's faith.[75] On the other hand, the common regular reminder has also been to watch out for possible elements that may disturb and undermine religious inclusiveness and tolerance.[76] The Singapore Government therefore adopts the stand of equal respect for all religions, and it treats all faiths equally. Places of worship for various religions are erected all across Singapore in an effort to show that Singapore is an all inclusive society. And many of these places of worship are often in close proximity of each other.

In this way, the Singapore model for managing faith matters parallels that of Zheng He's model; it is an example that illustrates the possible application of Zheng He's model in today's environment.

LEARNING FROM ZHENG HE'S FAITH PRACTICES

Zheng He's mission success seemed to draw significantly from his personal faith practices as well as those of his men. So while faith beliefs and practices are personal, they can add value to the success of the overall corporate mission.

Zheng He's faith practices also demonstrated his sensitivity, tolerance and acceptance of the different personal faith practices of his men. As the commander-in-chief of the grand voyages, his personal faith practices of tolerance and acceptance, and his desire to be one with his people, helped to facilitate an overall environment of corporate religious inclusiveness. And this had turned out to be most supportive for drawing out value from the varied personal faith practices of his men.

Zheng He's **PC** model of faith practices may therefore be deserving of a closer consideration by today's managers and leaders: *Personal Faith* can indeed be a *Significant Plus* for the organization, but *Corporate Inclusiveness* is an *Important Must*.

Endnotes

1. Edward L. Dreyer, *Zheng He: China and the Oceans in the Early Ming Dynasty, 1405–1433* (U.S.: Pearson Education, Inc., 2007), pp. 148–49 and 193.

2. Pamela Mortimer, "Religion in Business: Is it Faith or Suicide?" *Buzzle.com, Intelligent life on the web*, <http://www.buzzle.com/articles/religion-in-business-is-it-faith-or-suicide.html> (accessed 18 October 2010).

3. Martha Lagace, "Can Religion and Business Learn From Each Other?",

Working Knowledge, Harvard Business School, 2001, <http://hbswk. hbs.edu/item/3511.html> (accessed 10 October 2010).

4. Tan Ta Sen and Chia Lin Sien, eds., *The Zheng He Epic*, 1ˢᵗ edition in Chinese edited by Zhou Wenlin et al. (Kunming, Yunnan, China: Yunnan's Publishing House, Yunnan Fine Arts Publishing House, Auora Publishing House, 2006), p. 48.

5. Kallie Szczepanski, "Zheng He, Ming China's Great Admiral", *About. com Asian History*, <http://asianhistory.about.com/od/china/p/ zheng_he_bio.htm?p=1> (accessed 1 March 2011).

6. *Zheng He: China and the Oceans in the Early Ming Dynasty*, p. 11.

7. *Zheng He Epic*, p. 48.

8. Tan Ta Sen, *Cheng Ho and Malacca* (Singapore: International Zheng He Society, 2005), p. 2.

9. Louise E. Levathes, *When China Ruled the Seas: The Treasure Fleet of the Dragon Throne, 1405–1433* (U.S.: Oxford University Press, 1994), p. 62.

10. *Zheng He Epic*, p. 48.

11. *When China Ruled the Seas*, p. 62.

12. *Zheng He Epic*, pp. 55–57.

13. *Zheng He Epic*, p. 48.

14. *When China Ruled the Seas*, pp. 62–63.

15. *Zheng He Epic*, p. 175.

16. *Zheng He: China and the Oceans in the Early Ming Dynasty*, p. 12.

17. *When China Ruled the Seas*, p. 147.

18. Rosey Wang Ma, "I. Early Presence of Chinese Muslims — Zheng He, the Muslim Eunuch", *Chinese Muslims in Malaysia, History and Development*, <http://210.0.141.99/eng/malaysia/ChineseMuslim_ in_Malaysia.asp> (accessed 16 November 2010).

19. *When China Ruled the Seas*, pp. 147–48.

20. Tan Ta Sen, *Cheng Ho and Islam in Southeast Asia* (Singapore: Institute of Southeast Asian Studies, 2009), p. 197.

21. *Zheng He Epic*, p. 200.

22. *Zheng He Epic*, p. 201.

23. *Cheng Ho and Islam in Southeast Asia*, p. 197.

24. *Cheng Ho and Islam in Southeast Asia*, p. 154.
25. *Cheng Ho and Islam in Southeast Asia*, p. 195.
26. *Cheng Ho and Islam in Southeast Asia*, p. 179.
27. *Zheng He Epic*, p. 71.
28. *Zheng He Epic*, p. 42.
29. *Zheng He Epic*, p. 42.
30. *Cheng Ho and Islam in Southeast Asia*, p. 197.
31. *Zheng He: China and the Oceans in the Early Ming Dynasty*, p. 69.
32. *Zheng He: China and the Oceans in the Early Ming Dynasty*, p. 142.
33. *Zheng He: China and the Oceans in the Early Ming Dynasty*, p. 143.
34. *Zheng He: China and the Oceans in the Early Ming Dynasty*, p. 149.
35. *When China Ruled the Seas*, p. 93.
36. *Zheng He: China and the Oceans in the Early Ming Dynasty*, p. 69.
37. *Zheng He: China and the Oceans in the Early Ming Dynasty*, p. 187.
38. *Zheng He: China and the Oceans in the Early Ming Dynasty*, p. 12.
39. *Zheng He: China and the Oceans in the Early Ming Dynasty*, p. 5.
40. *Zheng He Epic*, p. 177.
41. *Cheng Ho and Islam in Southeast Asia*, p. 171.
42. *Zheng He Epic*, p. 175.
43. *Zheng He: China and the Oceans in the Early Ming Dynasty*, p. 197.
44. *When China Ruled the Seas*, p. 89.
45. *Zheng He Epic*, p. 201.
46. *Zheng He: China and the Oceans in the Early Ming Dynasty*, p. 148.
47. *Zheng He: China and the Oceans in the Early Ming Dynasty*, p. 192.
48. *Zheng He: China and the Oceans in the Early Ming Dynasty*, p. 196.
49. *Zheng He: China and the Oceans in the Early Ming Dynasty*, p. 196.
50. *Zheng He: China and the Oceans in the Early Ming Dynasty*, p. 197.
51. *When China Ruled the Seas*, p. 90; and *Zheng He: China and the Oceans in the Early Ming Dynasty*, p. 197.
52. *Zheng He Epic*, p. 71 and *Zheng He: China and the Oceans in the Early Ming Dynasty*, p. 69.
53. *Zheng He Epic*, p. 71.
54. The National Library Board, *Zheng He and Maritime Asia* (Singapore, 2005), p. 36.

55. *Cheng Ho and Islam in Southeast Asia*, pp. 172–73.

56. *Cheng Ho and Islam in Southeast Asia*, pp. 171–72.

57. *Zheng He Epic*, p. 200.

58. *Zheng He Epic*, p. 177.

59. *Zheng He Epic*, p. 175.

60. *When China Ruled the Seas*, p. 90; and *Zheng He: China and the Oceans in the Early Ming Dynasty*, p. 197.

61. *Zheng He: China and the Oceans in the Early Ming Dynasty*, p. 197.

62. *Cheng Ho and Islam in Southeast Asia*, p. 171.

63. *Cheng Ho and Islam in Southeast Asia*, p. 204.

64. *Cheng Ho and Islam in Southeast Asia*, p. 171.

65. *Cheng Ho and Islam in Southeast Asia*, p. 204.

66. *When China Ruled the Seas*, p. 147.

67. *Zheng He Epic*, p. 201.

68. *Zheng He Epic*, p. 175.

69. *Zheng He Epic*, p. 177.

70. 陈存仁，《被误读的远行：郑和下西洋与马哥孛罗来华考》，桂林市：广西师范大学出版社. Chen Cunren, *The misread Voyages: A Study of Zheng He's Voyages and Marco Polo's Trip to China* (Guilin, China: Guangxi Normal University Publication, 1998), pp. 44–45.

71. Rosey Wang Ma, "Zheng He's contribution on the spread of Islam in the Malay World and his legacy of an open-minded peaceful multi-ethnic, multi-religious community", International Conference on Zheng He and the Afro-Asian World, Malacca, 2010, p. 9.

72. *When China Ruled the Seas*, p. 100.

73. *Zheng He Epic*, p. 265.

74. *When China Ruled the Seas*, pp. 112–13.

75. "More Interaction to Strengthen Ties", *New Paper*, 21 July 2008, *Singapore United, The Portal for the Community Engagement Program*, <http://www.singaporeunited.sg/cep/index.php/chinese/node_313/Singapore-marks-Racial-Harmony-Day> (accessed 16 November 2010).

76. "Work on Racial Harmony is not done", *New Paper*, 21 July 2008,

Singapore United, The Portal for the Community Engagement Program, <http://www.singaporeunited.sg/cep/index.php/chinese/node_313/ Singapore-marks-Racial-Harmony-Day> (accessed 16 November 2010).

References

Dreyer, Edward L. *Zheng He: China and the Oceans in the Early Ming Dynasty, 1405–1433*. U.S.: Pearson Education, Inc., 2007.

Lagace, Martha. "Can Religion and Business Learn From Each Other?". *Working Knowledge*, Harvard Business School, 2001. <http://hbswk. hbs.edu/item/3511.html> (accessed 10 October 2010).

Levathes, Louise E. *When China Ruled the Seas: The Treasure Fleet of the Dragon Throne, 1405–1433*. U.S.: Oxford University Press, 1994.

Ma, Rosey Wang. "I. Early Presence of Chinese Muslims: Zheng He, the Muslim Eunuch". *Chinese Muslims in Malaysia, History and Development*. <http://210.0.141.99/eng/malaysia/ChineseMuslim_ in_Malaysia.asp> (accessed 16 November 2010).

———. "Zheng He's contribution on the spread of Islam in the Malay World and his legacy of an open-minded peaceful multi-ethnic, multi-religious community". International Conference on Zheng He and the Afro-Asian World, Malacca, 2010.

"More Interaction to Strengthen Ties". *New Paper*, 21 July 2008. *Singapore United, The Portal for the Community Engagement Program*. <http://www. singaporeunited.sg/cep/index.php/chinese/node_313/Singapore- marks-Racial-Harmony-Day> (accessed 16 November 2010).

Mortimer, Pamela. "Religion in Business: Is it Faith or Suicide?". *Buzzle. com, Intelligent life on the web*. <http://www.buzzle.com/articles/ religion-in-business-is-it-faith-or-suicide.html> (accessed 18 October 2010).

Szczepanski, Kallie. "Zheng He, Ming China's Great Admiral". *About.com Asian History*. <http://asianhistory.about.com/od/china/p/zheng_he_ bio.htm?p=1> (accessed 1 March 2011).

Tan Ta Sen. *Cheng Ho and Islam in Southeast Asia*. Singapore: Institute of Southeast Asian Studies, 2009.

———. *Cheng Ho and Malacca*. Singapore: International Zheng He Society, 2005.

Tan Ta Sen and Chia Lin Sien, eds., *The Zheng He Epic*, 1st edition in Chinese edited by Zhou Wenlin et al. (Kunming, Yunnan, China: Yunnan's Publishing House, Yunnan Fine Arts Publishing House, Auora Publishing House, 2006), p. 48.

The National Library Board. *Zheng He and Maritime Asia*. Singapore, 2005.

"Work on Racial Harmony is not done". *New Paper*, 21 July 2008, *Singapore United, The Portal for the Community Engagement Program.* <http://www.singaporeunited.sg/cep/index.php/chinese/node_313/Singapore-marks-Racial-Harmony-Day> (accessed 16 November 2010).

陈存仁,《被误读的远行：郑和下西洋与马哥孛罗来华考》,桂林市：广西师范大学出版社. (Chen Cunren. *The misread Voyages: A Study of Zheng He's Voyages and Marco Polo's Trip to China.* [Guilin, China: Guangxi Normal University Publication, 1998]).

INDEX

benevolence, 111
  being generous, 113
blank scrolls, 10, 16, 65, 143, 157
Boni (Brunei), 11
Buddha, 10, 46, 90, 117, 137,
    248, 255, 256, 263
  "Sanbao" (Buddhist "Three
    Treasures" or *Triratna*), 10,
    255, 256
  Buddhist law (*dharma*), 10,
    256
  community (*sangha*), 10, 256
Buddhism, 10, 252, 255, 258
Buddhist Classics, 255, 256
building trust, 48, 66

C

Calicut, 12, 29, 39, 40, 43, 69,
    74, 84, 86, 91, 148, 182, 185,
    208, 222, 224–26, 230, 231,
    259
capability in planning,
    organizing, directing and
    controlling voyages, 25
capable organizer, 143
Care for Crew as the Fuel for
    Performance, 183–85
castrated, 8, 16, 142, 251
CEO, 17, 33, 134, 149, 208
Ceylon, 12, 29, 39, 40, 45, 46,
    47, 82, 88, 90, 91, 117, 121,
    185, 208, 222, 223, 226, 230,
    263, 264
Champa, 11, 38, 39, 40, 42, 69,

71, 74, 78, 84, 85, 112, 182,
    185, 208, 211, 219, 220, 224,
    230, 259
  also see Zhancheng
Changle, 10, 17, 135, 136, 146,
    158, 163, 177, 185, 209,
    218–19, 230, 231, 256, 258
Chen Yicheng, Senior Medical
    Officer, 70, 177
Chen Zuyi, 31, 45, 81, 87, 88,
    115, 139, 140, 187, 188
Cheng Ho, 4
China
  close its door, 49
  gentle giant with enduring
    goodwill, 51
China's peaceful rise, 51
Chinese culture, 12, 19, 28, 35,
    108, 111, 112, 154
Chinese Muslims, 253, 254
Chinese traders, 62, 73
Christopher Columbus, 14, 15,
    19, 28, 164
clarity of strategic intent of
    voyages, 198
Clever HR Organizer, 172, 179–83
  Organization and Structures
    as the Required Enabler,
    179–82
  communications, 181
    fleet to sail with a formation,
    181
  departments, 180
  Command Centre, 180

D

Dabao'en Temple, 71, 80, 188, 255

Dazang Jing Buddhist Classics, 255

dazong, 40, 182

deception, 41, 66, 116, 118, 119, 121, 123

deep burden and responsibility for their safety, 185

deep care for crew, 185

Deng Xiaoping, 50

design and construction of massive, state-of-the-art fleet, 200

designing and building ships, 196

Desired Outcome, 110

detailed routes, 231

devout Muslim family, born into, 6, 10, 139, 248, 249

Dhofar, 12, 29, 44, 77, 230, 259

dichotomous strategies, 110

diplomacy of peace, 19, 28, 108, 187

diplomat, 5, 155, 164

duration of voyages, 5, 15, 18, 36, 133, 150, 172, 184, 195, 196, 204

E

East Africa, 14, 34, 70, 195, 217, 240

East and West King of Java, 89

East-West sea route, 222

eclectic nature of religious beliefs, 10

Efficient Consumer Response (ECR), 228

Emperor Gao Zong, 202

Emperor Hongwu, 3, 42, 63, 69, 72, 81

policy of *Haijin*, 72

Emperor Hongxi, 135

Emperor Hui (Jianwen), 9, 62, 72

Emperor Ming Taizu (Zhu Yuanzhang), founder of the Ming Dynasty, 7, 8, 9, 10, 11, 12, 27, 29, 142, 220

foreign policy, friendly and peaceful, 11

Emperor Renzong, 48, 64, 65, 122

Emperor Xuande, 12, 13, 28, 29, 136

Emperor Xuanzong, 48, 221

Emperor Yongle (Zhu Di), 9, 10, 11, 12, 13, 16, 17, 19, 26, 27, 28, 29, 31, 32, 33, 36, 41, 42, 43, 45, 61, 62, 65, 66, 67, 68, 72, 73, 80, 82, 83, 84, 85, 88, 108, 139, 141, 142, 143, 154, 155, 156, 157, 173, 177, 183, 187, 188, 189, 191, 199, 203, 204, 208, 220, 221, 225, 226, 252, 253, 255, 260

death, 48, 135

decree, 64, 65

foreign policy, 12, 28

Marco Polo, 203
maritime trade, 72, 73, 74, 203,
    225
market surveys, 34, 186, 232
"market" transactions, 123
"matou" or "great habour" of the
    Western Ocean, 224
Mazu, 160, 184, 259, 260, 262,
    263
  believer, 256
  practices, 256–58, 262
  see Goddess of the Sea
Mazu altars, set up, 184
Mazu belief,
  stemmed from Chinese
      traditional culture,
      traditional values and
      morality, 262
Mazu Temple, 28, 160, 256
Mecca, 6, 7, 14, 18, 32, 148, 195,
    217, 251, 259
medical officers, 33, 34, 46, 70,
    71, 90, 112, 150, 177, 180,
    181, 209, 232, 233, 236
medical services, 211
medical, cultural and religious
    services, 211
Mencius, 7, 32
message, 64, 67, 108, 109, 117,
    156, 252
Middle East, 8, 48, 254, 259
Middle Kingdom, 11, 12, 40, 154,
    161, 236
Ming Chengzhu (Emperor
    Yongle), 9

Ming China
  comprehensive capabilities in
      shipbuilding and maritime
      trade, 203
  financial position, 80
  projection of power, 63, 174
  splendor and glory, 89, 174
Ming Court, 4, 5, 8, 12, 16, 37,
    42, 64, 68, 69, 73, 79, 80, 81,
    82, 83, 88, 89, 90, 92, 115,
    142, 175, 188, 189, 199, 200,
    205, 218, 219, 221, 223, 224,
    225, 227, 251, 259
  vision of peace and stability,
      41, 67
Ming Dynasty, 7, 9, 10, 11, 13,
    27, 28, 62, 63, 143, 202,
    203
Ming Shi, 9, 43, 62, 63, 76, 88,
    89, 256
Ming Shi Lu, 12, 28, 221
Ming Taizong Shilu, 45, 68, 82, 88
Minghui Dian, 43, 76
mission, 12, 17, 19, 26, 27,
    28–30, 32, 33, 37, 40, 41,
    42, 47, 60–94, 108, 117, 138,
    140, 151, 154, 156, 164, 172,
    173, 174, 175, 178, 179, 182,
    183, 185, 186, 187, 191, 198,
    199, 200, 201, 209, 250
  success, 19, 178, 249, 250, 258,
      259, 260, 261, 264, 265,
      267
mission-critical, 172
mission of voyage, 12

ABOUT THE AUTHOR

Prof Hum Sin Hoon obtained his B. Commerce and B. Engineering (Hons) as a Colombo Plan Scholar from the University of Newcastle, Australia. He received his Ph.D. in Production/ Operations Management from the University of California, Los Angeles, USA.

Prof Hum is currently with the Department of Decision Sciences at the National University of Singapore (NUS). He currently serves as the Vice-Dean (Undergraduate Studies) of the NUS Business School.

Prof Hum had earlier completed his term as the Dean of the NUS Business School where he had earlier served as the Head of Decision Sciences Department. Prof Hum had been a member of the NUS Council and the NUS Senate. He had also served as a Board member of the East Asian Institute, and the Institute of Southeast Asian Studies (ISEAS). At ISEAS, Prof Hum had also served as the Chairman of its Audit Committee.

Prior to joining the University, Prof Hum worked as a Systems Engineer in the Ministry of Defence and participated in several studies aimed at optimizing the use of various types of training resources and systems. Prof Hum has conducted executive teaching and/or served as a consultant to both public and private organizations. Prof Hum's current area of active consulting work has been in helping companies and government agencies adopt and implement the Balanced Scorecard strategic measurement and management system.

Prof Hum's research interests are in the areas of operations strategy, modelling analysis of supply chains, production planning and control of bottleneck facilities and the strategic management of hotel and airline operations. His research papers have been published in various journals including *Operations Research, European Journal of Operational Research, Naval Research Logistics, International Journal of Operations and Production Management, Singapore Management Review* and the *Asia-Pacific Journal of Management.*